International Association for the Integrational Study of Language and Communication

2015

David Bade, Rita Harris, Charlotte Conrad. *Roy Harris and Integrational Semiology 1956-2015: A bibliography.*

2020

Sinfree Makoni. *Language in Africa. Selected papers* vol. 1
David Bade. *Efficiencies and Deficiencies: Cataloging and Communication in Libraries.*
Sinfree Makoni. *African Applied Linguistics. Selected Papers*, vol. 2
Sinfree Makoni. *Linguistic Ideologies, Sociolinguistic Myths and Discourse Strategies in Africa. Selected Papers*, vol. 3
Sinfree Makoni. *Languages and Language Planning in Zimbabwe. Selected Papers*, vol. 4.
David Bade. *Integrational Linguistics for Library & Information Science: Linguistics, Philosophy, Rhetoric and Technology*
David Bade. *Making Mongolians: Linguistics, Historiography, Fiction*

In preparation

Cristine Severo and Sinfree Makoni. *Language in Lusophonia: Perspectives from Bakhtin, Southern Theory and Integrational Linguistics*
David Bade. *Epistemologies of Rape and Revelation*

The International Association for the Integrational Study of Language and Communication

The IAISLC was founded in 1998. It is managed by an international Executive Committee, whose members are:

Adrian Pablé (University of Hong Kong), Secretary
David Bade (University of Chicago, retired)
Charlotte Conrad (Dubai)
Stephen J. Cowley (University of Southern Denmark)
Daniel R. Davis (University of Michigan)
Dorthe Duncker (University of Copenhagen)
Jesper Hermann (University of Copenhagen)
Christopher Hutton (University of Hong Kong)
Peter Jones (Sheffield Hallam University)
Nigel Love (University of Cape Town)
Sinfree Makoni (Penn State University)
Rukmini Bhaya Nair (Indian Institute of Technology)
Jon Orman (Brighton)
Talbot J. Taylor (College of William & Mary)
Michael Toolan (University of Birmingham)

Anyone wishing to join the Association can do so by email **apable@hku.hk** or by sending their name and address to the Secretary:

Dr Adrian Pablé
School of English
Run Run Shaw Tower
Centennial Campus
The University of Hong Kong
Hong Kong S.A.R

Making Mongolians:
Linguistics, Historiography, Fiction

by
David Bade

**International Association for the Integrational Study of
Language and Communication**

This collection ©2020. Corrected printing
Acknowledgements
Areal, Historical and Typological Aspects of South Siberian Turkic ©2013 Originally published in *Mongolian Studies*, v. 33, pp.119-125

The Past Tenses of the Mongolian Verb, ©2013 Originally published in *Mongolian Studies*, v. 33, pp.127-135

Dukhan, a Turkic Variety of Northern Mongolia ©2013 Originally published in *Mongolian Studies*, v. 33, pp.141-146

Janhunen's Mongolian ©2015 Originally published in *Mongolian Studies*, v. 35, pp.184-190

Studies in Mongolic Historical Morphology: Verb Formation in the Secret History of the Mongols ©2015 Originally published in *Mongolian Studies* v. 35, pp.191-193

On Quotation in Middle Mongolian: The Verb ke(m)e- 'to say' ©2015 Originally published in *Mongolian Studies* v. 35, pp.193-196

The Mongols in Javanese Historiography and Literature, ©2002 Originally published in *Mongolica*, v.13, pp. 283-291.

(Spi)Ritual Warfare in Thirteenth Century Asia? International Relations, the Balance of Powers and the Tantric Buddhism of Kertanagara and Khubilai Khan, originally published in Andrea Acri (ed.), *Esoteric Buddhism in Mediaeval Maritime Asia: Networks of Masters, Texts, Icons*. Singapore: ISEAS Press, 2016. pp.141-159

China as a Sea Power, 1127–1368. Originally published online by the International Institute for Asian Studies. Fall 2014: http://www.newasiabooks.org/review/china-sea-power

Eurasian Influences on Yuan China. Originally published online, International Institute for Asian Studies. Winter 2015: http://www.newasiabooks.org/review/eurasian-influences

A Monastery in Time, originally published in *Mongolian Studies* v. 36 (2014, published 2017), pp.82-86

Carl Robinson's Mongolia, originally published in *Mongol Survey* nr.26 (March 2013) pp. 5, 12

Imaginary Travels in Post-Socialist Mongolia, originally published in *Inner Asia* 2013, v. 15 nr.1, pp.135-164

Содном монгол ээждээ зориулав

Contents

Preface..9

Part I: Writing and Reading Mongolian Grammars

I. *Writing Mongolian Grammars from Schmidt to Janhunen: An Essay on the Object of Linguistic Description*..................13
II. *Areal, Historical and Typological Aspects of South Siberian Turkic*..35
III. *The Past Tenses of the Mongolian Verb*............................43
IV. *Dukhan, a Turkic Variety of Northern Mongolia*................55
V. *Janhunen's Mongolian*..63
VI. *Studies in Mongolic Historical Morphology: Verb Formation in the Secret History of the Mongols*.........71
VII. *On Quotation in Middle Mongolian: The Verb ke(m)e- 'to say'*...75

Part II: Writing and Reading Mongolian Stories and Histories

VIII. *Ramon Llull's Mongols*..81
IX. *The Mongols in Javanese Historiography & Literature*...151
X. *(Spi)Ritual Warfare in Thirteenth Century Asia? International Relations, the Balance of Powers and the Tantric Buddhism of Kertanagara and Khubilai Khan*.......167
XI. *China as a Sea Power, 1127–1368*....................................215
XII. *Eurasian Influences on Yuan China*................................221
XIII. *Mongolian Studies and Socialist Cooperation: the East European Scientific Expeditions to Mongolia*......227
XIV. *Carl Robinson's Mongolia*..257
XV. *A Monastery in Time*..265
XVI. *Imaginary Travels in Post-Socialist Mongolia*..............271

Preface

The seven papers reprinted in Part One are all related to a work in progress that will probably never be completed: a survey of the theoretical ideas underwriting the presentations of Mongolian grammar from the first grammars to the most recent work. An earlier version of "Writing Mongolian Grammars from Schmidt to Janhunen" was presented at the Annual Meeting of the Mongolia Society in 2009; revised, it is published here for the first time. The remaining six papers in Part One were published as book reviews in *Mongolian Studies*.

Part Two contains one paper (IX) that summarized my monograph *Khubilai Khan and the Beautiful Princess of Tumapel* and was presented at the 8th International Conference of Mongolists in 2002. Papers VIII, XIII and XVI were originally presented at meetings of the Mongolia Society, the first two of which are published herein for the first time in considerably expanded form. The remaining papers in Part Two were published as book reviews online by the International Institute for Asian Studies in Leiden (XI-XII), in *Mongolian Studies* (XV) and *Mongol Survey* (XIV), while X was written specifically at the request of Andrea Acri, an editor at the Nalanda-Sriwijaya Centre of the Institute of Southeast Asian Studies in Singapore. While the papers in Part One openly employ the writings of Roy Harris in the critique of modern descriptive linguistics, the papers in Part Two are less obviously related to the work of Roy Harris, but except for IX they were all influenced by his writings.

David Bade
Rachel's Farm
1 July 2020

Part I

Writing and Reading Mongolian Grammars

I

Writing Mongolian Grammars from Schmidt to Janhunen
An Essay on the Object of Linguistic Description[1]

Abstract

What does it mean to describe the/a Mongolian language? What should be included in a linguistic description or grammar? In this paper five recent works on Mongolian are examined with those questions in mind. Those five works (Kullmann and Tserenpil's *Mongolian Grammar* (1996); Legrand's *Parlons Mongol* (1997); Peyró García's *Introducción a la lengua mongol* (2000); Janhunen, ed. *The Mongolic Languages* (2003); and Janhunen's *Khamnigan Mongol* (2005)) are compared to previous works on Mongolian grammar with particular reference to their treatment of differences in spoken and written forms, the use of examples, and the sociopolitical aspects of language use and linguistic analysis.

---

[1] Revised version of a paper originally presented at the 2009 Annual Meeting of the Mongolia Society, Chicago, March 26.

1. Getting it all

In his paper on the history of grammars of African languages, Blommaert noted that one of the assumptions carried over into modern linguistics from nineteenth century philology was that "a good corpus of texts could yield all of grammar" (Blommaert, 2008: 293). Hockett mentions an anecdote involving Franz Boas that illustrates this attitude not only in Boas, but with Hockett and others as well in the later 20th century:

> It is rumored that when Newman returned to New York from his field work with the Yokuts, Boas asked him slyly, with no outward sign of humor, "Well, did you get the whole language?" Of course, the issue was not expressed clearly; but I, for one, was quite taken in, and assumed when I went to the Potawatomi that I did not have to strive for any measurable degree of practical control of the language in order to analyze and describe it. The facts could be stored in notebooks and file boxes as they were gathered. (Hockett, 1968: 30)

Boas's question implies that it is possible to completely describe a language, and that it can be described by someone who does not and cannot communicate via the language. It suggests that a language is something determinate that can be wholly known and thus described exhaustively once and for all, as the author of the Zirni manuscript described his own treatise: "The whole is finished complete and perfect." (Iwamura, 1961: 80)

Were it possible to completely (and perfectly!) describe a language, what would the existence of different descriptions of a given language mean? The question does not in fact depend upon the possibility of complete descriptions. Do variant descriptions imply the incompleteness or incorrectness of some or all of them? In that case differences in descriptions may perhaps be explained as differences in the data examined, differences in the linguistic competence (of the source of the data or of the linguist), or differences of the linguist's analysis of the language, i.e. a matter of ignorance or competing theories of language. Or perhaps the various descriptions of language *x* are not actually descriptions of the same language. If the descriptions are not of the same language—even though given the same name—the underlying question concerns the nature of a language, or more fundamentally, of the concept of language itself, a matter set forth bluntly by Lyons in 1977:

> What the linguist does when he describes a language, English for example, is to construct what is commonly referred to by scientists as a model, not of actual language-behaviour, but of the regularities manifest in that behaviour (more precisely of that part of language-behaviour which the linguist defines, by methodological decision, to fall within the scope of linguistics): he constructs a model of the language-system.
>
> (Lyons, 1977, v. 1: 29)

If methodological decisions determine the object of linguistic description, then it should be no surprise that there are so many differing descriptions, distinctions and classifications of languages. In this paper I propose to look at some of those methodological decisions of Mongolian linguists and explore the implications of those decisions for our understanding of the Mongolian language—or is it Mongolian languages?—and even of the nature of language itself.

2. *The* Mongolian language or *a* Mongolian language?

The question of what language is being described appears frequently in grammars of Mongolian, often explicitly in historical studies, descriptions of standardized languages and studies of local variation. The question itself, and how it arises, can take a variety of forms. For Schmidt in his *Grammatik der mongolischen Sprache*[2] the question of what language he was describing was clearly a matter of importance and an explicit decision on his part due to his reasons for writing the grammar.

---

[2] My thanks to Chris Hutton for his comments on this section.

> I am of the opinion that the Mongolian language and literature in no way deserve to be left out of account any longer, but that it is time to cultivate this language for the benefit and edification of Oriental studies...
>
> There are also other perspectives on the usefulness of studying Mongolian. I will not touch upon the practical benefits for Russia's trade and industry, nor its political contacts and interests ... but will approach the matter solely from the side of scholarship and the benefits such study would bring to its various branches. (Schmidt, 1831: vi-vii)

The Mongolian language—not *a* Mongolian language or dialect—concerns Schmidt, and in a later passage he further indicates that he understands *the* Mongolian language to encompass all sorts of variation, but that his interest is in a literary standard, and that for reasons which are for him very important:

> I find it necessary to note that the written language as it is found in the best writing accepted by *all* branches of the Mongols provides a quite admirable basis for this grammar. Regarding the many larger and smaller differences found in the words and spellings of the various groups themselves, and of the different words and phrases of the colloquial language of one or another of these same groups, I myself cannot deal with such matters here. For anyone who has had some practice with Mongolian grammar and writing it will be easy to observe and learn such things if you are led by profession or inclination into direct contact with Mongolian people; where this is not the case then knowledge of such matters will be of little value. Additionally, provincialisms and dialect differences belong nowhere less than in the grammar of a language where they would tend to distract rather than instruct. How different the skills and performance of the majority of our oriental translators would appear if along with better intellectual culture

they brought also a knowledge of the grammar and literature of the language to the work where their services are required! Instead, most of them, although familiar with the speech of the common people with all its vulgarity and its ramifications, demonstrate with regard to the language of their profession an aversion to its literature, since they do not understand it; and indeed their wretchedness is often so great that they desire to cover up their ignorance and indolence with scrupulosity. (Schmidt, 1831: x-xi)

Elsewhere in the introduction he mentions his intention of writing another grammar—of the Kalmyk Mongolian language, "this most noble adjoining dialect" (p. ix)—which has several distinct characteristics and uses an alphabet that differs from the Mongolian alphabet, yet like Mongolian, there is a significant literature written in this language which makes it worthy of his—and the reader's—attention. He also makes a revealing comment about his task as a linguist:

However my work would have been made much easier had the Mongols themselves systematically arranged their language and reduced it to its grammatical rules; but of this work as we understand it, they have no idea. (ibid.: viii)

Throughout Schmidt's introductory remarks we are presented with Schmidt's reasons for undertaking this work of writing a grammar and the nature and scope of the linguistic facts that he intends to "arrange systematically and reduce to grammatical rules." He does not give us "the whole language" because he does not want to. His entire project as he sees it is the production of just the kind of grammar that will present to the reader just the language he desires to present—without denying that there exists plenty of "the Mongolian language" elsewhere than "in den besten Schriften."

In Poppe's introduction to Iwamura's edition of the Zirni manuscript we find an entirely different situation:

> In this connection, one may ask: what kind of Mongolian language is presented in the Zirni Manuscript which is the subject of this book? Is it Middle Mongolian, i.e., the language of the XIII-XV (or XVI) century, the same as that represented in *Muqaddimat al-Adab* and other Moslem sources mentioned above? Or is it Moghol, i.e., the spoken language of the Mongols in Afganistan? (Iwamura, 1961: v)

Poppe then describes several phonological (actually orthographic) features common to both Middle Mongolian and Moghol, noting that "If we did not have other criteria it would be impossible to tell Moghol material from Middle Mongolian" (ibid.: vi). Poppe eventually identifies the language as Moghol based on the absence of any grapheme representing a development from the initial [p] of Ancient Mongolian. Where Ancient Mongolian presumably had an initial [p] Middle Mongolian has [h], Monguor has [f], and Moghol has no initial, and since the Zirni Manuscript has no initial in the corresponding words, it must be Moghol.

Poppe's analysis is interesting in its conflation of graphemes and phonological features, that is to say, assuming the identity or at least strict correspondence of spoken and written language as well as in basing the identification of the language on the lack (from a comparative perspective) of a certain grapheme in a particular set of written forms.[3] If the only difference between Moghol and Middle Mongolian (at least in the sample studied) is the presence versus the absence of a grapheme [h], why call them different languages?

---

[3] For a probing and remarkably insightful work on this matter see Harris (2000).

A further matter of interest is the relation of the language to time and space: 13th-16th century written texts on the one hand, and spoken Afghan Moghol of undetermined date on the other. Based on such statements as Poppe's, it appears that a language—in this case the Moghol language—can have a persistent identity however much it may vary from time to time and place to place, whether in spoken or—in the case of Middle Mongolian—written form. Yet if that identification is based upon a methodological decision made by the linguist, then what persists is not the language but the linguist's (in this case Poppe's) methodology.

The works discussed below each take a different approach to delimiting and justifying the linguistic object that they desire to describe. They write of "the Mongolian language" and "the Mongolian linguistic system," of spoken and literary standard languages, and of "Khamnigan Mongol" and "the Mongolic languages." Examining these authors' presentations and justifications of the object of their descriptions tells us much more about linguistics as it is theorized and practiced than it tells us about language, whether the Mongolian language, a Mongolian language or language understood as something that cannot be qualified by either the definite or indefinite articles.

3. The *Mongolian grammar* of Kullmann and Tserenpil

Kullmann and Tserenpil wrote of "the Mongolian language," noting that "this book could be revised forever, as the language is changing and so does its grammar" (Kullmann and Tserenpil, 1996: iii). Nevertheless, Tserenpil claims that it is "the first complete Mongolian grammar in English compiled in Mongolia which embraces both the Cyrillic and Classical scripts, and has an equal emphasis on pedagogy and science" (ibid.: iv). In addition to the Cyrillic and vertical script written forms, the introductory section on the Mongolian alphabets includes a transliteration (called transcription) of the vertical script examples into Latin letters. In this section the Cyrillic written form is identified as the pronunciation. We also read on page three that "The pronunciation of Classical Mongolian seems very difficult.

For this reason, the Cyrillic script was introduced in the 1940's. The aim was to create a script which would reflect common pronunciation in the twentieth century, making it easier for the average person." (ibid.: 3) The discussion which follows is from beginning to end a confusion of phonology with orthography. The vertical script is described as a "polyphonic alphabet", one in which "the same letter can symbolize different sounds" (ibid.: 5). Kullmann and Tserenpil apparently regard this as a defect or at least a problem for the statement is immediately followed by the remark that scholars have "attempted time and again to change the Mongolian alphabet to a monophonic one" but the persistent problem with these attempts is "that they only reflected the pronunciation of one dialect" (ibid.: 5). (We must add here, one dialect at a particular time.) In contrast, the classical Mongolian alphabet "gives all the Mongolian dialects one common script" (ibid.: 5) and I would add that this has served not only across the geographic range of Mongolian speakers but over a long period of time as well.

Another confusion is apparent in the section "The Mongolian Language and its Development" on page 2. Here we read that "the Mongolian language has steadily developed and the script has been revised several times. ... The language can be divided into the following languages and dialects" which the authors then list. They give ten languages and 39 dialects, with Darkhat and Dörvöd each appearing as dialects of two different languages. Both Ordos and Khamnigan are considered dialects of Southern Mongolian, while Minkhe and Khutsu are listed as dialects of Monguor. On the other hand, Moghol is not mentioned at all.

For these authors it appears that a grammar of vertical script Mongolian is or can be a grammar of *the* Mongolian language, whereas subsequent writing systems based on a particular dialect force the linguist to describe just one dialect. How can this be? In fact the vertical script is an orthographic standard, not a reflection of the varieties of the spoken language, and the Tod, Soyombo or Cyrillic orthographies would work just as well if they were adopted as a written standard rather than expected to be a reflection of pronunciation.

The authors state that as a consequence of their "indigenous approach ... this book is not necessarily user friendly" and I would agree, although only in a limited sense. While presenting many obstacles for all users, this grammar may well be the most useful grammar of Mongolian ever written for the simple reason that it includes not only both Cyrillic and vertical script for each example, but most of all an abundance of examples with translations and explanations. What the book lacks is any mention of political, cultural and social facts about the language, its forms, the history of its writing and standardization, and so on. For such matters, one must look elsewhere, for instance in the grammars of Legrand or Peyró García.

4. *Parlons Mongol*

Like Kullmann and Tserenpil, Legrand's description of Mongolian includes the standard Cyrillic and vertical script written forms but with these Legrand includes a phonetic transcription throughout the book to represent standard Khalkha pronunciation. Yet in spite of the near simultaneous appearance of these two books both based on the speech of late 20th century standard Khalkha dialect, his description and discussion of Mongolian differs greatly from that presented in Kullmann & Tserenpil.

Legrand also offers a few remarks on the Mongolian language in time and space:

> In a word, Mongolian of the 13th century is infinitely closer to contemporary Mongolian than is the French language of the same periods. (Legrand, 1997: 29)

> That proximity is further confirmed by the relative ease with which, after a short period of mutual adjustment, Mongols speaking different dialects manage to establish communication (e.g. the Khalkhas of Mongolia and the Kalmyks of the Volga). (ibid.: 30)

In a word, whether it is a matter of time or of space, to speak of "the Mongolian language" remains legitimate, even if the plural form "the Mongolian languages" may be used for perfectly respectable practical interests. Thus we use the term "the Mongolian language" with the caveat that while this will usually refer to the dialect of the Khalkha Mongols, the basis of the official language currently in use in Mongolia, we shall not thus confine ourselves, since the realities which we encounter in other dialects or of other epochs present only relatively minor variations. (ibid.)

Unlike Kullmann and Tserenpil (1996) and Poppe on the Zirni manuscript (Iwamura, 1961), Legrand is aware of the difference between written language and spoken language, and he presses this distinction upon the reader. He notes that we call written letters "consonants" and "vowels" but "consonants" and "vowels" are phonetic, not orthographic terms. The use of this nomenclature makes it "difficult to free ourselves of the certainty that there is a "natural" relation between the written form and the sound" (ibid.: 31).

Legrand's attention to the differences between written and spoken language is evident in his regular practice of writing all Mongolian examples not only in vertical and Cyrillic Mongolian scripts, but in IPA transliteration as well. It is even more clearly evident in his claim that vowel harmony, an important discussion in most Mongolian grammars, is "nothing but the insignificance of vowel quality in non-initial syllables." Many facts of the language that are "attributed to vowel harmony are in fact orthographic conventions regarding 'vowel letters' and have no relation to the sounds" occurring in spoken Mongolian. What the orthographic convention of "vowel harmony" does is to "play an important role in the demarcation and identification of words and therefore of comprehension" (ibid.: 37) for the reader. "The old uighur orthography" he notes, "and to a lesser extent the Cyrillic orthography, is an orthographic system and not a transcription intended to reproduce the sounds" of Mongolian. The orthography gives "each linguistic unit, each suffix a fixed and codified form" that permits the reader to identify and discriminate among various usages that vary or are indistinguishable in speech (ibid.: 97).

Another feature of Legrand's grammar that distinguishes it from all of the other works discussed here, is the lengthy section "Language and culture." If the object of a grammar is to describe a "linguistic system" (as Peyró García (2000) claims) or "linguistic structure" (as Janhunen (2003) assumes) what need is there for discussing culture? Although Legrand nowhere mentions his reasons for spending nearly 100 pages out of 400 on cultural aspects of language use, it is apparent from the materials included in this section that he does not think it possible to know the language unless one also knows the culture. He is in fact presenting a description of a cultural world focusing on its communicative devices and strategies.

A final note on *Parlons mongol*: the title of the book was clearly determined by the publisher, for the book is in a series of volumes all entitled *Parlons* something or other. It is ironic that the only grammar of Mongolian written to date by a linguist who sees clearly that a grammar will always be dealing with a written form of language, even when that writing is an attempt to describe the spoken form, should be entitled *Parlons mongol*, i.e. *Let's speak Mongolian*.

5. *Introducción a la lengua mongol*

According to the subtitle of Peyró García's description of Mongolian, the language that he describes is Cyrillic Khalkha Mongolian, i.e. the written standard language of modern Mongolia. Yet the book begins with a preamble on the Mongols in history followed by a chapter on dialects ("Extension and varieties"), a chapter on the Altaic Hypothesis, a "History of the language and of its writing systems" that includes discussions of nine historical systems of writing at one time or another in use among various Mongolian peoples, and a chapter on phonology—none of which chapters would seem pertinent for a description of the written variety of Mongolian adopted as the official written language of Mongolia in 1945.

The reason for this order and choice of presentation Peyró García makes clear in the chapter on the Altaic Hypothesis. Linguistic systems, he claims, are multidimensional realities, "the systems of oral communication utilized by human groups, the objects of linguistic study" while languages are "ideological constructions (as *discourses*) of cohesion and social homogenization, supposedly based on the lay speaker's consciousness of his linguistic system, but in reality defined by political and statist criteria, primarily articulated around the social myth of the nation" (Peyró García, 2000: 52). The distinction between linguistic system and language is reflected in the organization of the book, the first part being a description of the Mongolian *language* as something created and contested by linguists for social and political reasons and the object of reform and standardization by governments, while the second part is a more conventional treatment of the elements of grammar, i.e. what the author identifies as the Mongolian *linguistic system*.

The historical sketch of the Mongolian people and nation with which Peyró García's book begins is thus not something added onto his grammar, but a necessary element. His hypothesis of the different orders of linguistic realities underlies his decision to include the historical sketch in his grammar, as it does his decision to discuss in some detail the Altaic Hypothesis. While many grammars of Mongolian include material on both of these matters, whether the single sentence in Kullmann and Tserenpil or Schöning's chapter on Turko-Mongolic relations in Janhunen (2003), neither would be necessary for a description of linguistic facts, whether synchronic or diachronic, if the linguistic facts of a written language are assumed to be simply and solely the analysis of the orthographic, morphological, syntactic and semantic regularities found in the corpus examined as one would expect from a structuralist position, whether of the Sausurean, Bloomfieldian or Chomskian varieties.

One of the key ideas informing this grammar is explored in chapter three on the history of the language and its writing systems and in chapter four "Cyrillic Khalkha Mongol," which deals with the language, not the linguistic system (in Peyró García's terms). That guiding idea is that modern standard written Khalkha Mongolian was a creation of the Mongolian state, guided by its relations with the Soviet Union, the purposes of which were to unify the Mongols within the Mongolian People's Republic and at the same time to divide them from other Mongols who would become Buriats, Kalmyks, Dagur, Monguor etc. as these latter also became officially languages rather than geographical variants of the Mongolian language. He offers the case of Buriat as illustrative of the process:

> During the Stalin era and the policy of using the Cyrillic alphabet, the works of Soviet and Soviet influenced linguists stopped referring to Buriat Mongol or Mongol septentrional as they had until the 1930's and began writing simply of Buriat, cooking up an official grammatical model in which the differences between Buriat and Mongolian (that is written Khalkha) grammar received special emphasis. This process coincided with the change of the name of the republic from Buriat-Mongolia to Buriatia. (Peyró García, 2000: 79)

By dividing his grammar into two parts Peyró García makes the question of what a description of the Mongolian language ought to include disappear. For Peyró García, a linguistic system is a "multidimensional reality" that can be described, and even though he acknowledges that any description will have to follow some narrative order, he does not pursue this realization with the admission that this narrative will be no less a construction than the language constructed for political reasons. Peyró García states that he is giving a description of written Khalkha Mongolian, "a standard literary norm" created by government decree in 1941 and imposed upon the inhabitants of the MPR from then until 1994. A description of a norm is actually not a description of any "multidimensional reality" at all, but a prescription of a norm, and he acknowledges as much in the case of phonology: "The phonological analysis of a standard literary norm such as Cyrillic Khalkha necessarily means that it will be more prescriptive than descriptive" (ibid.: 16.) Yet what the author acknowledges in regard to phonology he apparently feels does not apply to morphology, syntax or the lexicon. The question of what a description of the Mongolian language (or, in Peyró García's terminology, the linguistic system of Mongolian) should involve remains open.

6. Janhunen, *Khamnigan Mongol* and *The Mongolic Languages*

Turning to an even more recent description we find Janhunen giving his reasons for "my third grammatical description of Khamnigan Mongol" (Janhunen, 2005, p. 5). He focuses on the bilingualism of its speakers and "its exceptional conservativeness as far as its linguistic structure and substance are concerned" (ibid.), noting that his field work was limited to "four relatively brief field periods between 1989 and 1994" and that his material was derived "from a few elderly informants" (ibid.). The available data "leaves even many trivial questions unanswered" and that this description is "another intermediate report" (ibid.). One of the important questions that he does wish to answer concerns the status of Khamnigan as a language.

> Khamnigan Mongol has been classified as a dialect of either Mongol proper (in Mongolia) or Buryat (in Russia). ... Linguistically, however, Khamnigan Mongol is a well-defined language, which can only be recognized as a separate member of the Mongolic family. (ibid.: 9)

That is not much of an argument. Janhunen narrates the historiography: Pozdneev (1880), Zhamtsarano, and the ethnic Khamnigan scholar Damdinov (1962) considered Khamnigan to be "linguistically" a dialect of Buriat, Uray-Kőhalmi (1959) considered it to be "linguistically" a dialect of Mongolian, and Janhunen himself devotes a section to Khamnigan"s relation to Dagur, noting that "Khamnigan Mongol and Dagur share a number of common features, which may be due to areal interaction," suggesting that "some of the features common to Khamnigan Mongol and Dagur are probably best explained as being due to the parallel influence of Ewenki" (Janhunen, 2005: 52). It would seem that "linguistically" we need to investigate what it means to be a dialect or a "well-defined language," but that is a question which Janhunen does not pursue.

What Janhunen does offer is a definition,

> *Khamnigan Mongol*, or simply *Khamnigan*, is the community language of an ethnolinguistic group that is best referred to as the Khamnigan. Genetically, Khamnigan Mongol belongs to the Mongolic language family, but areally it has evolved in close interaction with the Northern Tungusic Ewenki language. (ibid.: 9)

followed by an historical discussion of the term Khamnigan,

> The term Khamnigan ... has no satisfactory etymology, but it seems originally to have been used by the northern Mongols to denote the Northern Tungusic Ewenki speakers of the Baikal region. Due to the interaction between Mongolic and Tungusic populations, the term was transferred to denote also the speakers of Khamnigan Mongol many of whom were and are bilingual in Ewenki. (ibid.: 12)

and remarks on bilingualism:

> Much of the confusion that surrounds the concept of "Khamnigan" is connected with their widespread bilingualism. ... Within the bilingual sections of the Khamnigan community, the two languages (Ewenki and Kham-

nigan Mongol) are intertwined to the extent that it is impossible to tell which one is the actual vernacular. (ibid.: 15)

Yet these observations provide Janhunen with no reason for a moment's hesitation. He immediately proceeds with his declaration regarding the taxonomic status of Khamnigan:

> Although Khamnigan Mongol and Khamnigan Ewenki remain two completely distinct languages representing two separate language families, they belong historically to the same areal and typological complex ("Altaic"). Moreover, due to their coexistence as the ethnic languages of a single population, they have developed a number of special interaction phenomena, which have further increased their inherent phonological and morphological parallelism. (ibid.: 16-17)

And no sooner is the question of language settled than we learn that whereas there used to be distinct dialects of this language, only one survives today:

> The surviving Khamnigan Mongol dialect may be identified as (a descendant of) the historical Urulga dialect, which is thus combined in a bilingual relationship with both the Urulga and the Mankovo dialect of Khamnigan Ewenki (ibid.: 18)

Thus what appears to be a not-so-well defined ethnic and linguistic situation, Janhunen describes as the confusion of linguists, anthropologists, government classifications and even ethnic self-understandings in regard to the proper scope and use of the term Khamnigan. Perhaps we should ask instead whether anyone, including Janhunen, is using the term Khamnigan "correctly." Or should we go further and ask if there even *is* a correct use, and what does it mean that there is a question of correct usage at all?

In the preface to *The Mongolic Languages*, a collection of short uniform grammatical sketches of Mongolian languages edited by Janhunen, we find a discussion of many of the questions that I have asked of the other works discussed here. For instance the author states that because of the close similarities among Mongolian or Mongolic languages there are "a number of problems in the definition of what is a language in the Mongolic context" (p. xvi), with the author settling for mutual incomprehension as the criteria for identifying separate languages. Similarly, because of mutual similarities the "genetic taxonomy" of the Mongolian languages is difficult to describe. In some ways they "are more easily described in terms of the *wave* model of linguistic geography than the *family model* of conventional diachronic linguistics" (Janhunen, 2003: xvii), a point also made by Peyró García.

The most outstanding feature of the grammatical sketches in *The Mongolic Languages* is the standard list of topics and form of presentation which all follow rather closely. The table of contents alone reveals what are thought to be all the necessary elements of a "complete" description of a language, excluding the lexicon. Like the "grammatical sketches" discussed by Blommaert and similar to the Lincom series *Languages of the world—Materials*, the grammars here assume that "the fantastic variation that characterizes actual language in use can (and should) be reduced to an invariable, codified set of rules, features and elements" (Blommaert, 2008: 292). In the grammars Janhunen gathered together in *The Mongolic languages* there is no place for the cultural aspects that occupied such a large part of Legrand's book, written Mongolian is treated in a separate chapter—with all examples given only in transliteration!—and the ideological aspects of language identification so present to Peyró García are discussed as though they are simply theoretical issues for linguists to determine.

7. The production of Mongolian grammars

Why are there so many grammars of Mongolian? Because there are so many different questions to ask, so many different perspectives, for so many purposes. It would not be possible to write a grammar like Legrand's for any of the languages and dialects treated in Janhunen (2003) because Legrand is trying to describe *the* Mongolian language, not one of many, and his explicit purpose is to show that all of the Mongolian languages of Janhunen (2003) can be described with one grammar if one is writing of a literary standard from which actual spoken and written usage will differ more or less from time to time, place to place, person to person and even from one moment to the next within a single person's lifetime. Writing a grammar of written Mongolian is no different from writing a grammar of written English, Arabic or Chinese: either it is a prescriptive (i.e. standard) grammar or it will have to focus on a specific corpus of texts selected by the linguist for whatever reasons he or she chooses.

Different purposes for a grammar call for different kinds of treatments, presentation and selection of what facts to describe. A generative syntax such as that written by Binnick (1979) will not be anything like the structural view of Poppe (1951) nor like the functional syntax of Bittigau (2003). It is not the language that differs in such cases, but the theory which creates its own object by limiting the varied linguistic realities to just those specified by the linguist's theoretical necessities. Likewise, any description of a partial corpus, whether a single work such as the *Hua-yi-yi-yu* (Lewicki, 1949), the *Altan Tobchi* (Orlovsky, 1984) or the *Monggol-un niguca tobciyan* (Street, 1957), a grammar of spoken (Jagchid and Dien, 196-?) or written language (Godziński, 1985; Rakos, 2002) or the language of a particular place and time (Weiers, 1972) will focus on the differences and variety represented by that text or corpus.

From the one written Mongolian language described by Schmidt (1831) to the spoken language of a few elderly Khamnigans, the object of study is created by methodological decisions, that is, by the linguist. Neither the Mongolian language nor the Mongolian languages are natural facts to be picked up, examined and described by an objective scientist because all we have are individual speech acts or texts. As the products of human beings acting in concrete social circumstances that vary across communities, times and places, what the linguist is confronted with is chaos and variety as well as social norms concerning what are acceptable and desirable or prohibited linguistic practices. We conclude that there will be as many grammars of the Mongolian language as there are linguists who think that such a language can be described, and as many Mongolian languages as there are linguists who desire to distinguish one corpus of linguistic data collected for that purpose from all others. With a closed, methodologically delimited corpus, the linguist can indeed "get it all," but that "all" will be a linguist's fiction. If, on the other hand, one wishes to open the investigation to the actual variety found among any group of speakers or writers, in one or more places or times, then it will never be possible to "get it all" for that "all" will remain forever beyond any capacity for collection much less understanding in the context of its occurrence. Kullmann and Tserenpil did get it right by admitting that they could not possibly get it all.

Bibliography
Binnick, Robert I. *Modern Mongolian: A Transformational Syntax.* Toronto: University of Toronto Press, 1979.
Bittigau, Karl Rudolf. *Mongolische Grammatik: Entwurf einer Funktionalen Grammatik (FG) des modernen, literarischen Chalchamongolischen.* Wiesbaden: Harrassowitz, 2003. (Tunguso-Sibirica, 11)
Blommaert, Jan. "Artefactual ideologies and the textual production of African languages." *Language & Communication* 28:4 (2008): 291-307.
Дамдинов Д.Г. "Предварительные данные о языке хамниганов Читинской области." *Краткие сообщения Бурятского комплексного НИИ СО АН СССР* 4 (1962): 128-137.
Gáspár, Csaba. *Darkhat.* München: Lincom, 2006. (Languages of the World/Materials, 419)
Godziński, Stanisław. *Język średniomongolski: słowotwórstwo,*

odmiana wyrazów, składnia. Warszawa: Wydawnictwa Uniwersytetu Warszawskiego, 1985. (Rozprawy Uniwersytetu Warszawskiego)

Harris, Roy. *Rethinking writing.* Bloomington, Indiana: Indiana University Press, 2000.

Hockett, Charles. *The state of the art.* The Hague: Mouton, 1968. (Janua linguarum, Series minor, 73)

Iwamura, Shinobu, with the collaboration of Natsuki Osada & Tadashi Yamasak (1961). *The Zirni manuscript: a Persian-Mongolian glossary and grammar.* Kyoto: Kyoto University, Committee for the Kyoto University Scientific Expeditions to the Karakoram and the Hindukush, 1961. (Results of the Kyoto University Expeditions to the Karakoram and the Hindukush, 1955 v. 6)

Jagchid, Sechen, and Dien, Albert E. *Spoken Chahar Mongolian.* [Taipei]: Inter-university program for Chinese language studies, [196-?].

Janhunen, Juha (ed.). *The Mongolic Languages.* London: Routledge. 2003.

Janhunen, Juha. *Khamnigan Mongol.* München: Lincom, 2005. (Languages of the World/Materials, 173)

Kullmann, Rita; and D. Tserenpil. *Mongolian Grammar.* Hong Kong: Jensco Ltd., 1996.

Legrand, Jacques. *Parlons Mongol.* Paris: Harmattan, 1997.

Lewicki, Marian. *La langue mongole des transcriptions chinoises du XIVe siècle: le Houa-yi yi-yu de 1389.* Wrocław: Nakładem Wrocławskiego Towarzystwa Naukowego, 1949-1959. (Prace Wrocławskiego Towarzystwa Naukowego, Seria A. Nr. 29, 60)

Lyons, John. *Semantics.* Cambridge: Cambridge University Press, 1977.

Орловская, М. Н. *Язык "Алтан тобчи".* Москва: Наука, 1984.

Peyró García, Miguel. *Introducción a la lengua mongol.* Granada: Granada Lingvistica, 2000.

Poppe, Nikolaus. *Khalkha-mongolische Grammatik, mit Biblio-*

graphie, Sprachproben und Glossar. Wiesbaden: Franz Steiner Verlag,1951. (Veröffentlichungen der Orientalischen Kommission, Bd. 1)

Rákos Attila. *Written Oirat.* München: Lincom,2002. (Languages of the World/ Materials, 418)

Schmidt, Isaak Jakob. *Grammatik der mongolischen Sprache.* St.-Petersburg: Gedruckt in der Buchdruckerei der Kaiserlichen Akademie der Wissenschaften, 1831.

Street, John Charles. *The Language of the Secret History of the Mongols.* New Haven: American Oriental Society, 1957. (American Oriental Series, v. 42)

Uray-Kőhalmi, Katalin. "Der mongolisch-kamniganische Dialekt von Dadal Sum und die Frage der Mongolisierung der Tungusen in der Nordmongolei und Transbajkalien" *Acta Orientalia Hungarica* 9 (1959): 163-204.

Weiers, Michael. *Die Sprache der Moghol der Provinz Herat in Afghanistan (Sprachmaterial, Grammatik, Wortliste).* Opladen: Westdeutscher Verlag, 1972.

II

Areal, Historical and Typological Aspects of South Siberian Turkic[1]

In their preface to this volume the editors state that the contributors have "striven to throw light on the grammatical domains of a particular subset of the Turkic languages," and "to contribute to understanding these languages as a whole, and even to further our understanding of human language in general" (p. viii). The papers collected in this volume should be of interest to mongolists for the discussions of Mongolian found therein as well as for the broader topic of the relationships among these South Siberian languages and Mongolian in areal, historical and typological perspectives. While Ragagnin is the only one to focus her attention directly upon the relationships between Mongolian and South Siberian Turkic languages, a number of the other papers

---

[1] Review of: *Areal, Historical and Typological Aspects of South Siberian Turkic*. Edited by Marcel Erdal, Irina Nevskaya and Astrid Menz. Wiesbaden: Harrassowitz, 2012. (Turcologica, Band 94)

include sections on Mongolian or cross-linguistic comparisons in which material from Mongolian is included. Yet although the areal focus both invites and informs the interested mongolist, the theoretical assumptions upon which these papers are based raise many questions that the contributors either fail to ask or having noted, proceed as if those questions may be ignored.

The first sentence of the editor's preface presents at least four such theoretical problems:

> The South Siberian Turkic languages are a group of minor idioms which are in many ways archaic, because they developed in isolation in an area where the great Islamic literary languages had quite limited influence (p. vii)

First, there is the problem of the meaning of 'group', then the meanings of 'minor' and 'archaic', and finally the claim that "they developed in isolation." These languages are 'grouped' by the linguists according to areal, historical and typological analyses, but what besides the linguist makes these languages a group? And of languages rather than dialects? The problem with 'minor' I will leave aside as a comment on the social status of the speakers of these languages, but how is the claim that they "are in many ways archaic" to be understood? As another comment on the social status or conservativeness of the speakers, or a claim about their genetic inheritance? Furthermore, the explanation of this archaic nature as being a consequence of having developed in isolation apparently refers to their isolation from other Turkic languages given the reference to Islam in what follows, for language contact is a central focus in several of the papers that follow. In short, this first sentence demonstrates that many of the assumptions underlying modern linguistic theories are not questioned by the contributors to this volume, and this reviewer eventually concluded that the contributors failed "to contribute to understanding these languages as a whole," much less furthering "our understanding of human language in general." In the papers themselves we can see how this failure to question current theory leads to some questionable statements.

The first paper "Auxiliary verb constructions in Old Turkic and Altay-Sayan Turkic" by Gregory D.S. Anderson begins with the statement "Like all other Turkic languages, the language[s] of the Old Turkic sources..." (p. 1; bracketed [s] appears thus in the original). Right away we are presented with a formulation that equivocates on the question of whether we are dealing with a language (Old Turkic) or more than one language. The problem is clearly how to define a language in such a manner that we can in fact decide whether Old Turkic is one or more languages (and if more than one, how many and which ones). Yet by simply bracketing the plural, Anderson avoids the question of what 'a language' is, and proceeds as if that does not matter. Clearly he has not struggled with any of the questions Roy Harris raised in *The Language Makers* and *The Language Myth*.

If the question of what is meant by Old Turkic is neatly avoided, the question of what is meant by 'auxiliary verb' is dealt with directly. Anderson offers his definition of the term and in the next paragraph acknowledges that his definition is problematic.

> This definition of auxiliary verb is admittedly somewhat nebulous. There is no, and probably cannot be, any specific, language-independent criteria that can be used to determine the characterization of any given element as a lexical verb (including in serialized functions) or an auxiliary verb. As in all scalar, gradual, or gradient phenomena, clines of grammaticalization and semantic bleaching will have 'gray areas', where the element in question has accrued certain features generally associated with endpoints or focal points on the continuum, but perhaps not others. It seems likely that the degree of grammaticalization and semantic bleaching deemed sufficient to stop calling some particular verbal element Xv usages of lexical verb Xlv and start calling it auxiliary verb Xav

will vary from researcher to researcher, even when working on the same language (p. 2)

"There is no, and probably cannot be" Anderson states—but this does not provide him with any reason to engage in hesitation phenomena. In fact he proceeds to include in his description of auxiliary verbs the verb *yarliqa*, about which he remarks "Strictly speaking this is not a 'proper' AVC *per se*, as the 'auxiliary' verb is not really semantically bleached" (p. 25). Carry on, Mr. Anderson.

In a number of instances in this volume a language is said to have been 'contaminated' ("The rhetorical readings may be due to contamination with *erki(n)*." Lars Johanson in "Notes on Turkic stance particles", p. 56) or to have 'deteriorated,' ("the vowel harmonic systems of the Turkic and Mongolic languages have deteriorated," Marti Roos in "Western Yugur in the Qinghai-Gansu linguistic area" p.136) which ought to lead one to ask just what kind of thing language is if it can deteriorate or be contaminated. What is being discussed is the language evident in texts and among speakers of different eras. Did some group of speakers get contaminated or did their genetic equipment deteriorate? "Turkic and Mongolic languages display several common features, some of which may be considered as part of a common genetic inheritance," Elisabetta Ragagnin writes in "Turco-Mongolic relations: the case of particles". Are these metaphors innocent or seriously misleading? Are these authors following Mary Douglas (e.g. in her book *Purity and Danger*), Georges Canguilhem or Gobineau? None of the authors cite—and judging from the ideas presented, none appear to have read—Christopher Hutton's *Linguistics and the Third Reich: mother-tongue fascism, race, and the science of language* or his *Race and the Third Reich: linguistics, racial anthropology and genetics in the dialectic of Volk*.

That 19th century ideas about language and race in general are to be found just below the theoretical surface appears even more clearly in Irina Seljutina's papers. In "Consonant systems in the Turkic languages of South Siberia" Seljutina concludes that

> the positional length of low vowels before high ones, typical for Kipchak Turkic, as well as the prevalence of central-back vowels in the languages of Siberia show that Kipchak Turkic elements played an important role in the ethnogenesis of Siberian Turkic ethnic groups along with Ugric-Samoyedic ones. All this proves the complexity of the origin of the Altai-Sayan peoples.
>
> It is possible to assume a genetic relation between the substrates found in modern Northern Altai, Shor and Khakas, and there are indications that the Chik were hypothetical ancestors of the Tuvan people (p. 154)

Vowel length was a determining factor in the origin of the Altai-Sayan peoples? In another paper by Seljutina in this volume ("South Siberian Turkic vocalism as a reflection of language contacts") we read that the study of vowel systems reveals "the dominant characteristics of the articulatory-acoustic bases of ethnic groups" (p. 159). Seljutina then proceeds to discuss "general characteristics of vowel systems" (ethnic groups?), her research revealing

> a tendency towards the ideal Turkic symmetric pattern... Nevertheless, only the vowel systems in Tuvan, Standard Altay Turkic and the Tuba dialect reflect this pattern in full. The other dialects have incomplete subsystems (p. 160)

The South Siberian Turkic languages (peoples?) are striving to be ideal Turkic languages (peoples?) but unfortunately they are suffering from ethnic conflict:

> The present status of the vowel systems in the Turkic languages of South Siberia appears to be conditioned by a conflict between the articulatory-acoustic base of a non-

Turkic substratum language and that imposed by the superstratum language. The attempt of the substratum-language to accommodate its vocalism to the alien synharmonic system might have determined the tendency to level the phoneme markers relevant for this system and to strengthen the role of other linguistic means of semantics differentiation (p. 166)

Will the ideal Turk win or will those non-Turk underdogs in the substratum survive and prosper? Perhaps the Russian government could enact legislation limiting the power of the alien synharmonic system? Cannot those alien elements be deported and sent back where they belong?

Am I joking? Not really. In all the papers in this collection language is both actor and the one acted upon; the poor speakers of these "minor" languages are helpless bystanders of forces beyond their control: genetic inheritances, alien systems, languages in contact and even at war, the subversions of substrata and the impositions of superstrata and states, and the terrible seductions of ethnic impurities, Russian, Mongolian and Chinese.

Das Schorische befindet sich zur Zeit in einem Umwandlungsprozess, den es mit vielen anderen Minderheitensprachen gemeinsam hat: Unter dem Einfluss des Russischen als Mehrheits- und Statssprache verliert das Schorische viele seiner typisch türkischen Strukturen, und es steht zu befürchten, dass diese unter den zukünftigen Sprecher-generationen gar nicht mehr verwendet werden. (Monika Rind-Pawlowski, "Pragmatische Funktionen des Akkusativs bei der Redewiedergabe im Schorischen" p.119)

Conditional structures in South Siberian languages are semantically ambiguous Astrid Menz notes in her paper "The conditional in South Siberian Turkic," and in order to disambiguate "Siberian Turkic languages sometimes make use of conjunctions selectively copied from contact languages" (p. 72). Is it really languages that make use of conjunctions, or people? Do languages selectively copy from other languages? Or is it rather that the speakers/writers of these languages utilize their knowledge of communication strategies to avoid ambiguity when it seems to them to be a problem? Does it matter how we describe and theorize these activities? Menz almost points to the persons involved but stops short by invoking pragmatics:

> The comparatively rare use of forms other than the simple real conditional may simply have to do with pragmatics; statistically there might not be any communicative need to engage conditional forms that express meanings other than just neutral, open real condition and, to a significantly lesser extent, counterfactual unreal condition (p. 72.)

Once the "pragmatic" explanation is couched in statistical terms we know that the speaker is not being considered, but only a corpus of instances identified in the data collected.

Areal, historical and typological aspects of linguistic behaviour in southern Siberia are presented as though these matters have nothing to do with the people who made and make the language investigated. In the real world of southern Siberia—as everywhere else—people speak and write as they do because they deem such language suitable to their situation. People argue about what is good language, proper language and what is bad language, inappropriate language and harmful language. They teach their language, they encourage and correct those learning their language, and in doing so they make their language what it is, day by day, moment by moment. They may indeed feel that their language is "deteriorating" or that the speech of some persons or groups has been "contaminated," just as they may choose to engage others in their language, but these attitudes and actions indicate a social engagement or conflict among people for whom language matters and not an areal, historical, typological or genetic conflict among "languages."

The theoretical problems I have noted (as well as others not discussed) are not unique to this volume: they are the pressing problems of current linguistic theory in nearly all its varieties. Basing linguistic theorising on ancient assumptions without ever questioning them will never "contribute to understanding these languages as a whole"—whatever that may mean—nor will such research ever "further our understanding of human language in general." For those interested in the grammar of Turkic languages of South Siberia and comparisons with Mongolian languages, there is much of interest in this volume, but since neither the materials studied nor the manner of studying them led any of the contributors to question the theories they had previously adopted, there is nothing here of any theoretical interest.

III

The Past Tenses of the Mongolian Verb: Meaning and Use[1]

It has been thirty five years since Professor Binnick's *Modern Mongolian: a Transformational Syntax* appeared. Looking back at that book now it is obvious how much it suffered from the theory that determined not only the definition of "the language" studied, but the kinds of questions asked, the form of description, the analyses given, the explanations proffered and the arguments in support of those descriptions, analyses and explanations. A comparison of his new book with that earlier one shows that he delves much more deeply into Mongolian now than he did in 1979, although that appears to have much to do with the difference of focus: while syntax—even in the era of "generative semantics" and "deep structures"—was and remains by definition primarily a matter of structure rather than meaning and use,

---

[1] Review of: Robert I. Binnick. *The Past Tenses of the Mongolian Verb: Meaning and Use.* Leiden: Brill, 2012. (Empirical Approaches to Linguistic Theory, v. 1)

the present volume focuses on these latter matters which cannot be discussed in an adequate manner without taking into consideration a much greater range of linguistic phenomena than that which (apparently) sufficed for a syntactic analysis.

The wider range of phenomena discussed in the new book is evident in one of its nicest features, a feature that also distinguished the earlier book from much linguistic theory, namely Binnick's practice of noting the sources of (most) of his examples. This is what I LOVE about both of Binnick's books, and for a simple reason: it is not possible to decide on an appropriate analysis of any example, whether for syntax, meaning or usage, when that example is taken totally out of context and plopped bare naked into a theoretical context where that context itself directs one toward a certain interpretation. One splendid example of this problem may be found on page 43 in the new book. Here Binnick offers four examples of the use of *–lee*, all four taken from Ramstedt's *Über die Konjugation des Khalkha-Mongolischen*. For the fourth example "bid odoo xool idlee" which Ramstedt translated as "wir haben jetzt gegessen", Binnick adds a footnote:

> Sodnomdorj comments that this is incorrect; *odoo* 'now' renders the example future, not present perfect or past, and for the indicated sense, the modifier should instead be *saya* 'just now'. (p. 43)

The question here appears to be whether Ramstedt or Sodnomdorj is correct, but that is actually a question that can only be answered if we know in fact what was originally meant. Because Binnick has indicated his source for the example we might hope that the answer could be arrived at by asking Ramstedt, and of course Ramstedt has already indicated what he meant in his translation. The real problem is that Ramstedt did not indicate where his example came from. Did Ramstedt follow the practice of many (if not most) linguists and make up the example using his own speaker's intuition? Or did he take this example from a native speaker's actual discourse along with that speaker's explanation of its meaning? Did Ramstedt misunderstand something he heard and read, a misunderstanding that Sodnomdorj identified, or did he correctly understand an actual statement that Sodnomdorj misunderstood because the original context was not reproduced by Ramstedt? With the death of Ramstedt making it impossible to clarify any of these matters, we are left with a text the original meaning of which *we can never ascertain* and consequently it is an example that offers nothing to our understanding of the meaning and use of *-lee* because we do not know what it originally meant. All we can say is that Ramstedt wrote that it meant one thing and Sodnomdorj said it cannot mean what Ramstedt claimed it meant.

In other cases where Binnick asks a native speaker to identify the difference of meanings and possible uses of certain past tense markers, we find a very similar situation. Binnick apparently asked Sodnomdorj about the use of *bailaa* in a text and Binnick records his response that in that text "*baiv* could have been [the] same" as *bailaa*, that the difference was "*just stylistic*". The question here is of course what was meant? More to the point, what does it mean that someone can read a text and say that "it" could have been written another way and still have had the same meaning? A few pages later Binnick records an argument made by Wu that "in certain declarative sentences, *none* of the past tenses may be used (102), while in others (4) *any* of them may be" (p. 53). The question never asked in discussions of such examples is *what someone wants to say/write*. Wu apparently claims that you can use any of them in certain situations, but is that how anyone speaks or writes? Binnick himself argues that there is nothing optional (and I would agree with this) but does so on dubious grounds:

> The present work argues ... that the occurrence of the various past tense verb forms in different contexts is not in principle optional, but depends by and large on the inherent meaning of each particular ending. (p. 58-59)

He makes his point clearer a little later on:

> It would be wrong, however, to say that the choice of ending is an option of the speaker's, that the speaker is free to use whatever ending matches the way the speaker views the situation. (p. 91)

Thus, in order to understand the use and interpretation of the past tenses in Mongolian we must focus on what the markers mean, not on what the speaker means (and this is where Binnick, following all of modern linguistics, gets it completely wrong).

Clearly in the case involving Sodnomdorj he could not imagine the text meaning anything significantly different had it been written otherwise, but is that due to no difference in meaning in the text or to Sodnomdorj's lack of imagination? In fact neither the text nor the (absent) context could ever reveal that to any inquirer: the only way to know if the original author of the text would have meant something different with the two different verb forms would be to ask that original author—and that we cannot do. In the case of Wu, of course, there is no use asking anyone, for Wu clearly does not mean anything in particular. What we can do is read Binnick's footnotes and realize that native speakers can and do disagree about the meanings of examples taken from real spoken and written linguistic behaviour, whether presented with or without contexts.

Once we realize that disagreements concerning meanings of this or any other examples renders their analysis impossible — how can you analyze an expression if you do not know what it means?—we find ourselves faced with an enormous methodological problem. If we look back at Binnick's *Modern Mongolian* we see that the overwhelming majority of examples therein are not taken from any text that would provide sufficient context to clearly decide between alternative interpretations and therefore analyses, but are rather reproduced from grammars where they may have been nothing more than examples of non-native speaker's intuitions or even misunderstandings. Binnick's decision in 1979 to indicate his sources allows us now to evaluate the data upon which his syntax was based and to examine his examples in that light. The fact that Binnick's earlier work was largely limited to data taken from previous grammars suggests that its inadequacies go much deeper than its long ago abandoned theoretical framework. At one point in his new book Binnick faces this issue head on and immediately sticks his head in the sand to make it go away.

> In the first chapter of this book, the issue of the distinct characters of spoken, written, and "media" languages barely arose, because the grammatical tradition takes a rather unsophisticated view of what is a language as rich and complicated as any—Mongolian ... the second chapter of the present book largely ignored the issue and assumed that one could use print materials to reveal things about speech, and that there was no difference between asking a native speaker of Mongolian to perform tasks involving written language and asking him or her to perform ones involving speech.
>
> It should be clear by now that there are dangers in that approach. It obscures the linguistic realities, for not only do the past tenses not work in written Mongolian the way the traditional grammars claim, or imply, that they do, but they don't work in written Mongolian the way they do in Mongolian speech, either. (p. 130)

Given that the majority of the examples Binnick has discussed up to this point in his book are, as in the earlier book, taken from earlier grammatical treatises which neither indicate source nor context, we must ask what Binnick has been doing for 130 pages if the past tenses do "not work in written Mongolian the way the traditional grammars claim, or imply, that they do." In this context we should also note his attitude to native speaker's intuitions:

> While every textbook and grammar necessarily comments on the various "tense" endings, we shall see that there has been a wide divergence in opinions, often

> based on little more than naïve speaker intuitions and sometimes on mistaken comparisons with the quite different verbal systems of other languages. (p. 7)

> None of them [i.e. previous grammarians—DB] presents much (if any) evidence other than sheer native speaker intuition to support their accounts (p. 11)

And if at this point you are not already gaping in astonishment, note the way he treats the opinions of his guides in matters of native speaker's intuition. When Sodnomdorj objects to an example taken from Hangin (another native speaker), Binnick adds a footnote:

> Sodnomdorj calls *iree* here a mistake and comments that he would say *irj yavaa*. (This may reflect a difference in dialects.) (p. 30)

A few pages later Tserenchunt objects to two examples from Wu (Chuluu Ujeyidiin, another native speaker) and Binnick adds footnotes to each example:

> Tserenchunt comments (p.c., October, 2008) that "this example is practically impossible." This may reflect a dialect difference. ...
> Tserenchunt declares this sentence, too (cf. ex. 96) "practically impossible." Again, this may reflect a difference between dialects. (p. 52)

So we find linguists engaging in arguments about the grammaticality and hypothetical meanings of hypothetical examples that apparently originally never meant anything except "this is an example of one or another past tense morpheme." What do such arguments mean? Binnick avoids asking the question by dismissing the inconvenient "data" as belonging to a different dialect, and hence of no consequence. But how can Binnick so easily dismiss such disagreement among Khalkha speakers as insignificant dialectal difference when it is precisely meaning and usage that he is trying to determine? He argued on the very first page of the book that

> To discuss the problem purely within the context of Khalkha dialects and/or the Mongolian language written in the Cyrillic alphabet is to deprive oneself of insights from other members of the family and to artificially limit the scope of the inquiry at the outset. (p. 1)

and concluded this opening discussion with the remark

> Thus while the present work largely restricts itself to a discussion of, and principally draw[s] its data from Khalkha and relatively closely related Mongolic languages, we have occasion as well to refer to at least one other Altaic language, namely Turkish. (p. 3-4)

And contrary to his remarks on the differences between spoken, written and media languages in the third chapter, in these opening passages Binnick suggests that our problem is little more than a terminological quibble.

> To a certain extent there is only a terminological issue involved here, for it is often easier but not necessarily precise) to refer to aspects of a "Mongolian" grammatical system than to specify a more specific language or languages. The problem with this is that the term "Mongolian" has been used to refer to many different spoken and written languages, that the status of various members of the family as independent languages or as mere dialects is by no means clear, and the historical and classificatory relationships of the members of the Mongolic language family remain controversial. (p. 1-2)

Binnick's methodology reveals the profound dilemma of doing linguistics on the basis of terminology left deliberately vague so as to avoid the most difficult problems. Binnick wants to draw on data that confirms his analysis no matter what speaker, dialect, language or date characterizes that data ... and to dismiss the nonconforming data as belonging to a verbal system other than that under discussion (i.e. a different dialect, language, etc.). And his language here betrays his refusal to even consider the immensely consequential theoretical issues involved. We find grammatical systems contrasted with language, spoken language with written language, and independent family members versus "mere dialects." The situation only gets worse in chapter three where he claims to take seriously the distinction between spoken, written and media languages, treating them as indeed different languages or different grammatical systems or registers of a single language. Why? Because he cannot make a coherent case if he has to fit all of the evident differences into a single grammatical system. So if the data does not fit, it must either be a different dialect (Sodnomdorj vs. Hangin), or a different language (Spoken Mongolian versus Written Mongolian). But he cannot get off the hook so easily in either case.

As we have already seen Binnick dismisses differences of interpretation and opinions on grammaticality as "dialectal differences" rather than empirical data to account for when those differences do not fit into his analysis, but freely draws on those same native speakers (e.g. Hangin, Sodnomdorj, Tserenchunt, Wu) of different dialects when convenient, for he has argued at the beginning that "The verbal systems of these various 'dialects' and 'languages' are for the most part essentially the same" (p. 2). He manages to do this by writing about "the issue of what precisely is meant by 'Mongolian'" (p. 1)—avoiding the issue of what is meant by language and dialect—and then putting "dialects" and "languages" within quotation marks. He never questions the theoretical significance of the evident indefinability of these terms, or rather (what amounts to the same thing) the inability of linguists to advance any but an arbitrary definition for them.

While Binnick closes his eyes to the theoretical problems associated with the most basic terms of his discussion–language and dialect—he makes a different but equally unsatisfactory move when it comes time to deal with the issue of written and spoken language. In his discussion of writing in the third chapter, it is all too evident that Binnick has never thought through any of the theoretical issues that arise in considering the relation of speech to writing, and his bibliography suggests that he has read nothing on the topic either.

In his discussion of written Mongolian, Binnick makes a number of important observations without considering, much less pursueing their theoretical implications. First he describes the traditional view of linguists in which

> written Khalkha is simply the representation, using a version of the Cyrillic alphabet, of spoken Khalkha, which in turn is simply the modern development of older Mongolian in most of what used to be Outer Mongolia, just as Mongolian in Inner Mongolia is considered the written counterpart—using a modernized version of the old vertical script writing system—if not quite the written representation, of the corresponding spoken language that is the modern development of Mongolian in Inner Mongolia. (p. 114)

He then argues against this view that Khalkha Mongolian has "competing grammatical systems that distinguish spoken and written language" (p. 115). He notes that "much of the evidence for spoken language used not only by the older grammarians, but even in this present work, is drawn from written sources" (p. 115) and asks if this is justifiable. He then complicates the question by noting that what is at issue is not just the distinction between spoken and written language, but between formal and colloquial registers, concluding "For one thing, writing *is* used, sometimes, to represent speech, and sometimes it is not, but is independent of it" (p. 116). Binnick even realises that this leads to far deeper questions:

> Here sociolinguistics, pragmatics, discourse structure, and philology meet in a complex consideration of just what we are claiming when we speak of this or that feature of *the* modern Mongolian language...or even just of Khalkha. (p. 116, ellipse in original)

Yet instead of pursuing this question and the question of the relation between spoken and written language, Binnick simply declares that Mongolian—like English and other international languages—has two competing grammatical systems, one for the standard written language and one for the spoken language. In his third chapter "Past tenses in the written language" we find an astonishing concatenation of admissions, criticisms of the assumptions of past research and clearly formulated theoretical questions, all of which are simply dropped once the author sets up two competing grammars.

Things only get worse in Chapter Four, "The discourse functions of the tenses," but I have already written too much. So I shall skip to the concluding "Remarks in lieu of a conclusion" where Binnick really takes the cake:

> It became obvious in the course of the research for the present book that the tense system of spoken Mongolian is not the same as that of written Mongolian. (These labels of "spoken" and "written" should not be taken too seriously, for "spoken" Mongolian can be represented in writing, and informal writing approximates to speech in many ways, while "written" Mongolian can be spoken, and formal speech may approximate to the written language.) (p. 217)

All Binnick's fuss over two competing systems of grammar come to nothing when he insists that the distinction between spoken and written "should not be taken too seriously." It seems to this reviewer that Binnick needs to take spoken and written language much more seriously, and that it is Binnick that the reader should not take too seriously.

In these final pages Binnick not only takes the cake, he puts icing on it too. In the fourth chapter Binnick argued at length that the use and interpretation of the endings in the Mongolian tense system depend crucially upon context. On the third to the last page we are informed that "at its broadest, context includes everything the speaker knows, and all that he or she presumes that the addressee knows" (p. 218). If it is indeed the case that the use and interpretation of the Mongolian tenses are context dependent, then how can anyone write of "the inherent meaning of each particular ending" (p. 59) as though that exists independently of context, especially when context is everything that the speaker knows?

IV

Dukhan,
a Turkic Variety of Northern Mongolia[1]

The writing of a descriptive grammar presupposes that there is a valid reason for writing such a description, but in the grammars that I have read, those reasons are rarely mentioned, discussed, or justified by arguments. A rare instance of such discussion can be found in the introduction to Schmidt's 1831 *Grammatik der mongolischen Sprache*, where he mentions a number of possible reasons and makes clear why he has written his grammar:

> I am of the opinion that the Mongolian language and literature in no way deserve to be left out of account any longer, but that it is time to cultivate this language for the benefit and edification of Oriental studies...

---

[1] Review of: Elisabetta Ragagnin. *Dukhan, a Turkic Variety of Northern Mongolia: Description and Analysis.* Wiesbaden: Harrassowitz, 2011. (Turcologica, Bd. 76)

> There are also other perspectives on the usefulness of studying Mongolian. I will not touch upon the practical benefits for Russia's trade and industry, nor its political contacts and interests ... but will approach the matter solely from the side of scholarship and the benefits such study would bring to its various branches. (Schmidt, 1831: vi-vii)

adding a further note a few pages later:

> How different the skills and performance of the majority of our oriental translators would appear if along with better intellectual culture they brought also a knowledge of the grammar and literature of the language to the work where their services are required! (p. x-xi)

Schmidt was both a translator and a scholar, and these activities are offered as justification for writing a grammar. Ragagnin on the other hand offers no reasons and no justification. Her book is a revised version of her 2007 dissertation, and the dissertation written as part of the requirements for the degree but the publication of the book requires further justification. One may assume that the book has been published "for the benefit and edification of Oriental studies" just as Schmidt claimed for his work, but there are significant differences between the task Schmidt set himself and what Ragagnin has chosen to do. For Schmidt, there was a literature to study, and he insisted that the "provincialisms and dialect differences belong nowhere less than in the grammar of a language where they would tend to distract rather than instruct" (Schmidt, p. x). Ragagnin has no literature to study but only that spoken language that Schmidt dismissed.

This is indicative of the great reorientation of linguistics towards the spoken language that began with Saussure, but a number of remarks early in Ragagnin's book force the issue of Why? to the fore.

Her section on methodology begins with the claim "This study is a first systematic analysis of the sound system and morphology of Dukhan" (Ragagnin, p. 5). For many linguists, the description and analysis of linguistic systems is the whole point of linguistics, and this justification of linguistics is the justification of every particular description and analysis. Linguistic science is the accumulation of descriptions and the analyses based upon them, in a manner analogous to the description and analysis of chemical elements or biological organisms. Ragagnin is just doing science, and no justification or discussion is warranted because science is its own justification.

Although not explicitly stated, that this is how Ragagnin understands the what and why of her grammatical description seems clear from further remarks on this same page.

> The synchronic phonological description is taxonomic... The diachronic phonological dimension follows the model of Johanson... The impact of foreign languages on the lexicon, on the sound system and on the syntax of Dukhan is discussed in various sections of this study using the concepts and terms of the code-copying framework introduced by Johanson... the lexicon is discussed in terms of global, selective and mixed copying ... of a model code (p. 5)

Thus we are made aware of a number of important presuppositions, namely that we are classifying naturally occuring entities, that language is a code, and that this code exists in interaction with other codes. Summarizing her theoretical orientation, she offers her only justification for the book:

> it provides a substantial starting point for the analysis of Dukhan and a sufficient basis for further research. At the same time, this work is intended to be a contribution to the study of Siberian Turkic languages. (p. 6)

It is in this context, of language understood as a code interacting with other codes, that Ragagnin then launches into a discussion of the Dukhan people, "a Turkic-speaking nomadic group inhabiting the northernmost regions of Mongolia's Khövsgöl region" (p. 13). She uses "the English term Dukhan to refer to both the people and their language" (p. 13). The Dukhans have "adapted to changes in their environment due to outside forces", and "are subject to an ongoing process of Mongolization" (p. 16). Modern technology "should be considered as a positive factor for the preservation of their traditional lifestyle and the preservation of their native Turkic idiom" (p. 17). We learn that the Dukhan people "identify themselves as Dukha tu^hha, which is a phonetic variation of *tuva/tuba*, a designation common to various groups in the neighboring areas ... This name is generally connected with the *Du-bo ~ Tu-po* mentioned in Chinese sources" (p. 17). "The history of the Dukhan people before the twentieth century can not be traced independently of that of the neighboring peoples" she notes and then informs us of "the prevalent view of historians and Turcologists" that the "*tuva/tuba* were originally Samoyeds (i.e. speakers of languages belonging to the easternmost branch of the Uralic family) and Yeniseians (i.e. Paleosiberians) and were assimilated to Turkic in different historical times" (p. 18).

In these remarks we find the volatile mix of assumptions and associations that underlie her description and the linguistic theories that she reproduces. It is not only that she "follows" the Prague School and Johanson, nor that she uses the same term—Dukhan—for people and language, nor even that she traces this "self-identification" back to the sixth century. What is striking is that both language and ethnic group are treated as though they are natural phenomenon to be classified and analyzed when at the same time her ethnic groups (identified as originally Samoyeds on the basis of their language) turn into Turks and then Mongols. What kind of evolution is she presenting? Does changing one's language change one's ethnicity? Is this biolinguistics? Physical or social anthropology? An unquestioned carry-over from the 19th century?

Even more striking is that Ragagnin never once questions the theories she follows. Perhaps this has to do with the book's origin as a dissertation?

Matters change immediately when the author begins her discussion of the linguistic features of Dukhan on page 28. The people vanish and the code appears as a thing-in-itself. On page 28 Dukhan the code—not Dukhan the people—"displays those characteristics typical of the Turkic languages. ... Dukhan displays 16 vowel phonemes" (p. 28). Isn't a phoneme an artifact of Prague School analysis? If so, how can Dukhan "display" phonemes at all? The same question must be asked of the many other features found and "displayed" according to Ragagnin over the next few pages: "Dukhan displays the word classes nouns... The slot for aspect and mood can be filled by suffixes ... Dukhan displays an opposition of strong vs. weak consonants ... Dukhan displays the aspirated initial consonants ... " (p. 28-29) and on and on.

Is it just an infelicitous choice of words when Ragagnin describes Dukhan as "a well-behaved Turkic language" (p. 29)? What would a not so well behaved Turkic language do? Do languages in fact behave or misbehave?

Yet the matters discussed above did not strike me with nearly as much force as some statements in section 3.4 "Language status and use":

> Today, all Dukhans are bilingual in Dukhan and Darkhat Mongolian. Dukhan is used as the "in-group" language spoken within the narrow family circle. Darkhat Mongolian serves as the language for all spheres of communication outside the Dukhan community, especially in formal domains such as education and public administration. Dukhans freely switch from one language to the other, depending on the topic or the interlocutor. The high level of bilingualism allows speakers to copy Mongolic nominal and verbal elements and to integrate them into their basic code. ... They use one idiom or the other depending on the addressee. (p. 31-32)

The codes are understood to be natural objects "displaying" certain features which they may or may not share with other codes depending on ethnohistory, inbreeding, government policies and the use of modern communications technology. The situation as she describes it is entirely a social situation created by those codes, but her codes are at the same time presented as being threatened and endangered by that very situation in some cases, and positively affected in others.

> The fact that Dukhan people are quite famous in Mongolia (and beyond) as being the only reindeer herders of the country has the potential to positively affect the preservation of their native language. (p. 32)

If the Dukhan were originally Samoyedic, then Sayan Turkic, and now bilingual or monolingual Darkhat speakers, what does it mean to speak of "the preservation of their native language"? What sort of thing is language that it both defines and is defined by ethnicity as its speakers' understand it and at the same time endangered or protected by other people's speech, newspapers, education, government policy and reindeer herding? Ragagnin never considers the question, but she does note something that forced this reviewer to ask the question with which this review began: why describe Dukhan?

> Within the Dukhan community, there are many households where parents speak more Mongolian than Dukhan with their children. In mixed families, where one of the parents is Mongol, the children rarely master Dukhan. Only in rare cases do Mongols who are married to a Dukhan-speaking person learn the language. ... Today's mothers and father prefer not to speak Dukhan with their own children, in order to avoid the treatment they experienced in those days. Good knowledge of Mongolian is a necessary basis for acquiring a higher level of education in the city of Mörön or in the capital. (p. 32)

Thus it appears to be the case that Dukhan is not a well-behaved Turkic language after all and that rather than being threatened with extinction, it has been severely punished for its social failures, sentenced to death by the Dukhan people themselves.

If the Dukhan people do not want to speak Dukhan with their own children, why are linguists writing grammars of Dukhan? It cannot be—as it was for Schmidt—to enable scholars to read the literature, for there do not appear to be any texts available (Ragagnin mentions none). Nor is Ragagnin's grammar a pedagogical grammar: what use would there be for a pedagogical grammar of a language no one wants to speak?

What kind of linguistics offers us a 270 page description of a language that contains only one page on the status and use of that language? What Ragagnin provides us with is a description of what she heard of a language that no one wants to keep speaking, a description that linguists may enjoy reading but which tells us nothing at all about language as the Dukhan experience it. Had she spent her time and energies trying to understand and communicate to the reader why the Dukhan do not want to teach their language to their own children, we might have had a very interesting and important book. Yet such a description could not be based on an understanding of language such as that Ragagnin offers us, i.e. language as a code that interacts with other codes; it would have to be based on an understanding of language that is rooted in why people speak and to whom they are speaking, where and when. Ragagnin will have to subject the theoretical codes she has been reproducing to some probing scrutiny if she is to produce such a work in the future. Let us hope she does, for unlike most of us she can communicate with the Dukhan people, and that is the most important requirement of all.

V

Janhunen's *Mongolian*[1]

If I am not mistaken, Janhunen's first published paper on a Mongolian topic ("Preliminary notes on the phonology of Modern Bargut" *Studia Orientalia* (Helsinki) 64 (1988), pp. 353–366) caught the attention of my former professor Charles Kissiberth for he asked me in 1989 if I could find him any information on the Bargut dialect of Mongolian. Since that auspicious beginning Janhunen has published many more papers on Mongolian topics (42 as of 2012 according to Harry Halén's bibliography in *Suomalais-Ugrilaisen Seuran Toimituksia* vol. 264 (http://www.sgr.fi/sust/sust264/sust264_bibliography.pdf) with later publications listed on his web page on the Helsingin yliopisto website (https://tuhat.halvi.helsinki.fi/portal/en/persons/juha-janhunen(b535cfc7-918c-49a2-b61e-619e9706f1e)/publications.html).

---

[1] Review of: Juha A. Janhunen. *Mongolian*. Amsterdam/Philadelphia: John Benjamins Publishing Company, 2012. (London Oriental and African Languages Library, 19)

Of these many monographs and papers, I have only read the edited collection *The Mongolic Languages* (Routledge Language Family Series 5. London & New York: Routledge, Taylor & Francis Group 2003) and the monograph *Khamnigan Mongol* (Languages of the World / Materials 173. München: Lincom Europa 2005). The work reviewed here is the most substantial treatment of Mongolian that Janhunen has published.

The first thing that struck me in reading this book appears in the very blunt discussion that opens the Preface, namely Janhunen's almost complete lack of theoretical sense. The Preface begins with a statement of what he claims to be writing, namely a grammar that is a

> synchronic description of the Mongolian language. ... It differs from most of its predecessors ... by not being based on a specific dialect or standardized form of speech. Mongolian is a language spoken on a vast territory, written in two scripts and used orally in a large number of local forms. (page ix)

This is followed by a comment on the theoretical basis, or as he claims, the non-theoretical basis of his description:

> The description is focused on the qualitative analysis of the language in a rather strict form-to-function framework with no specific linguistic theory or quantitative corpus as a basis. (ibid.)

To write of "the language" is already making significant assumptions about what it is that he is describing; to acknowledge that there are multiple dialects, standard spoken forms and two written forms none of which form the basis of his description but all of which are to be understood as being "the Mongolian language" is simply to sweep aside all the fundamental theoretical issues of linguistics with one methodological decision while at the same time denying the theoretical import of that decision. A "strict form-to-function framework" also entails substantial theoretical underpinning, as does the comment that closes the paragraph, "diachrony is freely used as an explanatory tool, as it always should in a descriptive grammar" (ibid.). Having denied that he has any theoretical basis and admitting no quantitative corpus, he expects us to unblinkingly accept that he is offering us a qualitative analysis. If this is qualitative analysis, no wonder quantitatively oriented scientists want nothing to do with it.

The second matter that caught my attention may have some connection with the author's manner of writing English as a non-native speaker/writer, but I suspect the language he uses here signifies something more profound than a linguistic idiosyncracy and is in fact directly related to his attitute towards theory and the nature of descriptive linguistics. On page two we first encounter his use of the term "technically": "Mongolian is a member of a language family technically known as 'Mongolic'.'" On page three we are again confronted with the term: "the language of the historical Mongols once had relatives, today technically identified as the Para-Mongolic languages". If we inquire into the meaning of "technically" here and throughout the book, we find that we are to read the term as meaning in some instances "according to the theories espoused by Juha Janhunen," or, in those cases where he disagrees with another well-known analysis, according to the theories not espoused by Juha Janhunen, for there is no authority behind these technical explanations other than that Janhunen and other linguists, like-minded or not, have asserted them. Janhunen also uses other linguistic means to mask his assertions of scientific authority, for example when he uses a passive construction to justify the term "Common Mongolic":

> For the definition and delimitation of the Mongolian language, the branch of the most immediate relevance is Common Mongolic. Common Mongolic is probably best divided into six main entities, each of which is further divided into a number of local dialects and subdialects. The six main entities ... [etc.] (page 4)

Here we find descriptive linguistics at its worst: the linguist's methodological and theoretical assumptions and decisions are hidden behind "probably"s and passives, after which we move immediately into the strictly empirical (!?!) classification of those natural facts that the linguist calls "main entities," "dialects" and "subdialects". What is most astounding of all is that after writing the above passage, he follows it on the very next page with the dual admission that his definition of Mongolian "corresponds largely to the understanding of the ethnic Mongol layman" and Mongol linguists, but does not correspond to the views of Western linguists. "Ultimately, this is a matter of definition and terminology" (page 5) he states, and then concludes his discussion of Common Mongolic with the assertion

> It has to be concluded that Common Mongolic involves a complex network of isoglosses that allows several different taxonomic interpretations. For many purposes, Common Mongolic could also be described as a dialect chain, or a bundle of dialect chains, in which each individual can communicate with his or her neighbor, while many idioms separated by a physical distance may not be mutually intelligible. (pages 5-6)

Leaving aside whether his conclusions are as inevitable as he claims, we note that one key phrase here is "for many purposes." If linguistic descriptions and the taxonomy that underwrites them are dependent upon purposes, and those purposes may be political, religious or academic as his preceding discussion makes clear, what is the theoretical import of this recognition? Janhunen is oblivious to the theoretical consequences of his own theorising, and this is not surprising given his lack of awareness that he is even engaging in theoretical discussion: apparently the language of metalinguistics and of linguistic theory are intimately connected only for those who bother to think about it.

A second key phrase in the above quoted passage is that "each individual can communicate with his or her neighbor."

Here we must add a theory of communication into the very foundation of metalinguistic definitions, but nothing more about this from Janhunen and mutual intelligibility does not seem to have any importance to the definition of Mongolian, Mongolic or Common Mongolic.

In the next two sections, 1.4 *The Literary languages* and 1.5 *Dialectal division*, we are treated to this same mixture of authoritative assertations and definitions that betray no evidence that Janhunen has grasped any of the theoretical issues that such assertions and definitions require as a basis. We read of Written Mongol that "in its early form it was essentially identical with contemporary spoken Middle Mongol, complicated only by certain orthographical conventions" (page 6). Now I would like to know how anyone could possibly know how Written Mongol "reinforced by Chinggis Khan as a general medium of administration and literature" could in any way be identical to any spoken language of any date, given that we are dealing with two entirely different media, a semi-permanent written mark in Written Mongol, and an ephemeral audio-acoustic experience in any spoken language. Given that spoken Mongolian languages/dialects/subdialects/idiolects are characterized by tremendous variety over geographical space as well as time, one would have to assume that either at the time of the creation of Written Mongol no such variation existed or the speech of one man at one time and place was codified—and both of those hypotheses are untenable on the basis of the written records.

What clearly underwrites and informs Janhunen's assertions is a theory of the relation between speech and writing. Whatever may be the theory to which he subscribes, it allows him to write that "apart from the system of writing, the linguistic difference between Written Mongol and Cyrillic Khalkha is not great, and both written languages can be used to write down the same oral message" (page 7). This apparently indicates that the "oral message" precedes the written message and "the language" must therefore be a spoken form. However, in the following paragraph we find this:

> It follows from the preceding that the Mongolian language is best defined as the complex of Common Mongolic dialects that morphosyntactically correspond to the principles underlying Written Mongol and/or Cyrillic Khalkha. (page 8)

He continues with the remark

> the Mongolian language, thus defined, is not identical with any particular written language or uniform standard of speech, rather it is a complicated network of a diversity of oral idioms, which are in a dialectal relationship to each other. Written Mongol and Cyrillic Khalkha, as they are currently used, are best seen as artifacts whose function is to serve as the written mediums for all the underlying oral forms of speech. ...
> Neither Written Mongol nor Cyrillic Khalkha should therefore be assumed to correspond to the phonological structure of any actual dialect or subdialect of Mongolian; rather, they are simply two conventionalized ways to convey oral messages in writing. (page 8)

A few pages later we learn that Mongolian has "a structural identity" and that "this is, without doubt, connected with the unifying influence of Written Mongol" (page 12). Are the written forms of Mongolian simply conventionalized ways to convey oral messages? In writing this sentence alone Janhunen betrays not only a lack of theoretical perspicacity but a complete lack of reading and reflecting on writing. The "without doubt" that he writes in place of argument and analysis in his explanation of the "structural identity" of Mongolian does not hide the fact that the "structural identity" he claims for this "complicated network of a diversity of oral idioms" is due to "simply conventionalized ways to convey oral messages." What does it mean that the structure of a diversity of oral idioms is due to writing? Janhunen is totally confused on this and all related points precisely because he believes that theory is irrelevant to description, as though description does not entail analysis and analysis does not presuppose a theory of language.

While Janhunen posits a diversity of oral idioms/dialects/subdialects/idiolects he has no theory of variation. What are the consequences of declaring "the Mongolian language" to be "a complicated network of a diversity of oral idioms"? The very handy consequence for Janhunen is that he can then claim to offer "a dialectally unbiased presentation", a grammar that would "serve the purpose of fully describing the underlying language," something that he claims Svantesson's 2003 grammar cannot do. Unfortunately, it also means that his full description of the underlying language corresponds to no actually existing forms of any language or dialect, spoken or written (i.e. cannot be justified or critiqued on any empirical basis).

Given this definition of Mongolian (and presumably, any other language), it is strange to find the author refering to "Khalkha proper", "Khorchin proper" and "Mongolian proper, in the form of Khalkha." In similar fashion Janhunen argues that although Ordos is "strictly speaking a distinct (sub)-branch of Common Mongolic" and treated as a dialect of Mongolian, "linguistically this is questionable" (page 19). This stylistic preference for describing matters as technically, properly, strictly-speaking, etc. is a clear indication of Janhunen's avoiding theoretical questions, asking the reader to avoid them, and expecting his authority and knowledge to prevail over any questions that might arise.

The data he discusses are presented in phonemic transcription, which is to say he is presenting a post-analysis written form of an underlying unwritten language that is itself a linguist's abstraction from a disparate array of variants recorded by others and perhaps from time to time by the author himself. Yet even though he frequently comments on the possibilities of divergent analyses (for example on page 32 "there are many possible ways to describe the internal organization of the paradigm", on page 44 "a virtually identical phonetic sequence ... can be interpreted in two different ways", on page 62 it is "not immediately clear whether the vowel appearing at the morpheme boundary belongs to the stem or to the suffix", on page 105 "it is difficult to tell how many cases exactly there are ... The answer depends on what stand is taken with regard to the borderline between derivation and inflection...") all such cases are solved by a simple assumption without any discussion of the theoretical significance of each particular decision, much less the larger theoretical and methodological issue of presenting data that are constructed out of theoretical assumptions as much as (and often more than) any empirical data. Thus the analysis of the vowel paradigm is solved by an "it will be assumed", the divergent analyses of identical phonetic sequences is explained by two different dialects, the vowel at the morpheme boundary is explained by insisting that since synchronically the stem must end in a consonant, then the vowel must belong to the suffix, and the number of cases is dealt with by positing eight basic cases and a few marginal cases!

Janhunen's book offers the reader once again more of what so marred the earlier books of his which I have read. If a reader can tolerate all the assertions, the pompous style, the confusions and contradictions that follow from a lack of theoretical questions and clarity, there may be much to learn from this book. I am not such a reader and consequently cannot recommend this book to anyone.

VI

Studies in Mongolic Historical Morphology
Verb Formation in the Secret History of the Mongols[1]

In the study of the history of languages, two of the most common pursuits are etymology and the reconstruction of unattested forms; the latter are nearly always discussed as phonological reconstructions, but morphological and syntactic reconstructions are not unknown. Etymological researchers attempt to connect the meanings of what the etymologist assumes are earlier forms of a word with later meanings of the same word or with later and different forms that are assumed to have descended/developed from the earlier forms. Sometimes they also engage in proposing unattested earlier combinations of forms and meanings, hypothetical ancestors of a later attested word and its meanings. Problems of form and meaning go hand in hand in

---

[1] Review of: Béla Kempf. *Studies in Mongolic Historical Morphology: Verb Formation in the Secret History of the Mongols*. Wiesbaden: Harrassowitz Verlag, 2013. (Turcologica, 95)

etymology, as they do in phonological reconstruction, because the definition of a linguistic unit (at least within all theoretical positions ultimately relying upon Saussure) is a unity of form and meaning; the problems of synonymy and homonymy—which remain vexing to all who face them head on—usually being ignored in order to be able to proceed at all. In all such historical research and reconstruction concerning language prior to the 20th century, whether the history of meanings, of sound change, or of forms phonological or otherwise, the sole means of access to that language is through written documents for it is only since the late 19th century that anyone has produced sound recordings permitting us to listen to our predecessors rather than having to rely entirely on the written texts they produced.

As Kempf's treatise deals with derivational morphology, his analysis combines both semantic and phonological reconstruction on the basis of written documents, in particular the reconstructed text of the *Secret History*. His primary aim, he states, is "to examine the verbalization processes of Middle Mongol as it appears in the Mnt [=Mongol nuuts tovchoo]" (page 15) and to characterize the derivational elements he finds, which he does through an "examination in an empirical way, the starting point for the characterization being the text itself" (page 16). And here, alas, is where Kempf's theoretical troubles begin: an empirical study based on a reconstruction.

He suggests (on page 18) that "A very important failing of practically all periodization sketches of Mongolic language history is that they are strictly connected to the appearance of the written sources" but what he sees as their failure might be better described as the limitations of investigations that intend to be empirically based. The failure of the historical sketches Kempf has in mind surely cannot arise from their empirical basis, but from the theoretical assumptions made about that written basis and its relation to spoken language and the history of human communication. Kempf's failure is, if anything, far more serious than the earlier studies he criticizes.

Kempf proposes to base his periodization of Mongolian on "the period when a Mongolic linguistic unity existed. We may call this Proto-Mongolic, which may be approached via linguistic reconstructions based on all diachronic and synchronic material" (page 19). At some point, according to Kempf, "an extralinguistic factor entered the periodization: the use of writing" (page 19). With this starting point, Kempf grounds his entire project in a theoretical confusion rooted in two impossible assumptions: that there ever was or ever could be a linguistic situation characterized by an absence of variation, and that it is into this situation that writing as a representation of speech is first introduced. The theoretical problem was pointed out 50 years ago in a 1967 review of *Latino 'circa romançum' e rustica romana lingua*, a collection of 7-9th century texts:

> One is surprised to find that the discussion of scriptae is conducted without any reference to the complex problems of correspondence between written and spoken languages. The subject is touched upon only in the appendix, and there only in connection with phonetics. One would like to have seen in the preface a reminder of the variety of types of relation which may obtain between spoken and written discourse. For it is doubtful whether the beginner can make much of the notion of the development of a scripta at all, unless he is given some idea of the level or levels of abstraction involved. Without such guidance, he tends to be left with the impression that at one time (in some idealized Classical period) Latin was 'written as it was spoken', and that gradually the spoken language changed while the written language remained static, or lagged far behind, until the post-Carolingian period when the new vernaculars were again 'written as they were spoken'. ... Thus the fact that there is any linguistic problem as regards how changes in a spoken language may be expected to give rise to changes in a corresponding written language becomes obscured. (Roy Harris, *Medium Aevum* v.36 nr. 1. 52-54)

Kempf's introduction offers an interesting overview of some of the theoretical issues he sees involved in his project, and although brief, his criticisms of Janhunen's periodization (page 18) are important. The value of the monograph lies in his having drawn together information regarding verbal morphology that cannot be easily found by perusing a dictionary, but he does not—and cannot—provide the reader with anything that could shed light on pre-literate oral forms of Mongolian. What he knows of 13th century Mongolian is its written forms, the main source being a reconstructed written text derived from a much later text utilizing a different writing system. The morphological reconstructions he produces are themselves written representations of what he believes—and what he would have the reader believe—were the spoken forms that predated Mongol literacy, yet these have been produced on the basis of assumptions about the relationship between writing and speech that cannot stand up to any scrutiny. In the end, Kempf offers us a catalog of a linguist's fictions that in no way informs us about the linguistic situation of the Mongols prior to the introduction of writing. Instead of leading us forward in our understanding of linguistic prehistory, we are led further than ever backwards into theoretical confusion.

VII

On Quotation in Middle Mongolian
The Verb *ke(m)e-* 'to say'[1]

A caveat lector is in order for this review since the book reviewed was published by The Mongolia Society, the same as the publisher for this journal, and the Society's Managing Editor who accepted the book for publication was none other than the present reviewer. Generally such institutional self-promotion through self-review is inadmissable, but I hope to justify this review on other grounds than self-promotion, individual or institutional. It ought to be acceptable enough to simply indicate that the review that follows is not presented as an unbiased review but rather an open record of the reasons the Managing Editor agreed to publish the volume. My remarks are, however, more than that, for in fact I was thrilled with the book for reasons that

---

[1] Review of: John C. Street. *On Quotation in Middle Mongolian: The Verb ke(m)e- 'to say'*. Bloomington, Indiana: The Mongolia Society, 2013. (Occasional papers 27)

I want to make known and publishing those reasons here seems reasonable to me. Finally, there is yet another reason that I wanted to publish my remarks on this book even though I clearly have what other reviewers or readers might consider a conflict of interests: I enjoy and very much want to write about a book that I can recommend whole-heartedly, and any reader of my reviews of other books in the last two issues of this journal will know that I have not been lavish with my praise of recent linguistics treatises. In the remarks that follow I want to indicate not only why I thought the book deserved to be published, but what distinguishes Professor Street's approach to his topic from so much of linguistics as it is done today and makes his book more valuable than many other publications of the past few decades.

First of all, Street's book discusses the language of an historical linguistic document, not an hypothetical reconstruction or set of examples pulled out of his native or non-native speaker's intuition (although on pages 61-62 he does lay out two tables of examples that are mostly hypothetical and marked as such). This means nothing less than that any arguments about Street's analysis can be made upon the basis of the very same data upon which he relies, with no possibility of dismissing data as being due to different dialects, foreign influence or some other popular means of dismissing evidence.

Street is also very clear from the beginning that the language he is dealing with is a written document which has been reconstructed upon the basis of a much later document written in a script developed for purposes quite different from writing Mongolian. Nevertheless, his choice of topic—direct and indirect quotation involving the written verb *ke(m)e*/to say—forces him to confront matters concerning the relationship between spoken and written language, and Street's approach to this is markedly different from any other linguist whose works I have reviewed in the pages of *Mongolian Studies*. Read his remarks on "Full (onset-marked) direct quotation" on page 16:

> The clearest instances of quotation in Middle Mongolian are those in which the limits of a sequence purporting to be a repetition of some separate speech event are overtly marked by a prior preparatory converb in *–(U)rUn* and a concluding *ke(m)e-*. These two elements in effect act as the spoken equivalents of opening and closing quotation marks.

Now this passage either records a remarkable accident or a carefully worded statement of theoretical import; in light of the volume as a whole, I am convinced that it is no accident. Since what is being discussed in the original text is a speech event—an utterance about which someone is writing, and not a written passage about which someone wrote or spoke—the comparison of the spoken verbal forms to written quotation marks is appropriate. But note that these words are described as acting in effect as spoken equivalents of written symbols; written quotation marks are not and can in no way be described as representing speech anymore than the spoken verbs can be described as oral representations of written quotation marks. The difference in formulation and description is crucial: spoken language utilizes certain strategies to indicate to the hearer that some portion of the utterance was earlier spoken by someone else, while written language can and must use an entirely different kind of marker.

Another matter related to writing is found in his remarks on ambiguities. The book is full of discussions of possibly ambiguous passages, but theory rarely decides upon an interpretation. Instead, we find that Street suggests that the ambiguities are located in the written language but not necessarily present to hearers (the original hearers or those to whom the text may have been read). On page 19 for example, he notes that "it is not always clear whether one of these modifies the ...*ügüle-* clause or the entire clause ending in *kee-*. Presumably pauses in the spoken language would have clarified this for a hearer." This is followed later on with the remark that "Many passages that now seem potentially ambiguous may well have been disambiguated in the spoken language by features not represented in the writing systems." Here again, Street recognizes that the ambiguities a 20th century American reader finds in a (largely) decontextualised written document were not necessarily ambiguities for a contemporary hearer of the originally spoken passage, and that the spoken strategies for avoiding ambiguity do not necessarily have any counterparts in a written document recording that conversation.

The single most important reason that I liked this book so much was that Street focuses all of his attention upon what the passages in question mean, all of them selected for their inclusion of one particular written form. By focusing upon meaning he necessarily set his entire inquiry within the context of human communicative activity, a context vast enough to do justice to all of the facts of spoken and written language. What he examines and questions is how certain written forms can reveal the meanings that were the *raison d'être* of their production. This orientation led or at least permitted him to engage written language at its origin, the speaker or writer who has something to say or write, and who makes his meaning clear through, in this particular case, the written version of the *Secret History*. The only authority that peers through his prose is the authority of the author(s) of the *Secret History*, and this is something Street seeks to discover rather than merely assert. His treatment is in sharp contrast to Janhunen's analysis of Mongolian, for whom phonology and morphology count, but meaning and strategies for communicating meanings to others "should not be exaggerated at the expense of the actual grammar" (Juha A. Janhunen, *Mongolian*, Amsterdam: Benjamins, 2012: 289). For Street, actual grammar depends entirely upon what the writer/speaker meant, not upon the linguist's analysis, and that difference of theoretical orientation makes a world of difference to this reader.

Part II

Writing and Reading Mongolian Stories and Histories

VIII

Ramon Llull's Mongols[1]

I

Elizabeth Endicott opened her study of Mongolian rule in China with the following observation:

> The period of Mongolian rule in China, in its broadest sense 1206-1368, gives the historian an opportunity to examine the process by which two separate cultures and societies coexist, interact, and change one another.[2]

In this paper I would like to offer a brief sketch of one particular individual's response to Mongolian rule in China as an example of how two separate cultures and societies coexist, interact, and change one another in the space of one man's imagination and

---

[1] A paper originally read before the Mongolia Society at its Annual Meeting April Fool's Day 2005, here revised, with a bibliography and a selection of excerpts.

[2] *Mongol rule in China: local administration in the Yuan Dynasty*. Cambridge, Mass. : Council on East Asian Studies, Harvard University, 1989.

the limited knowledge and misinformation which informed it. Thus, it is not a work devoted to the history of the Mongols understood as what really happened (*res gestae*), nor is it a work of Mongolian or European history understood as the sort of thing that historians write about what they think actually happened (*historiae*); rather it is a study of public opinion (*opinio*): history as the non-historian knows and imagines it, since Llull was neither a historian nor a first hand observer of the Mongols. What Llull offers to the historian (and anyone else) is a glimpse of how 13th century Europeans thought, knew and imagined the Mongols, the origins of a legacy of thoughts and imaginations which remains evident in the ideas and attitudes towards the Mongols found frequently amongst non-mongolists and in the mass media in our time. It is because misinformation, the imaginary, falsehood and deception fashion the world as much as ideologies and truth that we must look back not only towards what really happened (the *res gestae*, which we can only imaginatively reconstruct as *historiae*) but to what really happened as that was known and understood according to the minds and imaginations of contemporaries. And for that we have a very clear record: we will never know for sure the whole story of what really happened, but we do know what certain people thought was happening and what they considered important.[3]

Ramon Llull (1232-1316) mentioned the Mongols several times in his early works, from the *Doctrina pueril* of 1275 through the 1288 dialogue *Liber Tartari et Christiani*, but it was in the latter part of his writing life and after that dialogue of 1288 that he returned again and again to the Mongols, in poems, in dialogues, in letters to kings and popes, and in treatises on science, theology, missions and the politico-military situation in the Muslim lands. What he knew about the Mongols and how much he knew is difficult to determine; why his remarks on the Mongols should be of interest to Mongolists is also difficult

---

[3] For these distinctions and the terminology I am indebted to the linguist Roy Harris for his typically brilliant insights in *The linguistics of history* (Edinburgh, 2004).

to assess, but I hope to convince at least some readers that his Mongols are worth investigating.

The importance of Llull in European intellectual history is difficult to evaluate; the appreciation of Llull in European intellectual history reveals vastly different responses to his work. One aspect of Llull's work which has attracted considerable attention, both admiration and repudiation, is his use of dialog as a literary form. It was in a study of Ramon's dialogues that I first stumbled upon a discussion of the *Liber Tartari et Christiani*, and it was my interest in both dialogue as a genre and in Llull as the author of the *Book of the Lover and the Beloved* that led me to pick up that book in early 2004. The ultimate goal of my own study of Llull's work is to understand just how dialogic were Llull's dialogues and just how Mongol were Llull's Mongols. Both of those questions seemed easy to answer at first: the dialogues were real dialogues, the Mongols imaginary fictions. Neither of those questions appear to be answerable after even a cursory reading of Llull and llullian scholarship. As in the most profound of dialogues, the reader of Llull is left with questions, not answers.

II

There are two salient characteristics of Llull's Mongols: they always appear in a religious context, and Llull's particular obsession is the possibility of forming a Mongol-Christian alliance to defeat the Saracens. This religious context, appearing as it does in the midst of the crusades, has led many to see in Llull's dialogues little more than a facade for medieval religious intolerance and crusading passions, a facade which was simply abandoned in his late dialogues and numerous proposals for a crusade in Palestine. On the other hand, Llull has been widely praised as the most tolerant of medieval thinkers and even the advocate of a postmodern liberalism. Let me begin with one remarkable passage from Ramon's novel *Blaquerna*, that novel in which the notion of a united nations organization and a binding international law first appear in European thought. The Mongols appear here in a prayer to the Virgin Mary:

> Ave María! Saluts taport dels sarraíns, jueus, grecs, mogols, tartres, búlgars, ongres de Ungaria la menor, comans, nestorins, rossos, guinovins: tots aquests e molts daltres infeels te saluden per mi qui som lur procurador. En la tua salutació los met, per ço que lo teu Fill los fulla remembrar e que tu acabtes ab ell com los trameta missatges quils endrecen a conèxer e a amar tu e ton Fill, en tal manera ques pusquen salvar e en est mon sapien e vullen tu e ton Fill, de tot lur poder, servir e honrar.
>
> Ave María! Aquests infeels per qui jot salut han innorancia de la tua salut e del honrament que Deus tà donat. Homens son. Semblant natura e figura han del teu Fill que tu tant ames e per quí tant est amada e honrada. En foc perdurable van per innorancia. La gloria perdurable de ton Fill perden, car no es quils preic ni quils demostre veritat de la santa fe catòlica. Boques han ab quet sabríen loar sit conexíen, cor han ab quet puríen amar, mans han ab quet puríen servir, peus han ab que poríen anar per les tues carreres. Tu est digna que per totes gents e que en totes terrres fosses coneguda servida amada loada. Saludente. Ajuda e gracia e benedicciò te demanen per mi.[4]

Hail Mary! I bring you greetings from the Saracens, the Jews, the Greeks, the Mongols, the Tartars, the Bulgars, the Hungarians of Lesser Hungary, the Comans, the Nestorians, the Russians, the Guinovins: all of these and many other unbelievers greet thee through me as their representative. I bring to thee their greetings, to the end that thy Son may desire to have remembrance of them, and that thou mayest beg Him to send to them ministers

---

[4] ORL v.9 p. 211-212.

who may lead them to know and to love thee and thy Son, in such manner that they may be saved, and in this world, may know and desire thee and thy Son, to serve and to honor him and thee with all their power.

Hail Mary! These unbelievers, on whose behalf I greet thee, have ignorance concerning thy salutation and the honor that God has bestowed upon you. They are human. They have the same nature and form as your Son whom you so love and by whom you are so much loved and honored; they go through ignorance to the eternal fire; they lose the eternal glory of your Son, for there is no one to preach to them nor to demonstrate to them the truth of the holy Catholic faith. Mouths they have with which they would praise you if they knew you, hearts they have which would love you, hands they have which would serve you, feet they have with which they would follow your path. You deserve to be known, served, loved and praised by all peoples. They greet you. Your help, grace and blessings they ask of you through me.[5]

There are two matters which struck me most in this prayer. First, the fact that the Mongols and the Tartars are both mentioned, as though Llull considers them two distinct peoples; in his entire works *mogols* appears in only one other passage, everywhere else he refers only to *tartres/tartins* or *tartars*, and when he gives any descriptive statements, it is clear that he is using *tartars* in the manner of his time, i.e. to refer to the Mongols. The second matter is the statement *Homens son* = They are human. This is another striking characteristic of Llull's treatment of the Mongols: in only two or three passages throughout Llull's entire corpus can one find the statement that the Mongols are barbarians or an implied comparison with the Romans who are a "bestial" people. For Llull, the Mongols are, categorically and emphatically, neither monsters nor demons but

---

[5] The translation is a slightly altered version of E. Allison Peer's translation (*Blanquerna*, 1926).

human beings. In the *Liber Tartari et Christiani* the principal character is a Mongol whom Llull describes as "very wise and knowledgeable in philosophy," a description which is rather unusual for 13th century European writers. More importantly, it should be noted that Llull's remark "They are humans" is followed by the reminder that these Mongols, Tartars and other gentiles have the same nature and form as Mary's Son whom Ramon of course believed to be the Son of God, with hands, feet, hearts and all the rest. I am reminded of the lines of a later fictional Jew:

> I am a Jew. Hath not a Jew eyes? hath not a Jew hands, organs, dimensions, senses, affections, passions? fed with the same food, hurt with the same weapons, subject to the same diseases, healed by the same means, warmed and cooled by the same winter and summer, as a Christian is? If you prick us, do we not bleed? if you tickle us, do we not laugh? if you poison us, do we not die? and if you wrong us, shall we not revenge? If we are like you in the rest, we will resemble you in that. (Shylock, in Shakespeare's *Merchant of Venice*)

This is one point in favor of declaring that Llull's Mongols, while perhaps imperfectly known by Llull, were certainly real Mongols because Llull understood them to be real humans and not mythical beasts from some apocalyptic vision.

III

Llull was also connected to numerous significant persons and events in Mongol-European relations, but his relationship to four particular moments are tantalyzing precisely because they are impossible to document. The first of these is the relationship of Llull to Rubruck: did Llull read Rubruck's report or otherwise gain familiarity with its contents? If he did, he paid selective attention to those contents. The second is the Second Council of Lyon, which Llull did not attend; the third concerns the mission of Rabban Shauma and the fourth Llull's relationship with Haytun of Armenia. Of these last two matters, much has been written in llullian scholarship, but I am unaware of this literature having been mined by mongolists. The Second Council of Lyon is of course, like the First Council of Lyon, well known among mongolists as a significant event in the history of European-Mongol relations; Llull's relation to the council is, I suspect, one of learning for it is only after this Council that the Mongols appear in Llull's writings. There are other matters of interest, such as Llull's plans for a school to teach Mongolian, but for my own interests, the relationship between Rubruck's report and Llull's passions, his art, his method and his life is the most tantalyzing of all.[6]

Rubruck was a Franciscan; Ramon was at once committed to becoming a Dominican but so attracted by the Franciscan order that he was never able to enter either order; he remained a layman his entire life. Rubruck was the instigator of the famous religious debates at the court of Möngke; Llull was the author of numerous interreligious dialogues, including the remarkable *Libre del gentil e los tres savis*. Rubruck's method in his debates were based upon his recognition of two requirements: the need to present a united front among the Christians and the desirability of beginning the debates by affirming the common ground between the Christians and the Muslims. Llull's *Art*, that method for logically demonstrating the truth which was revealed to him (he declared) by God on Mount Randa in 1274, was based upon beginning all discussion from a basis upon which all disputants could agree and in Llull's dialogues, that common basis

---

[6] Citations are rare in Llull's works, and those which appear in his late works cannot be assumed to have influenced his very early orientation towards missions, Muslims and Mongols. In the several publications devoted to the sources of Llull's thought Roger Bacon is frequently discussed as a possibility but Rubruck is never mentioned. The primary suspects in his early education (1263-1275) are the Franciscans of Mallorca and Montpelier and their libraries. See J.N. Hillgarth, "La Biblioteca de La Real: fuentes posibles de Llull" *Estudios Lulianos* 7 1963.

was assumed to underlie Judaism, Christianity and Islam. Rubruck did not proceed by arguing from scripture, since, he acknowledged, the Muslims do not share the same scripture; Llull's entire art of demonstration rests on the rational demonstration of the Catholic faith with no reliance on the authority of scripture. Rubruck's debates were sponsored by and keenly observed by the ruler of the world who established the rules of conduct; the gentile of Llull's *Libre del gentil e los tres savis* presides over the debate, being the one who asks questions, seeks clarification of concepts and explanations. At least one scholar has argued that in Llull's dialogues the unbeliever is *required* for the pacific and orderly proceedings as well as forcing the disputants to rely on logic and mutual agreement rather than scriptural authority.[7] In Rubruck's debates the participants are forbidden to speak injuriously or aggressively towards other participants, that each would speak in turn, and any violations of Möngke's stipulated conditions would be punishable by death. Llull's *Libre del gentil e los tres savis* is a debate in which the representatives of the three monotheistic religions—Judaism, Christianity and Islam—present their respective theologies with the utmost courtesy, each in turn acknowledging their points of agreement with what has been argued by the preceding debater(s) (e.g. concerning monotheism, the attributes of God).

No doubt some scholars would consider the possibility that it was not God but something that Llull read or heard which revealed the *Art* to him, or perhaps it was a simple product of the spirit of the times, "in the air" as we say of ideas like crusades, relativism and rationalism. The traditional date of that revelation is 1274; the Second Council of Lyon opened in 1274; Llull wrote or began writing his *Libre del gentil e los tres savis* probably in 1274. References to the Mongols in Llull's writings date from 1274 at the earliest; the first certain appearance is in a work of 1275. Since speculation can get us anywhere and thus

---

[7] The gentile of the *Libre del gentil e los tres savis* becomes a Mongol in the *Liber Tartari et Christiani*.

nowhere, I will not speculate on what he may have read and when he might have read it. The fact remains that the similarities between Rubruck's account of the manner in which the debates took place—and we know almost nothing more about Rubruck than his report to St. Louis—and Llull's lifelong preoccupations in his writing and missionary activities are remarkably similar. I would like to suggest that an understanding of Rubruck's debates and Llull's intellectual and spiritual project may be read as two realizations of a single project, whether these are based upon some work which I do not know, a Franciscan ideal, or perhaps Llull was directly inspired by Rubruck's report. If Llull was influenced by Rubruck's account, then we have a wonderful case of an event in Mongolia profoundly shaping European thought in a most positive manner.

IV

Amador Vega's recent book on Llull turns our attention from Llull's preoccupation with the compelling rationality which converts the Other to that other orientation of Llull's complex thought: the relationship between lover and beloved, the relationship of alterity which alters all persons involved, a relation which informs Llull's early writings as much as and—at least some have suggested—even more than his later works. My own interest in Llull was for many years rooted in an appreciation of his desire for and lifelong devotion to encountering the other. It may be that his insistence upon the Mongols as human beings actually arises from the revelation of the other as the beloved rather than being due simply to a logical analysis, the workings of his *Art*. In the case of Llull's attitudes towards Muslims, his knowledge and love of the Koran certainly played a determining role in his attention to the Muslim world, and the sources of his *Art* have been located in both Arabic philosophy and Jewish Cabala, an extensive knowledge of both of these distinguishing him from all of his Christian contemporaries.[8]

Vega noted that for Llull the lover and the beloved are necessary terms, and for Llull the Oriental Other shaped and made his entire post-conversion life. He quotes Llull from the *Book of the lover and the beloved*, one of the sections of *Blaquerna*:

> The secrets of the beloved are revealed in the secrets of the lover, and the secrets of the lover are revealed in the secrets of the beloved. And the question is, which of these two secrets is the greater occasion for revelation? (*Book of the Lover and the Beloved*, p.160)

and then continues with the following statement:

> The entire paradoxical world of Llull is contained in these verses. Just as we saw the impossibility of knowing any order of things in itself except through knowledge of another and different order, that is, beginning from the experience of alterity (which implies in this case a personification of the divinity), so here, too, the lover and the beloved are presented as distinct and necessary terms. ... Revelation takes place only in the encounter of the lover and the beloved, in the knowledge that their mutual love brings, and in the love that the knowledge of both makes possible.[9]

In the prayer to the Virgin quoted above, Llull's relationship to the Mongols is unquestionably one of lover to beloved;

---

[8] Llull's first book was on Ghazzālī and the model for his *Libre del gentil e los tres savis* is probably the *Hayy ibn Yaqzān* of the Andalusian philosopher Ibn Tufayl (d. 1185).

[9] Amador Vega, *Ramon Llull y el secreto de la vida*. Madrid: Ediciones Siruela, 2002. Cited from the Eng. translation by James Heisig: *Ramon Llull and the secret of life*. New York:Crossroad Publishing Co., 2003.

yet unless he met some Mongols during his travels in Lesser Armenia in 1301 or 1302, Llull's encounter with the Mongols was probably never face to face, his knowledge of the Mongols second hand at best.[10] Although probably partially informed through conversations with Franciscans who had traveled within the Mongolian domains, it is likely that Llull's knowledge was derived primarily from tales circulating during his lifetime and reading reports such as those written by John of Plano Carpini, Benedict the Pole and William of Rubruck or works based upon them (e.g. Roger Bacon). He may have met Haytun of Armenia; at any rate the similarity of Llull's remarks on the politico-military situation and proposals are repeated in almost identical fashion in Haytun's book a few years after Llull's visit to Armenia: perhaps they shared information with each other or held ideas and understandings in common or both. In addition, Llull almost certainly had some occasion to speak to Rabban Shauma and his entourage, or at least hear about this embassy from some of the participants while the ambassadors were in the same city as he was. The available information was abundant and Llull responded to it with treatises, proposals and travels.

What Llull brought to those oral or literary encounters was his passion for engaging the other, the foreign, the stranger, the non-christian; what he took from them and what he made of what he learned is directly revealed in only a few paragraphs in 23 of his written works (my count so far), yet the broad trajectory of his thought and certain recurring themes in his works suggest that what he had heard or read about the Mongols had a significant role in shaping the intellectual basis for the two salient orientations characterizing his entire career: the desirability of free, open, public debate concerning the truth about the world and God, and the idea of securing that possibility through

---

[10] However: Llull was a page at the Aragonese court of James I, tutor to James II and later his seneschal. Long ago I read somewhere that there were two Mongol captives at the court of James I in Aragon—I can no longer remember where I read about this, but it did catch my eye (DB, September 2020).

a secular power which would both demand mutual respect among debaters and prevent the suppression of debate by religious authorities.

For Llull, both preaching and missions were profoundly dialogic practices requiring respect for and protection of those engaging in them.[11] William of Rubruck's account of the religious debates held in the presence of the Mongol Khaan—or some later retelling of this story—may have been the good news that he discovered, the revelation of a hitherto unknown possibility: politically providing and securing the space for philosophical and religious debate, and perhaps even the nature of such debates. In the European and Judeo-Christian traditions forming the intellectual life of the time, neither political nor religious authorities had sought to protect much less promote religious and philosophical debate and the search for knowledge and truth: Socrates was killed, as was Jesus, the Inquisition and persecution of heretics was at its worst, and Llull himself was thrown in prison and condemned to death by the Islamic authorities in North Africa (saved from execution—as one legend

---

[11] But not always. The difficulties encountered in attempting to combine dialogue and alterity with a system of rational argumentation which (Llull believed) would be irrefutable and compelling are nowhere more evident than in the law which was passed giving Ramon Llull by name the right to preach in all mosques and synagogues in the kingdom. That right was combined with Llull's opinion that perhaps those Jews and Muslims who failed to be converted, i.e. convinced by the truth as set forth according to his *Art*, should be expelled from the kingdom since they must be enemies of the truth if they fail to be convinced. Llull has not been sainted and there are many reasons why he should not be. However, the compatibility or incompatibility of anyone's notions of truth and freedom has been a difficulty in virtually all religious, philosophical, political and scientific debate and Llull is in the same boat as Galileo, Marx, Freud, Wittgenstein, Chomsky and Osama bin Laden: those who know the Truth are rarely capable of allowing for the possibility that the Truth may be other than what they know. In his use of his *Art* and its compelling logic, Llull can be terrifying and totalitarian; yet his life as he lived it is an extraordinary story of encounter, dialog and intercourse with the many worlds of medieval difference. I plan to deal with this tension in Llull's thought in more detail in a work in progress.

has it—by the efforts of a Muslim philosopher who wanted to go to Europe without getting executed). Rubruck's account of his public debates, promoted, mediated and protected by the Mongol Khaan who himself listened to the entire proceedings must have been an astonishing tale to the 13th century Europeans. Llull's dreams of free and open, safe and respectful debates concerning knowledge and truth about the most important things, elaborated in detail from his earliest works, e.g. the *Libre del gentil e los tres savis,* were perhaps conceived in response to Rubruck's tale, or simply confirmed as possible because already realized in the great country of the Mongol Khaan. For Llull the Catholic (and perhaps also, as he once felt, Ramon the coward), seeking a European/Christian alliance with the Mongols was rooted in his desire to create the conditions within which that exchange of ideas could take place without undue dangers and martyrdom. The Mongols had proven that they could and would not simply tolerate debate but sponsor it and take a serious interest in the proceedings as well.

Llull makes no direct statements and no arguments drawing on the conditions of intellectual and religious debate among the Mongols. His attitude toward the Mongols is distinctly different than that of his immediate predecessors and contemporaries; given his orientation and attitudes, his attention to narratives concerning the Mongols may have provided the opening for the *Pax Mongolica* to influence the *Pax Christiana*. The parallels and possible links between Llull's thought and what was known about the Mongols in his age are easy to make and it is not far fetched—indeed I think it probable—that the influence of Rubruck's account on Llull's thought was profound. At the Mongol court Llull's dream was realized before Llull himself had dreamt it, and the story of those debates before the Khaan, known in Europe since Rubruck's return, did shape European understandings of the Mongols and therefore certainly also Llull's understanding even if only indirectly. Whether Llull's thoughts on preaching and missions simply arose within an intellectual climate in which the Mongols were ever present, or were directly inspired by tales of the Franciscan missions and debates at the Mongol court, or whether his existing ideas towards encounter and dialogue were merely altered and oriented by such reports, it is in any case well documented that Llull continually referred to the Mongols in contexts where he discussed the necessity of engaging the world beyond Christendom.

Llull's entire life was devoted on the one hand to convincing the intellectual community and ecclesiastical authorities of the necessity of engaging the non-christian others—"sarraíns, jueus, grecs, mogols, tartres, búlgars, ongres de Ungaria la menor, comans, nestorins, rossos, guinovins: tots aquests e molts daltres infeels" (*Libre de Blanquerna*)—through preaching and missions, and on the other hand the possibility of a politico-military means for securing a protected social space for that encounter and dialogue. His thought and activity during his early career focused exclusively on missions, preaching, dialogue and debate; in his later career, especially after the fall of Acre in 1291, he focused more and more on the politico-military means for securing the possibility for encounter and engagement with the others in missionary activity. The Mongols, perhaps, would make the world safe for religion.

For many 21st century readers, those goals seem not merely contradictory but both of them loathsome and in fact downright "medieval." For some scholars, however, Llull has been considered the first postmodern thinker ("the propagator of a wonderfully pragmatic way of thinking that we might call... a 'postmodern liberalism.'"),[12] the philosopher who laid the basis for the calculus and modern science,[13] the inventor of the first

---

[12] Stone, Gregory B. "Ramon Llull vs. Petrus Alfonsi: postmodern liberalism and the six liberal arts" *Medieval encounters* 1997 v.3 no.1, p.71

[13] In numerous publications by Erhard Wolfram Platzeck. See his "La combinatoria luliana" *Revista de filosofía* (Madrid) 1953 v.12 p.575-609 and 1954 v.13 p.125-165; *Raimund Lull: sein Leben - sein Werke: die Grundlagen seines Denkens (Principienlehre)*. Düsseldorf: Schwann, 1962-1964; "Gottfried Wilhelm Leibniz y Raimundo Lull" *Estudios lulianos* 1972 v.16 p.129-193.

computer[14] and a tireless laborer for the development of a logic which would transcend the distorting rationalism of the Enlightenment that followed him, leading him instead to an embodied, dialogic of differences and multiple perspectives, a search for truth based on the presupposition that truth is revealed only in the other as the beloved.

V

For a mongolist, one of the most interesting possibilities which is suggested by reading Llull on the Mongols is how this personal, embodied, dialogic orientation of thought towards the encounter with alterity is related to Rubruck's account of religious freedom and public philosophico-religious debates at the Mongol court. Nederman has described some of the most important moments in medieval European dialogic thought and she offers as most important among these Abelard's and Llull's dialogues, followed in a subsequent chapter by Rubruck's example of dialogic praxis. Of the first two, she notes what many have regarded a major shortcoming of these thinkers:

> In the works of Abelard and Llull, it was accepted as axiomatic that men of strong faith would nevertheless agree to enter into reasoned debate with one another and would subscribe to identical standards of rational argumentation. Moreover, it apparently did not occur to Latin medieval thinkers that the intellectual and linguistic matrix of Christianity was in any way short of universal. The Jew, the Muslim, and the Gentile are all made to

---

[14] Bexte, P.; Künzel, W. "Lullus oder was der Computer im Mittelalter konnte" *Frankfurter allgemeine Magazin* nr. 472 28 Okt. 1988; Künzel, Werner; Cornelius, Heiko. *Die Ars generalis ultima des Raymundus Lullus: Studien zu einem geheimen Ursprung der Computertheorie.* 5a. ed. Berlin: Künzel, 1991; Colomer i Pous, Eusebi. *El pensament als països Catalans durant l'edat mitjana i el renaixement.* Barcelona : Publicacions de l'Abadia de Montserrat, 1997.

speak (literally as well as figuratively) in the language of the Roman Church.[15]

She continues in her chapter on Rubruck's letter to St. Louis with a discussion of what she regards as "its most unique feature":

> its author's intensely personal struggle between his own zeal to spread the word of Latin Christian doctrine and his efforts to accommodate himself to the multireligious (and multicultural) world into which he has been sent. ... William looks often for opportunities to preach and discourse publicly on Roman Christianity, yet he is persistently thwarted—not by persecution or suppression, but by linguistic and cultural difference as well as by the need to compromise in a world that is not so much aggressively hostile as indifferent to his message. In a sense, William's narrative reveals many of the practical impediments to realizing interreligious dialogue while suggesting a strategy for negotiating a path through a society untroubled by the presence of religious diversity. His letter... illustrates how a devout medieval Christian might learn, in the face of circumstance, to conduct himself with a measure of tolerance, without surrendering his certainty about the ultimate rectitude of his own convictions. (p.55)

Nederman cited Rubruck's remark about how when he arrived among the Mongols he "felt as if he were entering some other world" and she continued with the comment that what Rubruck noticed was not military power but "the bewildering array of ethnic, racial, and cultural groups who live in relative peace and harmony under Mongol rule." (p.56). Like Rubruck

---

[15] Nederman, Cary J. *Worlds of difference: European discourses of toleration, c. 1100- c.1550*. University Park: Pennsylvania State University Press, 2000, p.53

and perhaps through him, Llull found in the Mongol attitudes towards religion something he had not found in either Catholic Europe or Muslim North Africa.

The Mongols were a part of Llull's world, a pervasive and powerful presence throughout European ecclesiastical, social, political and intellectual life. Among his immediate predecessors, the nature of the Mongols was debated: monsters, demons, Christians; were they even human beings? During Llull's youth Matthew of Paris had written of that monstrous inhuman race from Hell, yet in Llull's writings the nature of the Mongols was simple and clear from beginning to end: Mongols are human beings, rational creatures just like Christians and Muslims, and although living in theological error as gentiles, still they are intellectually capable and desirous of engaging others in the pursuit of the truth, exactly as they are portrayed in Rubruck's account. "Valde sapiens & eruditus in Philosophia" Llull wrote of his imagined Mongol. And the truth, Llull insisted, is revealed by love to the lover through the beloved. It is on this foundation that Llull began his engagements with the world, not just with the Christians, Muslims, Saracens and Jews of his native Mallorca, of Paris, Cyprus, North Africa and Armenia, but with the Mongols of his imagination as well. May our children also begin there.

VI

Only a few of Llull's writings in Catalan have been indexed; the new edition (NEORL, 6 volumes to date) includes only indexes to biblical references, not to topics. Indexes to his Latin works are in process of publication as are the Latin works themselves. The works by Llull listed and excerpted below are only those in which I have found references to the Mongols; it does not constitute a complete list of titles in which Llull mentions the Mongols as I have not had the time to go through all of the published works, let alone those yet to be published. The editions and translations identified are also not meant to constitute an exhaustive list.

The excerpts that follow each cited text provide the passages that I have located in which *mogols* or *tartres* are mentioned. Some adjacent text has been included to provide context. No selection from *Liber Tartari et Christiani* has been included here as the Tatar appears throughout that text.

Abbreviations
EA=*Escritos antiaverroistas (1309-1311)*. Porto Alegre: Edipucrs, 2001 (Pensamento franciscans, v.4)
NEORL=*Nova edició de les obres de Ramon Llull*. Palma: Patronat Ramón Llull, 1990-
Obras=*Obras deRamón Lull*. Palma de Mallorca, 1901-1903.
OE= *Obres essencials*. Barcelona, 1957-1960.
OLit = *Obras literarias*. Madrid: Biblioteca de autores cristianos, 1948.
ORL= *Obres de Ramon Lull*. Palma de Mallorca: Comissió Editora Lulliana, 1906-1950. Reprinted: Palma de Mallorca: M. Font, 1986-
Poesies. 2. ed. Barcelona: Els Nostres Classics, 1928.
RLO= *Beati Raymundi Lulli doctoris illuminati et martyris operum*. Mainz. 1721-1742. Facsimile reprint Frankfurt am Main,1965. The facsimile edition includes a separate title page with the title "Raimundus Lullus Opera."
ROL= *Raymundi Lulli opera latina*. v.1-5, 1959-1967, Palmae Maioricarum: Maioricensis Schola Lullistica del Consejo Superior de Investigaciones Científicas; v.6- 1975- Turnhout: Brepols
SW= *Selected works of Ramon Llull*. Princeton: Princeton Univ. Press, 1985. English translations by Anthony Bonner.

1. Libre de contemplació en Deu (1273-1274?)
Original text in Catalan:
Libre de contemplació en Deu. In: **ORL** v.7. Edited by M. Salvador Galmés.
Latin version: *Liber contemplationis magnus.* In: **RLO** t.IX-X (1740-1742)

Libre de contemplació en Deu (1273-1274?)
Catalan text as edited by M. Salvador Galmés in **ORL** v.7 (v. 6 of the individual title), p.84-93.

[Cap. 278. *Com es tractat de la amor que home ha en est mon e en lautre a la sancta humana natura' de nostre Senyor Jhesu Christ.*]
10.   *Oh vos, Sènyer, en lo qual van e venen mes amors e mos plaers!* Sensualment sentim e entellectualment entenem que en est mon son diverses sectes que no amen la vostra sancta humanitat, axí com tartres eretges ydolátrics ginoys e de moltes altres sectes qui adoren lo sol e les besties e les serpents e fan a aquells la reverencia que deurien fer a vostra deitat e a vostra humanitat.
♥ 11. On, com la vostra humanitat, *Sènyer,* no sia remembrada ni entesa ni amada per totes estes gents damun dites, e com tota la especia humana sia encarregada de remembrar e entendre e amar vostra sancta humana natura per so com murí e ac molt de treball per recrear aquella, per assò es significat al humá enteniment que tota la mellor obra que hom pogués tractar ni procurar en est mon, sería que hom se esforsás a remembrar e a entendre e a voler la art e la manera per la qual aquelles gens qui no remembren ni entenen ni amen vos, que us remembrassen e us entenessen e us amassen, per tal que vos aguessets l onrament que us tany aver de les creatures, e que en loc de vos los infeels no honrassen lo sol ni les besties ni les serpents. ♥ 12. On, beneit siats vos, *Sènyer Deus*: car enaxí com los infeels no amen la vostra humanitat per so car han defalliment en lo remembrament e enteniment e voler de lur ánima, enaxí, *Sènyer,* per so com los crestians no amen d aquella fervor que deurien, son los

infeels damun dits ublidosos e innorans e no amans la vostra sancta humana natura, la qual natura ha tant fet per lo poble dels crestians, que ha encarregat lur remembrament e lur enteniment e lur voler com la fassen remembrar e entendre e amar als pobles qui no la remembren ni la entenen ni la amen.

13. *Bo senyor sobre totes bonèes, gran Senyor sobre totes granèes!* Sensualment sentim e entellectualment entenem que en est mon ha molts crestians qui son molt culpables e molt peccadors de molt greus peccats. On, com assò sia enaxí, doncs lurs greus culpes donen significacio que ells no an amor a vostra humanitat segons que deuríen, car si amor li avíen no amaríen sino que vostra humanitat ama ni no ublidarien so que vostra humanitat ama ni no ublidarien so que vostra humanitat membra. ❤

14. On, beneyta si a la vostra humanitat, *Sènyer*: car enaxí com lo pintor qui a la figura fa aitants d ornaments e de afaisonaments com pot per tal que sia bellament vista a les gents, enaxí la vostra sancta divina natura ha aornada la vostra sancta humana natura en tal disposicio e en tal estament de vertuts, que digna cosa es que sia per tota la especia humana membrada e entesa e amada. Mas tant es gran lo defalliment el peccat nostre, que per assò desmembram so que deuríem membrar e membram so que deuríem ublidar, e per assò amam so qui no es digne de esser amat e desamam so qui es digne de esser amat. ❤ 15. *Piadós Senyor pacient!* Com ajam encercada la amor que hom ha en est mon a la vostra humanitat gloriosa e com no la ajam atrobada en los jueus, ni los sarrayns a vostra humanitat no agen amor acabada, ni en los crestians peccadors no sia aquella amor que deuría, ni en los tartres ni en los eretges ni en los ydolátrics ni en les altres sectes, e doncs, *Sènyer*, on es anada ni que s es feita la gran amor que tuit deuríem aver a la vostra humanitat sancta qui tant nos ha amats e qui tan carament nos ha comprats e qui tan gran loc nos té ab la vostra misericordia divina?

2. Libre del gentil e los tres savis (1274 to 1276?)
Catalan version:
1) *Libre del gentil e los tres savis.* In **Obras**, t. 1, p.1-305.
2) *Llibre del gentil a dels tes savis.* In: **NEORL** v.2. 1st ed. 1993; 2nd ed. 2001.
Latin version: *Liber de gentili et tribus sapientibus.* In **RLO** t. II (1722), treatise ii, pp. 21-114.

Neither *mogols* nor *tartres* appear in this work, but an otherwise unidentified *gentil* is the protagonist.

3. Llibre contra Anticrist (1274 to 1283?)
Original text in Catalan:
1) *Llibre qui és contra Anticrist.* In: Josep Perarnau i Espelt, "El *Llibre contra Anticrist* de Ramon Llull: edició i estudi del text" *Arxiu de textos catalans antics* 1990 v.9. p.7-182. Includes index.
2) *Llibre contra Anticrist.* A cura de Gret Schib Torra. In **NEORL** v.3 p.115-160.
[Latin version, probably from ca. 1290-1292, remains unpublished. Hillgarth (1971) in Appendix II cites a Latin manuscript from the *First Catalogue of Lull manuscripts in Paris, drawn up in August 1311: the collection at the Chartreuse de Vauvert.* The *Liber Antichristi* is nr.19. In Appendix III The *Electorium magnum* catalog has a work entitled *[Liber] contra Anticristum* (item 137).]

Llibre qui és contra Anticrist (1274?)
Text as edited by Perarnau (1986), p.155 line 1514 to p.156 line 1525.

[De guerres e de batalles]
...

    Per sperièncía de les guerres e de les batalles, que·ls reys christians, prínceps e grans batons, cavallers e altres hòmens, han fetes contra·ls sarraÿns, pot hom conèxer e sabr que per altre manera pus alta e pus noble és possíbol cosa a convertir lo món e a conquerre la sancta terra d'Oltramar, que no és ceylla que·ls christians han presa contra·ls infaels per guerres e per batalles sensuals contra les intel·lectuals batalles, la qual manera és semblant a la primera segons que los sarraÿns han començada e muntiplicada lur secta. E açò matex se segueix dels tartres e dels infaels, qui per armes de fust e de ferre alcien los hòmens, sens que no·ls endreçen ni·ls vençen ab armes de fe, sperança, caritat, justícia, prudència, fortitudo, temprança, veritat e passiència.

4. Doctrina pueril (1275)
Original text in Catalan
1) *Doctrina pueril.* In **ORL**, v.1, p.1-199
2) *Doctrina pueril.* Barcelona: Barcino, 1972.

Doctrina pueril (1275)
Text as edited by Gret Schib in *Doctrina pueril.* Barcelona: Barcino, 1972. p.166-167, lines 1-21.

LXXII. De gentils.

Gentils són gents senes lig e qui no han conexença de Déu. On, per la ignorància que han de Déu, cor segons cors de natura tot hom deu haver conexença de son creador, per açó los gentils, jatssia que no coneguen Déu, almenys fan alguna honor a algunes creatures a significança que alguna cosa sia pus nobla que éls.

Amable fill, per la ignorància que·ls gentils han de Déu, són en diverses errors e oppinions, e per açó són diversses pobles: los uns adoren ýdoles, los altres adoren lo sol e la luna e les esteles, e los altres adoren les bèsties e les aus, e los altres adoren los elements, e cascuns han diversa manera dels altres en ço que creeguen.

Mogols, tàrtins, búlgars, ongres d'Ongria la menor, comans, nestorins, rosos, ginovins e molts d'altres són gentils e són hòmens qui no han ley; a enaxí com flom d'aygua qui per costuma va a enjús e no fa mas de córrer en la mar, e enaxí tots aquests decorren e no sessen de perdre Déu e de anar en foch perdurable; e a penes és negú qui sia lur procurador ne qui·ls ajut a demostrar via perdurable.

5. Libre d'Evast e d'Aloma e de Blaquerna (1283)
Commonly referred to in the shortened and hispanisized form *Blanquerna*.
Original text in Catalan:
1) *Libre de Blanquerna.* In **ORL**, v.9 (1914).
2) *Libre de Evast e Blanquerna.* Barcelona: Els Nostres classics, 1935-1954.
Spanish translation: *Libro de Evast y Blanquerna.* In **OLit**, p.143-596.
English translation: *Blanquerna: a thirteenth century romance.* Trans. E.A. Peers. London: Jarrolds, 1926.

Libre de Blanquerna (1283)
Text as edited by Antoni Ma. Alcover in **ORL** v.9, p.211-212; 300; 302; 345

[Cap. 61. *En qual manera labat Blanquerna fé lo libre de Ave María.*]
4. Ave María! Saluts taport dels sarraíns, jueus, grecs, mogols, tartres, búlgars, ongres de Ungaria la menor, comans, nestorins, rossos, guinovins: tots aquests e molts daltres infeels te saluden per mi qui som lur procurador. En la tua salutació los met, per ço que lo teu Fill los fulla remembrar e que tu acabtes ab ell com los trameta missatges quils endrecen a conèxer e a amar tu e ton Fill, en tal manera ques pusquen salvar e en est mon sapien e vullen tu e ton Fill, de tot lur poder, servir e honrar.
5. Ave María! Aquests infeels per qui jot salut han innorancia de la tua salut e del honrament que Deus tà donat. Homens son. Semblant natura e figura han del teu Fill que tu tant ames e per quí tant est amada e honrada. En foc perdurable van per innorancia. La gloria perdurable de ton Fill perden, car no es quils preic

ni quils demostre veritat de la santa fe catòlica. Boques han ab quet sabríen loar sit conexíen, cor han ab quet puríen amar, mans han ab quet puríen servir, peus han ab que poríen anar per les tues carreres. Tu est digna que per totes gents e que en totes terrres fosses coneguda servida amada loada. Saludente. Ajuda e gracia e benedicciò te demanen per mi.

[Cap. 80. *Gloria in excelsis Deo*]
9. Esdevencse un dia que lo cardenal de Domine Deus Agnus Dei Filius Patris, tramès en una terra per espiar la captinença del bisbe e del príncep daquella terra. Dementre que la espía estava en aquella terra, manament fo fet de part de lapostoli al bisbe que precuràs tots anys .1. tartres e .x. frares que lapostoli trametía en aquell bisbat per ço quels tartres mostrassen lur lenguatge als frares, e los frares lo lur als tartres, segons que era ordenat en cort; e que lo bisbe feés un monestir fora la ciutat on esteguessen, e hom los donàs certa renda per tots temps. ...

... Esdevencse un jorn que lapostoli hac tramès un cavaller prevere, qui era de lorde de sciencia e cavallería, a un rey sarraí. Aquell per força darmes vencé .x. cavallers la un aprés laltre per diverses dies, e en aprés vencé per raons tots los savis de sa terra e a tots provà la santa fe catòlica esser vera. Daquests benauyrats missatges e de molts daltres inluminava lo mon lordenament damunt dit quel Sant Pare Havía establit.
12. Esdevencse una vegada que dels .l. tartres qui aprengueren nostre lenguatge e qui enteneren nostra fe, se convertiren los. xxx., e lapostoli tramès los ab .v. frares al gran ka. Aquells .xxx. ab los .v. frares qui hagren après lenguatge tartaresc, foren denant lo gran ka, e preycaren la fe dels crestians e convertiren moltes gents en sa cort, e lo gran ka gitaren de la error en que era e meterenlo en dubte; e per lo dubte esdevenc aprés un temps a via salutable.
13. En una terra estudiaven .x. jueus e .x. sarraíns ab .x. frares religioses; e com hagren apresa nostra lig e nostra letra, convertirense a nostra lig la meytat, e preycaren als altres jueus nostra

lig e a sarraíns la santa fe cristiana denant aquells qui no seren convertits, e açò faíen tots jorns e continuament; e per ço car la cort apostolical faía son poder, e per la continuació de la disputació, Deus, per ço car veritat ha poder sobre falsetat, donà gracia que tots los jueus e los sarraíns daquella terra se convertiren es batejaren, e la santa fe als altres preycaren.

[Cap. 88. *Domine Fili unigenite Jesu Christe*]
5. En Turquía venc un missatge on atrobà quatre frares qui havíen après lenguatge turquesc, e los turcs nols lexaven preycar en la terra; e lo missagte escrisc aquesta cosa al cardenal, e foren elets missatges quel papa tramès ab gran joyes al senyor dels tartres qui havía subjugada a sa senyoría Turquía. Lapostoli pregà per sos missatgers lo tartre que ell sostengués que los quatre frares poguessen preycar per tota Turquía la honor del Fill de Deu; e lo tartre per los precs e per les joyes quel papa li tramès, sostenc aquella cosa; e los turcs no gosaren vedar als frares lur preycació daquí en avant.

6. Liber Tartari et Christiani (1288)
Original text in Latin:
Liber super Psalmum Quicumque vult sive Liber Tartari et Christiani. In **RLO**, tomus IV (1737), treatise V, p. 347-376. Latin text with Catalan translation: *Llibre del tàrtar i el cristià, o bé, Llibre sobre el salm Quicumque vult*. Edició bilingüe a cura de Josep Batalla, Óscar de la cruz Palma ; amb la collaboració de Francesc Rodríguez Bernal. Turnhout : Brepols ; Santa Coloma de Queralt : Obrador Edèndum, 2016. Series: Traducció de l'Obra Llatina de Ramon Lull ; v.4.

(No selection is presented here as the Tatar appears throughout the text.)

7. Libre de meravelles (1288/1289)

1) *Felix: de les Maravelles del Mon*. In **Obras** t. 3-4 (1903)
2) *Libre de meravelles*. Barcelona: Editorial Barcino, 1931-1934. Series: Els nostres classics. Col·leccio A, v.34, 38, 42, 46-47.
French translation: *Félix, ou le Livre des Merveilles*. Monaco: Éditions du Rocher, 2000.
Spanish translation: *Felix, o Maravillas del mundo*. In **OLit**, p.597-1000.
English translation: *Felix, or The book of wonders*. In **SW** v.2 p.647-1105.

Libre de meravelles (1288/1289)
Text as established by Salvador Galmés in the editon of *Els nostres classics*, 1931-1934, v. 4, p.107 line 16 to p.108 line 18.

[LXXXIX. De créixer e de minvar]
... Sènyer—dix Fèlix—, ¿com poria hom créxer en lo món la sancta Sgleya, e aminvar la error qui és en aquells qui li contrasten?—.
—Fill—dix lo ermità—, ·I· hom qui lonch temps havia trebayllat en la utilitat de la Sgleya romana, vench a París, e dix al rey de França e a la Universitat de París que en París fossen fets monestirs hon fossen apreses los lenguatges de aquells qui són infaels, e que hom en aquells lengatges treledàs la *Art demostrativa*; e que ab aquella *Art demostrativa* hom anàs als tartres, e que a aquells hom preycàs e la *Art* mostràs; e que de aquells hom a París hagués, e que la nostra letra e lenguatge lurs mostràs, e que puxes a lur terra lurs trematés. Totes questes coses e moltes de altres demenà aquest hom al rey e la Universitat de París, e que fos confermat per lo sant apostoli e fos obra perdurable. Per aquesta manera, fill, se poria créxer la fe romana; car qui convertia los tartres e aquells de Licònia e·ls altres gentils, aquells destrouiren los sarrayns; e enaxí, per via de martiri e per granea de caritat, tot lo món poria ésser donat a crestianitat.—

Con Fèlix hac entesa la manera per la qual la fe més podia muntiplicar que per neguna altra manera, desijà molt aquella manera, e meraveyllà's de tots aquells qui a aquella manera de muntiplicament de fe contrestaven.

8. Epistola Raymundi Lull ad Universitatem Parisiensem (1288/1289)

Martene and Durand date this letter "ca. 1300" while the *Chartularium Universitatis Parisiensis* gives the dates 1298-1299, these latter dates generally accepted until Bonner's research suggested 1288-1289.

Original text in Latin: *Epistola III Raymundi Lullii ad universitatem Parisiensem.* In: Martene and Durand, *Thesaurus novus anecdotorum*, Paris, 1717, t.1 p.1317-1319. Reprinted as: *Epistola Raymundi Lull ad Universitatem parisiens., quam laudibus extollit, quamque hortatur ad porrigendum preces suas regi, ut fundetur Parisiis studium Arabicum, Tartaricum et Graecum.* in: *Chartularium Universitatis Parisiensis.* Parisiis: Ex typis fratrum Delalain, 1891. v.2 p.83-84.

English translation: *On the study of oriental languages.* In *University records and life in the Middle Ages,* ed.and trans. by Lynn Thorndyke. New York: Columbia University Press, 1944, p.125-127. Reprinted in: *University of Chicago readings in Western civilization* / general editors, John W. Boyer and Julius Kirshner. Chicago: University of Chicago Press, 1986-. v. 4, p. 357-359.

Epistola Raymundi Lull ad Universitatem Parisiens., quam laudibus extollit, quamque hortatur ad porrigendum preces suas regi, ut fundetur Parisiis studium Arabicum, Tartaricum et Graecum (1298-1299)
Complete text as printed in *Chartularium Universitatis Parisiensis,* v.2, p.83-84.

Deo fidelis est ac summa caritate successus qui in cognitionem et dilectionem summe sapientie et amoris, ignorantes dirigens, cecos illuminans, mortuos in viam vite reducens, pro testamento Dei sui adversitatis et corporalis mortis pericula non formidat. Gloriam et magnum decorem ejus quis enarrabit? Generationes infidelium qui hodierna die Deum nesciunt quis enumerabit? Quot ab erroris cecitate in infernorum tenebras labuntur quis excogitabit? Proh dolor! tanta damna merito plange devota plebs fidelium christiana. O fons superne scientie, qui Parisius tot tante auctoritatis professores inebriasti doctrina mirifica, extende torrentes tuos ad terras infidelium, et irriga errantium corda penitus arida rore celi, et pelle tenebras, aperi eis radia eterni luminis. Heu, quando ambulabunt omnes gentes in lumine tuo, et omnis homo ambulans in splendore solis tui videbit salutare Dei? Desiderio desideravi hoc ego Raymundus Lull quod summe desiderabile est omnibus fidelibus christianis, et ab his perfectibile, quorum intellectus summa sapientia divinitus illustravit. Felix est illa Universitas, que tot gignit fidei defensores, et felix illa civitas, cujus milites armati sapientia et devotione Christi possunt barbaras nationes subdere summo regi. Quando adorabit te omnis terra, Deus, psallet et benedicet nomini tuo, et omnis tribus et lingua servient tibi? Considerate hoc, reverendi patres et domini, intellectibus et voluntatibus, quorum est objectum summa veritas et summa bonitas. Quoniam sicut Deus est intelligibilis et amabilis quia summe verus et summe bonus: sic ubique et multum, quia immensus, et in omni tempore assidue, quia eternus. O quam felices fuere apostoli et martyres, quia in omnem terram exivit sonus corum, et in fines orbis terre verba eorum predicantium Jesum Christum. O quam pretiosa mors eorum in conspectu Domini, qui multos de morte revocarunt ad vitam. O utinam essent modo multi tales viarum illorum reparatores, quoniam valde gloriosum et necessarium esset toti populo christiano, quia sicut ego scio, quoniam expertus sum, multi sunt philosophi Arabum, qui ad perfidiam Macometi christicolas pervertere nituntur, et improperant nobis infideles filii dicentes: Ubi est Deus eorum? Et preterea Judei et Saraceni, prout possunt, conantur Tartaros in suas sectas inducere; et si contingat, quod absit, Tartaros esse

Judeos vel Saracenos, vel cos condere per se sectam, timendum est ne cedat in totius christianitatis incomparabile detrimentum, sicut accidit de secta Macometi, qua inventa Saraceni irruerunt super nos, et quasi tertia pars christianitatis cecidit. Innumerabilis est illa Tartarorum generatio, in brevi quidem tempore multa sibi regna et principatus manu bellica subjugavit.

Videte, reverendi patres et domini magistri, imminere periculum toti ecclesie Dei, et nisi sapientia et devotio vestra, qua tota chriestianitas sustinetur, Saracenorum perfidie opponat clypeum salutarem, et si negligat impetuosum torrentem Tartaricum refrenare—nolo ulterius dicere—sed pensate quid poterit evenire. Et mirum est quod plures sint adversarii Dei, quam defensores, et plures homines vituperent illum, quam laudent: et Deus homo propter homines factus est, et ipse homo mortuus, ut cos vivificaret; et multi etiam ab unitate ecclesie jam declinaverunt, ut Greci et multi alii schismatici. Considerate quantum malum pro bono deo redditur, et quantum opprobrium ab eis qui ad laudandum Deum creati sunt, et quanta persecutio nobis fidelibus immineat, et de qua questione simus Deo in extremo judicio responsuri, cum requiret a nobis mortem eorum qui nostris predicationibus et exemplis debuerant vita perfrui sempiterna.

Hic conscientie stimulus me remordet, et coegit me venire ad vos, quorum summe discretionis et sapientie interest ordinare circa tantum negotium, tam pium, tam meritorium, tam Deo gratum servitium et utile toti mundo, videlicet quod hic Parisius, ubi fons divine scientie oritur, ubi veritatis lucerna refulget populis christianis, fundaretur studium Arabicum, Tartaricum et Grecum, ut nos linguas adversariorum Dei et nostrorum docti, predicando et docendo illos, possimus in gladio veritatis eorum vincere falsitates, et reddere populum Deo acceptabilem, et inimicos convertere in amicos. Quod si fiat et placeat Deo, quod sit, maximam quidem pro nobis suscipiet christianitas exaltationem et dilatationem. Et hujus rei tam inestimabilis eritis fundamentum, et tu Parisius Universitas nequaquam eris minima in doctoribus tuis, ex te enim exiet lux universis gentibus, et perhibebis testimonium veritati et confluent ad te

magistri et discipuli, et universi aurient de te scientias universas.
Quid habebunt boni Greci et Arabes in fvoluminibus suis quin
sit tibi notum, cum sine interprete linguas eorum intellexeritis?
Quis estimabit quanta laus, quantus honor Deo, quanta caritatis
compassio erga miseros errantes, et quantum bonum in hoc et ex
hoc loco sequetur? Et hoc leviter fieri potest, si illustri regi
Francie preces vestras porrexeritis, ut ipse, qui nobilissimus est
inter reges terre, huic nobilissimo negotio inter omnia negotia
largiri dignetur suam bene meritam elemosynam, videlicet predictum studium seu studia fundare et dotare, et exaudiet vos, ut
confido, postquam hujus negotii cognoverit auctoritatem.

9. Liber de Sancta Maria (1290)
Original text in Catalan: *Libre de Sancta María*. In **ORL**, v.10 (1915), p.1-228.
Latin version: *Liber de Sancta Maria*. In **ROL**, v.28 (2003), p.1-241.

Libre de Santa Maria (1290)
Catalan text in **ORL** v.10 p.9-10; p.143-144; p.185-186.

[Del pròlec]
16. Lausor amiga! dix Oració: No cal que tragats exempli dels romans de comuna utilitat, car en aquest temps en que som, son unes gents qui son appellats tartres, los quals ha poc de temps que son venguts, e auells comencen a senyorejar tot lo mon per so car amen comuna utilitat de lur secta e manera, la qual han presa a honor daquell loc don son exits, e dien que ells deuen senyorejar tot lo mon, e son geng sens fe e sens ley e no han sciencia ni han conexença de Deu ni de nostra Dona; per que es perill que no conquiren tots aquells qui comuna utilitat no amen. E dic vos aytant Lausor, dix Oracio, que gran raó par que pus los homens qui han conexença de nostra Dona e de Deu, no fan a aquella honor a Deu e a nostra Dona que deuríen, que Deus los faça tots esser sotsmesos de gents bestials e ue son sens enteni-

ment, per ço quels punesca del falliment que fan a Deu e a nostra Dona.

[Cap. 19. De honrament]
8. Comença Oració e dix a nostra Dona que bé conexía que los sarraíns la honren en quant lapellen sancta e verge e mare, per Sant Esperit, de Jesu Christ, emperò desonor li fan en quant neguen e descreen que siats mare de Deu. Encara, reyna, quels jueus vos fan desonor car no us apellen verge e mare de Deu, eus apellen fembra corrumpuda e mare de hom fill daltre hom. E reyna! dix Oració: Los tartres els pagans e aquells qui Deu no creen, vos fan desonor, car mare e verge nous apellen e nous amen; e bé atorc, reyna, quels mals cristians vos fan desonor, car en vos servir e honrar no fan lur poder, e car per amor de la vostra honor nos lexen de fer peccats e no han totes les virtuts que haver poríen. Tot açò fan mes greu e de tot som despagada, e tot sesdevé per ço car ells amen més lo lur honrament quel vostre ni cell de Deu vostre fill. Emperó nou faç jo, reyna; ans vos dic que a mi plau e més desig vostre honrament e cell de vostre fill, quel meu e tot altre, e som aparillada de soferir tots treballs e de lexar totes benanances e penre mort per honrar vos e vostre fill. On, si en aquesta petita de bona volentat e sencera e sens tot encamerament e maestría podía un petit vos honrar, plagués a la vostra gran bontat virtut santetat e amor, que moguesseu los peccadors a honrar vostre honrament de totes lurs forces.

[Cap. 24. De pietat]
6. Començà Oració a pregar nostra Dona, e dix aquestes paraules: Piadosa reyna! Vos sots font flum e mar de pietat, e car ho sots prec vos de obres de pietat; car pus que havets pietats, cové que najats les obres, e les obres de pietat son, reyna, que vos preguets vostre fill que li prena pietat de tots los homens qui van en foc perdurable ignorantment, com son sarraíns jueus tartres els altres pagans. Tots aquests, reyna, han fretura de fè e de sciencia, e hauríen mester homens savis e que fossen cristians qui los mostrassen veritat de la sancta fè romana. Daquests

homens, reyna, vos prec que per pietat e per mercè los nos trametats e que per tot lo mon los escampets, car gran mercèe farets. E consirats, gloriosa, com gran pietat es aquesta que un home sia núu e mort de fam de set e de fret, e que sia a la porta de un home ric qui en su casa ha molts draps e molts diners e moltes viandes; e enaxí, reyna, es gran pietat e molt major pietat encara, que en la sancta Esgleya sia tant savi home e devot e quels homens infeels nagen tan gran fretura. Ah reyna, e per Deu no sia! Movets los savis cristians a devoció e a amor e a pietat, e vagen per tot lo mon fructificar e recontar los honraments del fill vostre e los vostres.

Liber de Sancta Maria
Latin text as edited by Blanca Garí and Fernando Domínguez Reboiras in **ROL**, v.28 (2003), p.52-54, lines 181-211; p.171, lines 151-172; p.205-206, lines 115-137.

[De prologo]
—In illo tempore, cum Roma toto dominaretur in orbe, diligebant Romani publicam utilitatem, et inerat ideo uirtus Romae dominandi super totum orbem, quem diu possedit, quoniam utilitatem publicam dilexerunt. Confestim autem cum utilitas publica diuisa fuit et Romani proprias utilitates dilexerunt potius quam communes, tunc Roma suam uirtutem dominandi perdidit, tendens in declinum.

Heu, quomodo ipse Caesar et Romani erant corde nobiles! Quomodo Roma inclitos habuit pugnatores tunc cum publicam dilexit utilitatem! Et quam multiplici laude digni fuerunt, pro eo quanto commune commodum dilexerunt! Et si isti uiri infideles, qui de beata Maria cognitionem non habuerunt, fuerunt tam alti cordis, quid esset nunc temporibus istis si catholici in tantum utilitatem publicam amarent (ita ut per uniuersum orbem facerent amari et cognosci beatam Mariam uirginem et benedictum filium eius, quem ipsa tam diligit, et e conuerso) et resumerent Romani dominium, quod soliti fuerunt possidere?

—Laus amica—dixit Oratio—, super utilitatem ublicam te non oportet exempla trahere de Romanis, quoniam modo a modico tempore citra quaedam gens, uidelicet Tartari surrexerunt, qui super totum orbem iam incipiunt dominari, quoniam communem utilitatem diligunt suae sectae, quam sibi sumpserunt ad honorem illius loci unde processerunt. Isti sunt sine fide et sine lege, scientiam non habent, Deum et eius beatissimam genitricem non cognoscunt. Quare omnes illi, qui communem non diligunt utilitatem, ex illis sibimet minatur ruinam.

Et dico tibi Laus —ait Oratio—, quam, ex quo homines, qui Deum et beatissimam matrem eius cognoscunt, non exibent illis ipsum honorem, quem decet utrumque, iusta quidem ratio mihi uidetur esse, quod Deus subiciat eos gentibus bestialbus et puniat eos pro defectibus, quos inferunt et Deo et ipsius genitrici.

[XIX. De honorificentia]

Incepit Oratio et dixit beatae Mariae:
—Bene quidem perpendo, gloriosa uirgo, quod Saraceni te honorificant, cum te apellant sancta uirgo, sancto spiritu mater Iesu Christi. Verumtamen dedecus tibi faciunt negantes te esse Dei matrem. Iudaei autem uituperium tibi faciunt, quia uirgnem et matrem Dei te negant et affirmant te mulierem esse corruptam, matrem hominis a uiro generati. Tartari quoque et pagani et omnes illi, qui Deum negant seu non credunt, faciunt tibi dedecus, quoniam te penitus ignorant. Et bene concedo, quod mali christiani te inhonorant, quoniam ad seruiendum tibi et honorandum te totis suis uiribus non laborant, ac etiam quia ad honorem tui non abstinent a peccatis et, quibus possunt, uirtutibus non adhaerent. Hoc autem totum accidit eis, quia plus honorificationem suam diligunt quam tuam honorificentiam, et filii tui. Sed ego, domina mea, plus desidero honorificationem tuam et filii tui, quam meam seu cuiuscumque alterius, parata omnes ferre labores et dimittere cunctas mundanas prosperitates, mortemque subire ad honorandum te et filium tuum. Igitur si ego in hac modica bona uoluntate, sincera, sine fraude et sine aliqua mali labe possum aliquantulum te honorare, placeat tuae magnae

bonitati, uirtuti, sanctitati et amori mouere peccatores ad honorandum honorificentiam tuam uiribus totis.

[XXIV. De pietate vel compassione]
Orauit Oratio beatam Mariam dicens:
—Tu, regina piissima, cum sis fons, flumen et mare pietatis, oro te pro pietatis operibus. Nam ex quo pietatem habes, opera quidem eius oportet te habere. Opus quidem pietatis est, ut ores filium tuum, ut ipse pro pietate sua misereatur tot hominum, qui ignoranter in ignem corruunt sempiternum, uidelicet Saracenorum, Iudaeorum, Tartarorum et ceterorum infidelium. Omnes autem isti fide indigent et scientia, et sapientibus christianis, qui fidei Romanae ueritatem eis ostendant. Pro istis igitur pietatem tuam inuoco, ut nobis eos transmittas. Disperge illos per orbem uniuersum, quia sic magnam caritatem nobis impendes.

Vide et considera, mitissima domina, quanta pietas est ista: Sit quidam homo nudus et afflictus fame, siti et frigore, iacens ad portam cuiusdam diutis, habentis in domo sua multos pannos, multam pecuniam et epulas multas. Numquid est pietas magna super pauperem istum? Multo quidem maior est pietas multos dare uiros deuotos et sapientes in ecclesia Dei, de quorum scientia et doctrina maxima infidelium multitudo mendicet lumen fidei et cognitionem Dei omnipotentis et gloriosae uirginis matris eius. O piissima regina! Miserere super his, moue sapientes christianos ad amorem, ad deuotionem et pietatem, fluant per uniuersum orbem fructificantes, et omnibus annuntiient filii tui et tuas honorificationes.

10. Liber de passagio (1292)
Original text in Latin: *Liber de passagio (Quomodo Terra sancta recuperari potest* et *Tractatus de modo convertendi infideles)*. In **ROL**, v.28 (2003), p.255-353
French translation of *Tractatus de modo convertendi infideles*: *Traité sur la manière de convertir les infidèles*. In **Sugranyes de Franch (1954)**, p.129-143.

Liber de pasagio (1292)
Text as edited by Blanca Garí and Fernando Domínguez
Reboiras in **ROL** v.28 (2003)
First part: *Quomodo Terra sancta recuperari potest*, p.329 lines
23-31; p. 330, lines 60-69; p.331, lines 80-83.

[p.329 lines 23-31]

Isti autem uiri sancti conentur, quantum possint, ad uniendum scismaticos ad catholicos et ad destruendum scismata eorum, quae leuiter destrui possunt. Et, unitis scismaticis, ad fidem catholicam Tartari leuiter acquiri possunt, quia sine lege existunt. Et, unitis scismaticis et Tartaris conuersis, omnes Saraceni leuiter destrui possunt. Multum cauendum est, ne Tartari accipiant legem sicut stetit Mahometus, qui quasi medietatem christianorum destruxit, quia, si accipiant legem per se uel si Saraceni eos ad sectam eorum inducant, in magno periculo erit tota christianitas.

[p. 330, lines 60-69]

Saraceni habent auantagium ad bellandum contra christianos, quia possunt ire et redire; christiani non, propter nimias armaturas. Habent tamen auantagium christiani contra Saracenos manendo in campo. Vnde, christiani habeant modum bellandi dupliciter, ita quod in eorum exercitu sint similes Saracenis in bellando et in armaturis. Et, fugantes Saracenos, recursum habeant ad illos, qui campum teneant; et per istum modum possent Saraceni expelli de campo. Bellatores autem ad eundum et redeundum, ut dictum est, possunt haeri ad solidum de Graecis, Ermeniis, Tartaris et Iorianis.

[p.331, lines 80-83]

Si autem ista ordinatio praesens in breui tempore non fiat uel alia, quam fecimus hic infra, quae magis generalis est quam ista, timendum est, quod Tartari uel Saraceni acquirant Graecos, et tunc erunt uicini, quod absit Latinis, quia magnum periculum esser.

Liber de pasagio (1292)
Text as edited by Blanca Garí and Fernando Domínguez
Reboiras in **ROL** v.28 (2003)
Second part: *Tractatus de modo convertendi infideles*, p.340-341, lines 1-35; p.345, lines 28-41; p.346, lines 60-67.

[III. De tertia partia, quae est de modo convertendi]
    In principio fiat registrum de sectis uariis, in uniuerso, quae sunt contra fidem catholicam. Et fiant studia plura in quibus addiscantur idiomata infidelium. Addiscentes sint uiri sancti et religiosi, desiderantes mori propter Christum, instructi bene in theologia, philosophia et in moribus bene ordinati; et successiue mittantur ad praedicandum et disputandum cum infidelibus, habentes ita rationes necessarias, quod positiones, quas infideles facere possent, destruantur, et obiectiones eorum, et positiones, quas fideles faciunt, et obiectiones permaneant. Istae autem rationes in sacrosancta pagina sunt seminatae et in multis uiris sapientibus, quod quidem sum expertus. De istis rationibus fiant libri et transferantur in linguis uariis, ut infideles in ipsis studere possint et suos errores cognoscere. Etiam fiant libri de erroribus scismaticorum et soluantur rationibus necessariis, quae leuiter inueniri possent. Et illi libri tradantur scismaticis, ut per ipsos notitiam habeant de ueritate, in qua Ecclesia sacrosancta consistit. Ad uniendum scismaticos Ecclesiae sanctae multum dominus Papa cum suis fratribus debet laborare, quod per eorum unionem possent leuiter deuinci Tartari et omnes aliae nationes.
    Studium unum fiat Romae, quia est caput ecclesiae. Studium autem aliud unum fiat Parisius, cum ibi sit plus de scientia quam in aliquo alio loco, et quia plures studentes conueniunt ibi, et gaudebunt scholares de modo studii et de intentione et de rationibus necessariis, quas uidebunt contra infideles. Aliud studium fiat in Hispania propter Saracenos. Aliud Ianuae, aliud Veneriae, quia uadunt plus inter Saracenos et Tartaros quam alii homines. Et aliud in Pruscia, aliud in Vngaria, aliud i Capha, aliud in Herminia, aliud Taurus et in pluribus aliis locis competentibus ad addiscendum linguas diuersas et ad disputandum

cum infidelibus. Studia inter Latinos magis idonea sunt quam inter infideles ratione securitatis, perpetuitatis et propter examinationem addiscentium. Studentes autem in praedictis locis habeant sufficienter sua necessaria.

[IV. De quarta parte quae est de rationibus, quare posita in isto tractatu debent fieri]
3. Et, quia Saraceni occupant terram ecclesiae christianorum, licitum est ipsos impugnare et terras, quas iniuste possident, recuperare. Saraceni multum conantur Tartaros inducere ad sectam eorum et dant eis filias, sorores et de bonis suis. Et per istum modum multos Tartaros ad sectam eorum inducunt, maxime cum secta eorum sit facilis ad credendum et delectabilis, quia promittunt in alia uita fiminas, et comestiones, et potum et multa alia sensibilia, sicut in lege eorum continetur. Et, quia Tartari sunt homines rudes, periculum est, quod ueniant ad sectam eorum. Et, si ueniant, aut quod per se sectam faciant aut quod Iudaei possunt eos habere, in maximo periculo erit tota christianitas. Vnde, ad cauendum istud periculum ita magnum, Ecclesia debet conari super ordinationem praedictam et, si posset Tartaros ad fidem conuertere, faciliter omnes Saraceni destri possent.

...
5. Saraceni, Tartari aliaeue nationes quaecumque per se non habent ita magnam potestatem ordinandi et persequendi publicam utilitatem sicut christiani. Et hoc ratione maris, in quo christiani sunt potentiores; et etiam ratione multiplicationis clericorum et scientiae et potestatis eorum. Et in armis et in pecunia et in moribus sunt potentiores et nobiliores quam aliqui alii, et maxime quia christiani sunt in ueritate et idonei ad recipiendum gratiam et adiutorium a Deo ratione fidei; alii non, quia sunt sine fide et in errore.

11. Petició de Ramon al Papa Celestí V per a la conversió dels infidels (1294)

Original text in Catalan published by Josep Perarnau i Espelt: "Un text català de Ramon Llull desconegut: la *"Petició de Ramon al Papa Celestí V per a la conversió dels infidels"*: edició i estudi" *Arxiu de textos catalans antics* 1982 v.1 p.9-46. Includes index.

Latin version:
1) *Petitio Raymundi.* In **RLO** t. II (1722) p.174-175. Text is appended to his *Liber de quinque sapientibus.*
2) *Petitio Raymundi (pro conversione Infidelium) ad Coelestinum V et ad Cardinales directa. Neapoli an. 1294*. In **Golubovich (1906)** v.1 p.373-375.

Petició de Ramon al Papa Celestí V per a la conversió dels infidels.
Catalan version edited by J. Perarnau i Espelt.

Con Déus aya creat home principalment a membrar, conèxer e amar, honrar e seruir si mateix; e con sien tans infeels qui no·l membren ni·l coneixen ne·l amen e asò depús que aquest món fo creat entrò a aquest temps en què som, anant aquels a foc perdurable; e encara con sien tans, que per I cr[e]stià que sien cent o plus qui no són crestians, molt seria couinent cosa que uós, subirà sant auesque Celestinus quintus, qui per Sant Spirit sots elet a papa, e que ls seynors honrats e discrets cardenals obríssets lo trezor de sancta esgleya a procurar con aquels qui són en error e Déu no coneixen ni amen venguesen a lum de veritat e seguissen la fi per què són creats.

Aquest trezor de sancta esgleya concitam en dues maneres: trezor speritual e trezor corperal. Espiritual, que ls sants hòmens religiozes e seglars, qui per, nostre seyor a honrar desígien pendre mort e qui són de doctrina sacra il·luminats, aprezessen diuerses lengatges que anassen prehicar los euuangelis per tot lo món e que uós, sant pare, e uosaltres, seynors cardenals, assignàssets vn seynor cardenal, qui tractàs aquest negoci e qui feés sercar aquels per totes les terres dels cristians, qui a aquesta sancta predicatió couinens seran e éser voltan, e que a aquels fossen mostrats tots los lenguatges del món, e que d'assò fossen estudis fets en les terres dels crestians e dels tartres; e que l seynor cardenal qui aquest offici auria feés la mescíó dels estudis e dels estudians, e assò contínuamen entrò que tot lo món fos de crestians.

Lo trezor corporall és que uós, pare sant apostoli, e vós, seynors cardenals, asignàssets per tots temps la dècima de la esgleya, e que n fos feta decretal, a conquerre les terres dels infeels e la sancta terra d'oltramar. E assò per forsa, d'armes. E d'aquesta dècima fos dada mescìò al seyor cardenal, qui tractaria los estudis, e l remanent fos dada al seynor altre cardenal, qui feés les mescions de les gerres, assò contínuament tro que tot lo món fos de crestians.

Couendria, encara, que la esgleya recobràs los sismàtics e aquels vnís a ssi, los quals pot recobrar ab disputatió e ab mostrar veritat que éls són en error e ls latins en veritat; car ab éls puria hom mils destrir los saraÿns e ab los tartres auer partissipació e amistat.

Seria, encara, cuuinén cosa que la esgleya que feés son poder a conquerre los tartres per disputació, lo qual conquerimén seria leuger per so cor no an ley e car sostenen que en lur terra pot hom prehicar la fe de Christ e encara que quisuol pot éser crestià sens que non an paor de seynoria; e aquest tractamén és molt necessari, car si ls tartres fan ley axí con fo Maffomet, o ls saraÿns o ls jueus los poden conuertir a lur ley, en gran peril serà tota crestiantat.

Si uós, sant pare e seynors cardenals, trametíets als reys dels saraÿns que us tramezessen savis, als quals mostràssets so que nós de Déu creem, e ls feÿets aplaer, éls, enteses nostres rahons, per uentura consentrien a aqueles o duptarien en lur fe, car éls no s pensen que nós creegam so que creem de la trinitat e de la encarnatió. E éls, tornats en lurs terres, dirien so que entès aurien de nós e puria éser que aquels qui u ohirien d'éls consentissen a les nostres rahons o duptassen en lur creensa. E aquesta manera que hom tengués ab éls puria éser molt proffitable. Aquesta mateixa manera puria hom tenir ab los sismàtics, als quals couendria que hom dixés tan forts rahons e tan nescessàries, ab les quals hom vensés totes lurs obieccions e posicions e que éls no poguessen soure nostres obieccions ni destruir nostres posicions; e d'aquestes rahons enaxí necessàries és molt bé garnida la sancta esgleya; e yo, Ramon Lul indingne, ne cuyt auer moltes segons alcuna noua manera que Déus m'a donada a vensre tots aquels qui contra la fe cathòlica vulen neguna cosa prouar o improuar.

Concirats, pare sant, e uós, seynors cardenals, con sots en gran càrrec a tractar en la honor de Déu, qui tant uos ha honrats e del món vicaris vos a fets, e con per aquest tractament damunt dit se pot sequir gran bé e si l negoci és lonc, él s'és bo e amable; e, si per la prolexitat e difficultat és jaquit, serà iaquit e meinspreat lo bé qui se'n pot seguir. E concirats con los hòmens d'aquest món per los béns temporals enprenen grans fets e de trebail, en qui són molt perilozes, axí con reys qui enprenen grans guerres; e anxexins, qui scientalmén se liuren a mort per so que lurs parens pusquen gitar de la seruitut en què són. E encara vos plàssia concirar con los crestians perden lurs terres e la audàcia que sulien auer contra saraÿns. E concirats con pública vtilitat és poc amada e con tuit clamen contra clergues; per què, seria gran escusa als clergues en tractar les cozes damunt dites, car bon exempli darien de si mateis e de lurs obres.

Si alcun diu que totes aquestes cozes se faran con a Déu plaurà, concirats si Déus uol la fi per què a creat home e si·n a dat exempli Ihesu Christ e·ls apòstols e ls màrtirs a sseguir aquela fi per què són; e qui dirà que Déus contínuament no vula éser amat per son poble?

Moltes d'altres rahons puria dir, mas tem trop parlar; e, si trop parle, soplec e clam mercè que·m sia perdonat e, posades aquestes coses que deman en orde, clam mercè a uós, sant pare, e a uosaltres, seynors cardenals, que us plàssia mi indingne trametre dels primers als saraÿns per honrar en éls nostre seyor Déus.

Data aquesta petició en la citutat de Nàpols al sant pare Celestinus e als honrats seynors cardenals en l'ayun de mil e CC XC quatre.

Petitio Raymundi (pro conversione infidelium) ad Coelestinum V.
Latin version from Golubovich.

Cum Deus principaliter creaverit hominem, ut homo ipsum recolat, intelligat, amet, honoret, et ipsi serviat, et cum sint tot infideles euntes ad ignem perdurabilem, qui illum non recolunt, nec cognoscunt, nec amant, et hoc quamprimum hic mundus fuit creatus usque ad hoc tempus, in quo sumus: et etiam cum sint tot, quod credo, quod pro uno Christiano sint centum vel plures qui non sunt Christiani, multum esset conveniens, quod vos supreme sancte Episcope Coelestine Quinte, qui per Sanctum Spiritum estis electi in papam, et Domini honorati et discreti Cardinales aperiretis thesaurum S. Ecclesiae ad procurandum, quomodo illi, qui sunt in errore et Deum non cognoscunt nec amant, venirent ad lumen veritatis, et sequerentur finem, propter quem sunt creati.

Hunc thesaurum sanctae Ecclesiae consideramus *duobus modis*, scilicet *thesaurum spiritualem* et *thesaurum corporalem*. *Thesaurus spiritualis est*, quod sancti homines religiosi et seculares, qui ad honorandum nostum Dominum Deum desiderarent sustinere mortem, et qui sacra doctrina sunt illuminati, addiscerent diversa linguagia, qui irent praedicare Evangelia per totum mundum; et quod vos sancte Pater, et vos Pater, et vos Domini Cardinales assignaretis unum Dominum Cardinalem, qui tractaret hoc negotium, et quod tales faceret quaeri per omnes terras Christianorum, qui huic sanctae praedicationi essent convenientes et vellent esse, et quod illis monstrarentur omnia linguagia mundi, et quod de illis fierent studia in terris Christianorum et Tartarorum, et quod ille Dominus Cardinalis, qui hoc officium haberet, faceret missionem studiorum et studentium, et hoc continuo, usque dum totus mundus esset Christianorum.

Thesaurus corporalis est, quod vos sancte Pater Papa, et vos Domini Cardinales assignaretis semper decimam Ecclesiae, et quod fieret Decretum ad conquirendum terras infidelium, et Sanctam Terram ultramarinam, et hoc per vim armorum; et de hac decima daretur missio Domino Cardinali, qui tractaret studia, et residuum daretur alteri Domino Cardinali, qui faceret missiones guerris, et hoc continuo, usque dum totus mundus esset Christianorum.

Conveniret etiam, quod Ecclesia recuperaret *Schismaticos*, et illos sibi uniret, quos potest recuperare cum disputatione monstrando veritatem, et quod illi sint in errore, et latini in veritate; quia cum illis melius possent destrui *Saraceni*, et haberi participatio et amicitia cum *Tartaris*.

Etiam esset conveniens, quod Ecclesia faceret suum posse ad conquirendum *Tartaros* per disputationem; quae conquisitio esset facilis, quia non habent legem, et quia permittunt in illorum terra praedicari fidem Christi, et etiam quicunque vult, potest esse Christianus absque timore dominii: et ista ordinatio est multum necessaria, quia si *Tartari* faciunt legem sicut fecit *Mahomet*, vel *Saraceni* vel *Judaei* poterunt illos convertere ad illorum legem et tota Christianitas erit in magno periculo.

Si vos sancte Pater et Domini Cardinales mitteretis ad Reges *Saracenorum*, ut vobis mitterent sapientes, quibus monstraretis hoc quod nos de Deo credimus, et illis faceretis placitum, et illi intelligerent nostras rationes, forte consentirent illis, vel dubitarent in sua fide; quia non putant, quod nos credamus hoc quod credimus de Trinitate et Incarnatione, et quando redirent in suas terras, dicerent hoc quod intellexissent de nobis; et posset esse, quod illi, qui hoc audirent ab illis, consentirent nostris rationibus, aut dubitarent in sua credulitate: et hic modus sic procedenci cum illis posset esse multum utilis. Hic idem modus posset teneri cum *Schismaticis*, et esset conveniens, quod illis dicerentur tam fortes rationes et tam necessariae, cum quibus vincerentur omnes illorum objectiones nec destruere nostras objectiones nec destruere nostras positiones, et quod illi non possent solvere nostras objectiones nec destruere nostras positiones: et istis rationibus ita necessariis est multum bene munita sancta Ecclesia. Ego *Rayundus Lullus* indignus, aestimo me multas tales [rationes] habere secundum aliquem novum modum, quem Deus mihi dedit ad vincendum omnes illos, qui contra Fidem Catholicam aliquid volunt probare vel improbare.

Considerate sancte Pater et vos Domini Cardinales, quod etis in magna via ad tractandum pro honore Dei, qui vos tantum honoravit, et vos fecit Vicarios mundi, et quod per supradictum tractatum potest evenire magnum bonum; et si negotium est longum, illud est bonum et amabile; et si propter prolixitatem et difficultatem abjicitur, spernitur bonum, quod inde potest sequi: et considerate, quomodo homines hujus mundi propter bona temporalia sustinent magnas defatigationes et labores, in quibus sunt multi in periculo, sicut Reges, qui sustinent magna bella, et *Anxexini*, qui scienter se tradunt morti, ut suos parentes possint eripere de servitute, in qua sunt: et etiam placeat vobis considerare, quod Christiani perdent suas terras et audaciam, quam solebant habere contra Saracenos; et considerate, quod publica utilitas parum ametur, et quod omnes clament contra Clericos; quare esset magna excusatio Clericis in tractando supradicta, quia darent bonum exemplum de se ipsis, et de suis operibus.

Si dicitur, quod omnia ista fient, quando Deo placuerit, considerate, utrum Deus velit finem, quare creavit hominem, et utrum

Iesus Christus dederit exemplum, et Apostoli et Martyres, ad assequendum illum finem quare sunt: et quis dicet, quod Deus non semper velit amari per suum po[po]lum?

Multas alias rationes possem dicere sed timeo nimium loqui, et si nimium loquor, supplico et peto veniam, ut ihi remittatur; et ponendo ista, quae peto, in ordine, peto veniam a vobis sancte Pater et a vobis Dominis Cardinalibus, ut vobis placeat me indignum primum mittere ad Saracenos ad honorandum inter illos nostrum Dominum Deum.

Data est haec petitio in civitate Neapolitana sancto Patri Coelestino Quinto, et honoratis Dominis Cardinalibus Anno MCCXCIV.

12. Disputació de cinc savis (1294)
Original Catalan text: *Disputació de cinc savis*. In: Josip Perarnau i Espelt, "La *"Disputació de cinc savis"* de Ramon Llull: estudi i edició del text català" *Arxiu de textos catalans antics* 1986, v.5, p.7-229. Includes index.
Latin version: *Liber de quinque sapientibus.* In **RLO**, t. II (1722), treatise IV, p. 125-174.

Disputació de cinc savis (1294)
Catalan version *Disputació de cinc savis.*
Text as edited by Perarnau (1986), p.23 line 1 to p.25 line 27.

Déus abondós de tot bé, en vertut de la tua gràcia, comensa aquesta disputatió de cinc sauis.

En vna gran selua, a ombra d'un bel arbre, prés d'una gran fontana, estauen quatre sauis, qui longamén auien estudiat en philosophia; la vn era latí, l'altre era grech, l'altre nestorí, l'altre jacopín. E parlauen de Déu. En làgremes e·n plors estauen, car gran tristícia auien per raó del món, qui és en tan torbat estamén, e car Déus era tan poc conegut e amat per son poble, com sia so qu·él sia dingne de gran amor e honor e gran mal sia no conèxer Déus ni amar ni fer a él la honor que li coué.

Dementre que los quatre sauis enaxí de Déu parlauen, éls veeren uenir un sarray, qui en la sciència de philosophia auia longament estudiat. E dix la un d'éls: "Ha! Con gran dampnatge és de crestians e gran deshonor pren Déus en est món en so que los sarayns, qui són en error, prenen nostres terres e tenen aquela sancta terra on Ihesu Xrist fo nat, crucificat e mort per nosaltres peccadors!" Respòs un dels sauis que él deya veritat e, encara, que era gran peril que si los sarrayns conuertien los tartres a lur ley, lo qual conuertimén és possible e·ls sarraïns hi fan tot so que poden, leugera cosa seria als sarraïns de destruir quaix tots los crestians.

Plorà vn dels sauis e dix aquestes paraules: "Com crestianisme sia en tan gran perill, per què tots los crestians del món no han unitat, pus que han concordança en creure la sancta trinitat de Déu e la sua encarnació? E si en alcunes coses han contrast, per què no·s concorden? Car, si s'unien, leugeramen purien vencre e destruir tots los sarraïns del món e, aprés, los tartres e·ls altres pagans purien sobiugar a la sancta fe cristiana.

Liber de quinque sapientibus
Latin text in RLO t.2 (1722) treatise III, p.1-2.

Deus, qui es abundans & perfectus in omnibus bonis, in virtute tuæ gratiæ Incipit Liber *de Quinque Sapientibus*.

De Prologo
In quadam magna silva sub umbra cujusdam pulchræ arboris juxta magnum fontem sedebant quatuor Sapientes, qui longo tempore studuerant i Philosophia: unus erat Latinus, alter Græcus, tertius Nestorinus, quartus Jacobinus, qui omnes cum suspiriis & lachrymis invicem loquebantur de DEO, multum dolentes de perturbato & misero statu mundi, & etiam de hoc, quod Deus adeo parum cognosceretur & amaretur a suo populo, cum sit dignus omni amore & honore, & sit magnum dedecus ac malum, ipsum non amari, nec cognosci, nec honorari ut decet.

Cum quatuor Sapientes sic invicem loquerentur de DEO, viderunt quendam Saracenum venientem, qui erat peritus in Scientia

Philosophiæ; dum ipsum videbant, unus ipsorum incepit dicere: heu! quantum damnum imminet Christianis, pro dolor, quantum dedecus & vituperium recipit Deus in hoc mundo, videlicet in hoc, quod Saraceni, qui sunt in errore, capiant & occupent nostras terras, & teneant illam sanctam terram, in qua Jesus Christus pro nobis peccatoribus fuit natus, crucifixus & mortuus.

Alter euorum respondit ei: quod diceret veritatem; & adhuc de alio periculo esset timendum, ne scilicet Saraceni convertant Tartaros ad sectam eorum; nam cum sit facile Saracenis, fieri hujusmodi conversionem, si Tartari essent conversi ab eis (quod absit) leve quid esset Saracenis destruere quasi totum populum christianum.

Dixit tertius: adhuc est timendum aliud periculum, scilicet, quod, si Saraceni vel Tartari possent devincere Græcos, faciliter possent debellare Latinos.

Quartus vero tristis plorando dixit hæc verba: cum Christianitas sit subjugata in tot & tantis periculis, quare non omnes Christiani hujus mundi habent unitatem, postquam habent concordantiam credendo in sanctisimam Trinitatem Dei & suam Incarnationem? & quare non concordant, si usque nunc inter eos fuit discordia super aliquibus Articulis? nam si concordarent, leviter possent devincere omnes Saracenos, & postea illos convertere, & illos & Tartaros & alios Paganos subjugare christianæ Fidei.

13. Lo desconhort (1295)
Original text in Catalan:
1) *Lo desconhort.* In **Poesies**, p.69-105.
2) *Desconort.* In **ORL** v.19 (1936), p.217-254.
Bilingual editions (selected):
Catalan and French: *Le desconort, ou, Le Découragement de Ramon Llull.* Étude littéraire et historique, édition critique et traduction française Amédée Pagès. Toulouse: Édouard Privat; Paris: Henri Didier, 1938. Pagès' introduction provides some interesting remarks on the influence of Ibn Tufail's *Hayy ben Yaqdhan* on this work and Llull's thought in general.

Catalan and German: *Lo desconhort* = *Der Desconhort*. Mit einer Einführung versehen von Johannes Hösle und Vittorio Hösle. München: W. Fink, 1998.

Lo desconhort (1295)
Text as edited by Ramon d'Alòs-Moner in **Poesies**, p.86, lines 385-396 and p.101-102, lines 745-756.

XXXIII
Ramon, segons que auig dir, mant hom és anat
preïcar als tartres e pauc han enançat,
e encara als sarraïns, d'on són meravellat
can així estats forts en vostra volentat,
car de tot fait on hom se sia fadigat,
e majorment con tantes vets l'haja assajat,
se deu tot hom partir, pus que sia senat
e si no se'n parteix faf-se'e tenir per fat;
per què us consell, germà, que hajats pietat
de vostre cors mateix que tants havets hujat,
e estats en un lloc on sia reposat,
e de vostres dammnatges estiats consolat.

LXIII
N'ermità—dix Ramon—,bé havets consirat,
car per aital cercle pot ésser acabat
lo fait que és tam bó a crestianitat;
e digats ça e lla, a rei e a prelat
que si el fait tost no es pren que ja és ordenat
per sarraïns que els tartres a el síon girat,
e ja n'han convertits una gran quantitat;
e els tartres convertits en sarraïnitat
lleu poran destruir quaix tota cristianitat
en tant que no serà cristià qui haja regnat
ni negú prelat haurà cavall sejornat.
Vejats, doncs, n'ermità, lo món a què és tornat.

14. Petitio Raymundi pro conversione infidelium et pro recuperatione Terrae Sanctae ad Bonifacium VIII (1295-6)

Original text in Latin: *Peticio Raymundi pro conversione infidelium*. In: Helene Wieruszowski, "Ramon Lull et l'idée de la Cité de Dieu: quelques nouveaux écrits sur la croisade" *Estudis Franciscans*, 1935 v.47 p.87-110. Reprinted in: *Miscellanea Lulliana. Homenatge al Beat Ramon Lull en occasió del VII centenario de la seva naixença*. Barcelona, 1935, p.403-426 and in her *Politics and culture in medieval Spain and Italy*. Roma: Edizioni di storia e letteratura, 1971. (Storia e letteratura: raccolta di studi e testio, 121), p.161-164.

Petitio Raymundi pro conversione infidelium et pro recuperatione Terrae Sanctae ad Bonifacium VIII (1295-1296)
Text from Wieruszowski (1971), p.161-164.

  Advertat sanctitas vestra, sanctissime pater, domine Bonifaci papa ac vos reverendi patres domini cardinales, quod, cum Deus creaverit homines, ut eum cognoscant, diligant et honorent et recolant in veritate et cum infideles sint multo plures quam christiani, qui a mundi principio usque nunc persistentes in errore, non cessant descendere ad penas perpetuas infernales, quantum deceret, quod vos, sanctissime pater, qui per Dei gratiam primatum tenetis in populo christiano, et vos reverendi domini cardinales, aperiretis ecclesie sancte thesaurum ad procurandum, quod omnes qui verum Dei cultum ignorant, ad veritatis lumen perveniant, ut finem valeant assequi, ad quem Deus eos ex sua benignitate creavit.

  Thesaurus iste quem pro divini cultus multiplicatione ipsis infidelibus dicimus reserandum, duplex est, spiritualis videlicet et corporalis.

  Thesaurus spiritualis potest ipsis infidelibus communicari, hoc modo scilicet, quod in diversis locis ad hoc aptis per terram christianorum ac in quibusdam locis etiam tartarorum fiant studia idiomatum diversorum, in quibus viri sacra scriptura competenter imbuti tam religiosi uam seculares, qui cultum divinum per orbem terrarum desiderant ampliari, valeant ipsorum infidelium ydiomata diversa addiscere et ad eorum partes pro predicando evangelio Dei utiliter se transferre, et quod uni dominorum cardinalium hoc pium Dei negotium committatur, de cuius ordinatione et licentia illi tales ponantur in studiis et ad predicandum mittantur, ui eis, prout decens fuerit, provideat in expensis.

Thesauro corporali uti poteris, isto modo scilicet, quod similiter uni domino cardinali ordinatio committatur ad procurandum et tractandum passagium pro terra sancta laudabiliter acquirenda et acquisita etiam conservanda, potenter ordinato ad hoc certo numero bellatorum et quandocumque contiget mori aliquos corundem, totidem vel plures vel pauciores, secundum quod expedire videbitur, sine dilatione mittantur per ordinationem dicti domini cardinalis eisdem in expensis necessariis provisuri.

Cum autem predicta sine magnis sumptibus non valeant adimpleri, decimam ecclesie pro acquisitione et aliam competentem collectam ut ubique terrarum perpetuo reddatur honor debitus summo Deo.

Multum etiam expedit, quod Greci et alii scismatici reuniantur ecclesie sacrosancte, quod fieri poterit disputando per auctoritates et rationes necessarias, quibus per Dei gratiam ecclesia latina sufficienter habundat, ipsis enim ecclesie reunitis facilius poterimus eorum subsidio mediante, qui viciniores existunt, impugnare et de terra iure nostra expelle sarracenos ac etiam, quod non est modicum, participare cum tartaris, ad quorum conversione, debemus per predicationem et disputationem viriliter laborare. Ipsi enim cum adhuc gentiliter sint viventes, ad legem nostram, quam possumus inter eos libere predicare, faciliter possunt trahi, cum etiam non sit cure principibus tartarorum, cuiusque secte sint eorum subditi professores, quod vere nulatenus est a fidelibus negligendum. Nam iudei et sarraceni, qui sunt dominationi tartarice subiugati, trahere illos ad sectam propriam quilibet elaborant. Qui si traherentur ad aliquam illorum, quod absit, vel tertiam per se ipsos, sicut Mahometus fecit, instituerunt, possent ecclesie Dei maximum dampnum inferre.

Si vos, sancte pater, quibusdam sarracenorum regibus scriberetis, quod vobis mitterent aliquos sarracenos eorum, qui discretiores et subtiliores inter alios repuntantur, tales, prout credo, vobis mittere non different, quibus inter nos per aliquot annos commorantibus, possemus disputando benigne et amicabiliter conferendo veritatem ostendere, quam de fide nostra tenemus. Ipsi enim estimantes nos irrationabiliter et fatue de Deo et eius operibus secundum articulos nostre fidei credere et sentire, cum viderent nos valde rationabiliter et sapienter supra quamcumque aliam credulitatem humanam de Deo et eius operibus secundum articulorum nostre fidei invicibilem veritatem credere et sentire ac nos esse promptos ad ostendendum rationes, quas infideles apponunt contra fidem nostram, non esse necessarias nec aliquid contra nos secundum veritatem concludere, rationes vero nostras pro fide sic esse invincibiles, quod nullum ex ipsis omnino inconveniens sequitur, immo sublimitas ineffabilis divine essencie et eius operationum gloriosior humane intellectui declaratur, ex quo valde convenientes et necessarie comprobantur. Que quidem rationes in sacra pagina seminate sunt et plantate et per philosophiam significate, prout apparet intuentibus diligenter, in quibus scientes quendam modum novum inquirendi et inveniendi ad hoc ex divina beneficiencia noviter mihi R. Lulii licet inmerito et valde indigno concessum possunt copiosius habundare unde infideles vel reciperent fidem nostram aut multum hesitantes de secta sua recederent et suis compatriotis, quid et quomodo sentimus et credimus de Deo et eius operius recitarent.

 Consideretis igitur, sancte pater, et vos reverendi domini cardinales, quomodo pre ceteris hominibus tenemini honorem Dei et ecclesie utilitatem totis viribus procurare, cum Deus vos pre ceteris honoraverit, vos suos vicarios et gregis sui pastores constituens et quomodo per tractatum predictorum potest universali ecclesie magna utilitas evenire et licet sic longum negocium, est tamen exsecutione dignum, cum sit amabile et Deo gratum ac valde omnibus fructuosum.

Nec est pretermittendum propter eius prolixitatem a viris magnaminis tantum bonum considerantibus, quomodo mundani homines agrediuntur laboriosa et valde ardua propter transitoria acquirenda et quomodo reges terre guerras maximas et valde periculosas assumunt, quomodo etiam Anicessini seipsos morti scienter exponunt et ad hoc faciendum ab infantia nutriuntur, ut genus suum tradere valeant libertati.

Consideretis etiam si placet, quomodo christiani terras amittunt et audaciam quam contra sarracenos habere solebant at quomodo perit respublica et sint fere ab omni christiano neglecta at quomodo clamant layci contra clerum.

Quare ex predictorum ordinacione haberent in vobis et vestris bonis operibus exemplum layci ad bona publica procuranda ex quo sufferetur grande honus a vobis, cum dampnum et detrimentum christianitatis pro maiori parte vestre negligentie imputetur.

Si autem dicat quis, quod fiet infidelium conversio non modo sed alias, quando Deo placuerit, meditetur diligenter et recogitet ille talis utrum Deus velit quod semper et ubique sibi in veritate a suo populo serviatur et utrum velit omnes homines salvos fieri et ad finem, ad quem eos creavit, venire ac si de hoc dedit dominus Jesus Christus exemplum et sui discipuli per mundum universum laboriosissime discurrentes ad cultum Dei in omnibus hominibus statuendum.

Plures ad hoc possunt adduci rationes auctoritates et sanctorum exempla et plura alia particularia sunt in christianitate necessarie ordinanda, que devotioni aliorum dimitto, cum merito timeam in tantorum dominorum presentia plura loqui.

Et si in hiis que proposui nimis presumptuose in aliquo sim locutus flectens cordis genua veniam postulo et requiro humiliter quantum possum, me paratum exhibens predictis omnibus ordinatis, que, prout per se patet, possibilia sunt, laudabilia sunt et decentia et ipsis ordinatoribus inestimabiliter meritoria, primum mitti vel inter primos ad terras sarracenorum, quorum linguam didici, ad cultum divinum ampliandum domini nostri Jesu Christo subsidio mediante.

15. Arbre de sciència (1295-1296)
Original text in Catalan:
1) *Arbre de sciencia*. In: **ORL** v.11-13 (1917-1926).
2) *Arbre de ciència*. **OE** v.1, p.547-1046.
Latin version: *Arbor scientiae*. In: **ROL** v.24-26 (2000)

Arbre de sciencia (1295-1296)
Text as edited by Galmés in **ORL**, v.2, p.5-6; v.3, p.159-160

[Del' Arbre apostolical.
I. De les rayls del Arbre apostolical.]
4. Lo papa cové que haja aquella fe que hac sent Pere, pus que es son vicari. E aquella fe cové que la haja sots hàbit de bontat, enaxí quel papa sia bo, car la fe es bona; el papa cové que haja gran fe, per ço car la fe de sent Pere fo gran, e cové que la fe del papa sia tan gran que respona a la fe de son poble; e la fe del papa cové que sia durable, pus que es general, car en la privació de la causa general son privades les duracions particulars; e la fe del papa cové que sia forts, per ço que la força daquella enfortesca la fe de cascún home; e per açò fo ma per ço que ab braç seglar fos lo papa forts a contrastar deu esser clara a les gents per bon exempli, car aquella claredat illumina a cascún home la sua fe, enaxí, car aquella claredat illumina a cascún home la sua fe, enaxí com lo sol qui illumina moltes esteles, illuminant gran lum molts lums petits; e la fe del papa deu esser caritativa e amable, per ço que mova los seus sotsmeses a caritat e a calor damor per gran fervor; e la fe del papa deu esser irtuosa per ço que sia contra vicis. E la fe del papa deu esser vera, per ço que sia contra falsetat e error , e per açò dix Jesu Christ a sent Pere que si lamava, que donàs a menjar a les sues ovelles; e açòli dix .iij. vegades, a significar que les ovelles son de Deu Pare, e de Deu Sant Esperit e de Deu Fill e home, un Deus tots .iij., un Christ qui eleg un pastor a les sues ovelles, per ço quels donàs a menjar veritat de la fe, ab la qual veritat viuen; e en persona de sent Pere son comenades les ovelles a la fe de cascún papa: e per açò fa mal aquell papa qui no exampla la fe en moltes ovelles,

per ço que sia molt general e que en ella viuen moltes ovelles, car assats es major gracia de vida espiritual que de corporal. E encara, la fe del papa deu esser repòs de la fe de cascún home, enaxí com los particulars bens qui en los generals han repòs; e encara, en la fe del papa no deu esser differencia della jni de la fe de son poble, car una deu esser la fe en ell e en ses ovelles. E encara, lo papa ab la sua fe se deu concordar ab la fe de cascún home; e ab la sua fe lo papa deu esser contra les causes qui son contra la fe, per raó de la qual contrarietat se deu esforçar de destrovir les errors qui son sembrades en los sarrasins tartres e juseus qui son contra la fe cristiana, e encara deu destrovir les cismes sembrades en los crestians desviats a la fe crestiana. E encara, la fe del papa deu esser començament e lum per bon eximpli e anar davant a les ovelles, per ço que venguen en lo loc on son les pastures e les aygues de vida eternal; e la fe del papa deu esser mijà en qui s prenga lo lum de Deu e quel do a son poble, enaxí com la luna qui pren la virtut del son e la dona sajús a les plantes e a les substancies sensuades; e encara, la fe del papa se deu haver a la fi per que ell es papa, ço es saber, per ço que ab la sua fe illumín les carreres per les quals los sants van a santa vida e contemplativa e a penitencia. E encara, la fe del papa deu esser enaxí major, com es lo pastor major que less ovelles; e encara, la fe del papa deu esser egual ab la fe de ses ovelles en creure de Deu veres coses; e encara, per çoquel papa es pastor e es en una metexa fe ab les ovelles, se deu enclinar a les menoritats daquelles, per ço que les pug a ensús en reebre beneffici de la sua majoritat, axí com lo foc qui s enclina al àer qui no es de tan gran virtut com ell, el puja a ensús en quant lo majorifica en virtut; e açò metex fa lo sol qui puja a ensús lo foc en quant li multiplica sa calor.

[Del Arbre questional.
III. De les questions de les branques.
8. De les questions de les branques del Arbre moral viciós, e primerament
58. De les questions de mentir e dels vicis ab ella mesclats

Questió. Mentir e maldír, per que havets feta companya? — Sol. Digueren que havín fet companya per ço que destrovissen bontat e veritat qui son amigues.

766 Quest. Per que los homens mentifors son pus impacients que altres? — Sol. Home mentidor, tota hora que hom lo reprèn, s escusa.

767 Quest. Mentir, de que es lo vostre fundament? — Sol. Dix quel seu fundament era de ergull enveja e avaricia e ypocresía

768 Quest. Demanà ermità a la boca si era tan sutza per mentir com la camisa del lebrós per lebrosia? — Solució. Dix la boca que ho demanàs a ypocresía qui es pus leja que la camisa del lebrós.

769 Quest. Mentir, còm fets falsía? — Sol. Respòs e dix que symonía e ypocresía ho sabíen.

770 Quest. Mentir, havets diligencia? — Sol. Dix que per tot lo mon havía sembrada la sua sement.

771 Quest. Mentir, havets ensenyament? — Solució. Respòs e dix que ell havía apresa rectòrica per ço que pogués enganar la gent.

772 Quest. Mentir, sots estat obedient? — Sol. Dix mentir que ho demanàs als tartres e als jueus e als sarrains, e al argent dels cristians e al hàbit de ypocrisía.

16. Cant de Ramon (1299)

Original text in Catalan:
1) *Cant de Ramon*. In **Poesies**, p.30-33.
2) *Del cant de Ramon*. In **ORL**, v.19 (1936), p.255-260.
French translation: *Cant de Ramon*. In **Sugranyes de Franch (1954)**, p.143-145.

Cant de Ramon (1299)
Text as edited by Ramon d'Alòs-Moner in **Poesies**, p.31, lines 25-36

Lo món era en damnació;
morí per dar salvació
Jesús, per qui el món creat fo.

Jesús pujà al cel sobre el tro,
venrà a jutjar li mal e el bo:
no valran plors querre perdó.

Novell saber hai atrobat,
pot-n'hom conèixer veritat
e destruir la falsetat:
sarraïns seran batejat,
tartres, jueus e mant orat,
per lo saber que Déus m'ha dat.

17. Liber de praedicatione (1304)
Liber de praedicatione. In **ROL**, v.3-4 (1963)

Liber de praedicatione (1304)
Text as established in **ROL**, v.4, p.336-337.

LXXXV. [De sanctis XVII]
Sermo de beato Stephano Protomartyre (26. Dec.)
...
II.
Hic sequitur pars, quae est de applicatione. Et haec in tres partes dividitur, secundum quod ad tria applicabimus supra dicta. Primo ad infideles. Secundo ad malos christianos. Et tertio ad detractores. Et primo de prima parte dicemus sic:
1. Infideles fidelibus contradicunt, scilicet christianis, sicut Iudaei, Saraceni, Tartari et huiusmodi. Iudaei dicunt, quod Iesus fuit malus homo; et ita malus, quod numquam fuit ita malus, nec unquam erit ita malus. Christiani dicunt, quod Iesus est melior homo, qui unquam erit. Et tamen christiani cum istis Iudaeis participant maledictis; ipsos salutant in via, et cum ipsis mercaturas faciunt, de quo miror. Saraceni occupant Terram sanctam; ipsi negant sanctissimam incarnationem Filii Dei Patris, negant etiam beatissimam trinitatem, bellando interficiunt christianos, et deprimunt quantum possunt. Et sic de Tartaris potest dici.

18. De fine (1305)
Latin text:
1) *Der liber de fine*. In **Gottron (1912)**, p.64-93.
2) *De fine*. In **ROL**, v.9 (1981), p.233-291.

De fine (1305)
Text as established in **ROL**, t.IX, p.266-269, lines 532-617.

I.5. Contra Tartaros

Tartari, et sic de aliis gentibus, non habent scientiam, neque legem. Legem non habent, nam eis deficiunt praedicantes. Scientiam non habent, quia intellectus eorum est de rebus sensibilibus occupatus et imaginabilibus. Et sic ecclesia praedicatores deberet eis dare, qui eos instruerent in sancta lege catholica cum rationibus probatiuis. Et quod de iure et de medicina et de philosophia et de moralibus eis darent scientiam; et hoc continue et expresse.

Quo ad theologiam libri nostri supra dicti essent ualde boni, et inter alios *Liber gentilis*; in quo christianus, Saracenus et Iudaeus coram quodam gentili de ueritate disputant. Et de fide per illum librum possent cognoscere, si uolebant, quod sancta fides catholica obtinet ueritatem, et quod Iudaei in errore sunt, et etiam Saraceni.

Ego uero fui in partibus ultramarinis, et audiui, quod Cassanus, imperator Tartarorum, pluries dicebat, quod uolebat de fide christianorum esse certus. Quoniam si de ipsa habebat certitudinem, ipse se faceret christianum, et faceret, quod tota sua militia esset omnimode baptizata. Et quia certitudinem non hauit, factus fuit cum tota sua militia Saracenus. Et sic in Dei ecclesia contritio magnam habet materiam et subiectum ad corda eorundem remordendum.

Vlterius: Accidit, quot Tunicio fuit quidam rex Saracenus, qui Miramamoli uocabatur. Et adhuc non est diu, unus religiosus christianus arabice huic probauit, quod Saracenorum lex erat falsa; et hoc est facile ad probandum. Tunc rex sibi dixit, quod christianorum fidem approbaret; et ipse deinde se faceret christianum, et omnes alios de sua patria faceret baptizari.

Dictus religiosus non erat multum literatus in philosophia nec in theologia, et respondit, quod christianorum fides non erat probabilis, sed credibilis tantum. Et tunc rex pro trufa habuit dicta sua; et dixit ei, quod nolebat credere pro credere dimittere, sed bene credere dimitteret pro intelligere ueritatem. Et ideo, si religiosus ille de nostra fide tales dedisset rationes ita cogentes, quod rex non posset soluere ante dictas—quae rationes sunt in sacra pagina implicatae; et sum certus etiam, quod in libris meis supra dictis sunt, ut patet in eisdem—tunc rex fuisset christianus, et una cum eo suae gentes, quoniam sanctus rex Franciae Ludouicus iuit tunc Tunicium cum exercitu suo magno; et si praedictus rex Saracenorum consensisset, tota sua patria fuisset iam fidelis. Et sic recuperata fuisset Terra sancta. Et ideo conscientia spectet habere iudicium contra illos, qui possunt agere bonum, et ad hoc deputati sunt, et non agunt; nam quasi ab illis penitus est neglectum.

Vlterius: Dico et etiam iuro, quod Ianuae accidit mihi semel, dum cum quodam Iudaeo de fide per rationes cogentes uolui disputare, et ipse dixit, quod non licitum mihi erat, quoniam summus pontifex hoc nolebat. Et tunc ego dixi, quod cum talibus cogentibus rationibus cum ipso uolebam disputare, cum quibus omnes suas el soluerem rationes, et meas ipse dissoluere non posset ullo modo. Tamen non "propter quid" nec "per quia", sed "per aequiparantiam"; de qua fecimus unum librum, superius in principio nominatur, et per modum etiam plurium aliorum, superius iam dictorum. Et finaliter disputauimus, sicut dixi. Et in fine fugiuit, ita quod coram me causa disputationis non fuit ausus postea apparere.

Tartari, et sic de aliis paganis, omnes mundum esse aeternum quasi credunt, et ad praedestinationem multum stant siue ad iudicium astronomiae. Sed quod mundus nouus sit, satis est in sacra pagina implicatum. Et per rationes cogentes est etiam probatum in pluribus libris meis, in tanto quod intellectus humanus non potest tenere contrarium bono modo. Et ad hoc etiam bonus est unus liber, quem fecimus, qui *De praedestinatione* nominatur. In quo probatur, quod liberum arbitrium homo habet bonum aut malum simpliciter ad agendum. Etiam fecimus unum librum, *De astronomia* nominatum; in quo probamus astronomorum iudicium non in omnibus fore certum. Et sic de multis aliis, qui boni essent ad conuertendum Tartaros et paganos; et illis conuersis coran christianis nullus Saracenus esset ausus postea apparere. Sed si Saraceni conuertant ipsos, et iam multus, ut supra dictum est, conuerterunt, nullus christianus habebit faciem coram ipsis.

Et oh, ecclesia sancta catholica, uideas, quot inimicos habes et habebis, si in tua otiositate permanes, et aliud non pertractas. Nam septuaginta anni sunt elapsi, quod Tartari a montibus descenderunt; et habent plus de dominio in hoc mundo, quam inter Saracenos et omnes etiam christianos. Et ideo, ecclesia, quare dormis, et non laboras, postquam tantus thesaurus est tibi commendatus per spiritualem gladium et etiam per gladium corporalem? Forte non poteris, dum uolibis.

Finita est prima distinctio huius libri. In qua multa alia possent dici ad conuersionem infidelium ordinandam. Sed causa breuitatis, quae dicta sunt, sufficiant quo ad praesens.

Et ista distinctio gladium spiritualem significat, uidelicet ueritatem contra falsitatem, ignorantiam et errorem. Modo sequitur de secundo gladio, uidelicet corporali. Et quia homo non est compositus, nisi ex corpore et anima, gladii sufficiant isti duo.

19. Liber disputationis Raimundi christiani et Homeri saraceni (1308)

Original text in Arabic, now lost. Two Latin editions available:
1) *Disputatio Raymundi christiani et Hamar saraceni.* In **RLO**, tomus IV (1737), treatise VII, p. 431-477.
2) *Liber disputationis Raimundi christiani et Homeri saraceni.* In **ROL**, v.22 (1998), p.159-264.

Liber disputationis Raimundi christiani et Homeri saraceni
(1308)
Text as established in **ROL**, t.XXII, p.262-263, lines 39-60.

III. De tertia parte: Quae est de ordinatione siue de fine libri.

Item: Tres sunt imperatores Tartarorum. Quibus maior imperator, nuncupatus Magnus Canis, et possidet terram presbyteri Iohannis. Et ultra istum imperatorem uersus partes orientales nescitur alter dominus nisi ipse. Et alter dominator est uersus partes septentrionales, cuius nomen est Totay [ms. variants: Totan; Cotay]; Saraceni sunt sui scriptores et dispensatores, ut ratione participationis ipsos possint conuertere. Tertius imperator est dominus Persiae usque in Indian, et uocator Carbenda. Et ipse et omnes sui milites facti sunt Saraceni; et hoc fuit factum tempore Casani, fratris sui. Et sic non oportet regem Franciae ire in Syriam, neque etiam aliquem alium, cui Persia ets uicina; alioquin Carbenda et Soldanus essent contra christianos.

Amplius: Dicitur, quod non sunt nisi septuaginta anni aut parum plus, quod Tartari exiuerunt a montibus. Et isti tres imperatores possident maiores terras in duplo et plus, quam omnes reges christianorum et Saracenorum.

Adhuc dicitur, quod Nestorini et Iacobini, odientes Latinos incipiunt iam praedicare et conuertere Tartaros. Et ideo considerent maiores, quid erit in fine. Deus namque multum est amabilis et timibilis; idcirco dedit potestatem Latinis, quod ipsi totum mundum possent acquirere, si uellent; ut figuratum est in *Libro de fine*.

[Borrás (1908) translates this passage from *Liber disputationis Raimundi christiani et Homeri saraceni* into Spanish and follows his translation with seven paragraphs of comments.]

20. Liber de convenientia Fidei et intellectus in obiecto (1309)

Latin text: *Liber de convenientia Fidei et intellectus in obiecto.* In **RLO**, tomus IV (1737) treatise XII, p.571-575 Some manuscripts, including that used for the published edition, have the date March 1304, others March 1309, both according to the Florentine system used by Llull.

Liber de convenientia fidei & intellectus in objecto. **RLO** t. 4 (1737), treatise 11, p.1 and 5

Deus cum tua Sapientia & Charitate, Gratia & Benedictione incipit Liber, qui est *de Convenientia, quam habet Fides & Intellectus in Objecto.*
De Divisione hujus Libri.
Iste Liber dividitur in tres pPartes. Prima Pars est de quibusdam dicendis contra illos, qui dicunt, quod Fides non debeat probari. Secunda Pars est de Probatione aliquorum Articulorum Fidei. Tertia Pars est de Narrationibus Damni, quodsequitur ex eo, quia est infamia ab Infidelibus ad Fideles, qui decunt, quod Sancta Catholica Fides non possit probari. ...

[Pars III.
4. Sunt tres Imperatores Tartarorum, quorum Major dicitur magnus Canis; & alter in Persia & nominatur Carbenda; tertius vero apud Septentrionem, qui Cotan appellatur: Carbenda cum tota sua Gente factus est Saracenus, & Saraceniu conantur pervertere majores Imperatores, & alium etiam, qui Chaspar est dictus; & isti tres Imperatores multo plus possident de terra, quam omnes Christiani, & etiam omnes Saraceni, quid esset de nobis minimis Christianis? & non sunt adhuc octoginta anni, quod Tartari exierunt a montibus.

21. Liber de acquisitione Terrae Sanctae (1309)
1) *Liber de acquisitione Terrae Sanctae.* Edited by É. Longpré, *Criterion* 3 (Barcelona, 1927), 265-278.
2) *De acquisitione Terrae Sanctae: modus recuperandi Terram Sanctam.* Edited by E. Kamar. In: *Studia Orientalia Christiana Collectanea* 6 (Cairo, 1961), 103-131.

Liber de acquisitione Terrae Sanctae (1309)
Text from Kamar (1961), p.116, 124-125, 129-130.

[p.116]
De secunda distinctine.
De modo praedicandi.

Distinctio ista est de praedicatione sive de disputatione cum infidelibus, et est divisa in sex partes:
Prima pars est de ordinatione.
Secunda de Sarracenis.
Tertia de Judaeis.
Quarta de Haereticis.
Quinta de Schismaticis.
Sexta de Tartaris sive Gentilibus.

[p.124-125]
De sexta parte secundae distinctionis.
Tartari sive Gentiles sunt homines rudes et non habent legem, et ideo in disputatione cum ipsis recurrendum est ad moralia, videlicet ad virtutes et vitia et, ipsis illuminatis, recurrendum est ad divinas rationes et ad actus earum, per modum inducere ipsos ad legem sine qua virtutes non essent sufficientes ad acquirendum viam paradisi nec ad evitandum viam inferni: nec sapientia, potestas et caritas possunt habere in nobis subiectum ex ipsis habituatum, et per talem modum homo reduceret ipsos ad credendum legem esse necessariam quantum ad bene esse; et hoc facto, recurrendum est ad leges Christianorum, Judaeorum et Sarracenorum, et probare quod oportet illam legem esse veram in qua divinae rationes magis possunt exercere actus suos et per quam homo posset se magis disponere ad habendum virtutes et ad evitandum vitia, et haec est lex Christianorum, ut per se patet. Nos autem hoc probavimus in libro qui dicitur de Gentili et in libro de disputatione Raymundi christiani et Hamari sarraceni.
Diximus de secunda distinctione et datus est modus et doctrina per quam totus mundus potest reduci ad bonum statum, posito quod ecclesia Dei viriliter et festinanter aperiat thesauros suos, scilicet pecunialem, corporalem et spiritualem, sicut supra iam est tactum.

[*De secunda parte tertiae distinctionis.*]
p.129-130
Tres imperatores tartarorum qui de terra plus possident quam inter christianos et omnes etiam sarracenos et tamen non prae-

terierunt anni octoginta quod ab eorum montibus exiverunt; et talis subita infidelium multiplicatio multum periculosa est naviculae Sancti Petri. Nam unus ex illis cum tota sua militia factus est sarracenus et dominus Persarum, qui Carbenda nominatur, et sic ille magis posset impedire acquisitionem Terre Sancte quam aliquis homo vivens; ratione cuius esset bonum quod dominus papa festinaret creare illos religiosos litteratos, in secunda distinctione superius nominatos ad convertendum illum cum sua militia de novo perversum antequam essent indurati in secta Mahometica et imbuti, et quod aliqui istorum religiosorum essent sub habitu religiosi militis magistri generalis. Sarraceni sunt valde cautelosi et multum zelant ad exaltandum sectam sive legem eorum et, quia Tartari sunt homines in scriptura rudes et grossi, faciunt se eorum scriptores et bajuli, ut cum eis valeant participare et convertere ad legem eorum. Quare est dubium quod alii duo imperatores ad cautelas illorum pervertantur et postea periclitaretur in decuplo dicta nauicula Sancti Petri.

Imperium Constantinopolitanum de facili posset a Tartaris conquestari et si ab illis conquestaretur, quid esset postea de passagio Terrae Sanctae? Nec quis posset eos postea retrocedere quin venirent Romani et ulterius conquestatum. Ah! potestas, sapientia et caritas, festinetis vigilando et non dormiatis, nam inimici vestri sunt prope vigilantes.

22. Vita coaetania (1311)

Original text in Latin: *Vita coaetania.* In **ROL**, v. 8 (1980), p. 268-309.

Latin and Catalan versions, parallel text: *Vida coetanea de Ramon Llull.* In **OLit,** p.41-77.

English translation: In **SW**, v.1, p.13-48. (Interspersed with commentary and copious notes.)

Vita coaetanea (1311)
Text as edited in **ROL**, v. 8 (1980), p. 294-295, lines 500-510.

VIII

...

Sed uidens se parum uel nihil super talibus obtinere, regressus est Maioricas. Vbi trahens moram, conatus est tam disputationibus quam etiam praedicationibus trahere Saracenos innumeros ibi morantes in uiam salutis. Fecit etiam ibidem libros nonnullos.

33. Factum est igitur, dum Raimundus talibus insudaret laboribus, ut noua discurrerent, uidelicet quod imperator Tartarorum Cassanus regnum Syriae fuisset aggressus, illudque totum suo dominio ambiebat.

Quod cum audisset etiam Raimundus, inuenta naui parata transfretauit usque Cyprus. Ibique reperit noua illa penitus fore falsa.

23. Liber disputationis Petri et Raimundi sive Phantasticus (1311)
Liber disputationis Petri et Raimundi sive Phantasticus. In **ROL**, v.16 (1988), p.1-30.

Liber disputationis Petri et Raimundi sive Phantasticus (1311)
Text from ROL v.16 (1988) p.28 line 534 to p.30 line 610.

[V. De ordine]
534. Ait clericus: Constantinus, imperator romanus, dedit imperium ecclesiae. Spiritus autem sanctus fecit homines in ecclesia deuotos, sanctam fidem catholicam ueram esse cognoscentes.

Ait Raimundus: Clerice, uerum dicis. Nam uniuersa catholicorum ecclesia duos gladios habet, ut in euangelio dictum est, scilicet gladium corporalem, ensem uidelicet, et spiritualem, scilicet scientiam et deuotionem. Cum istis autem duobus gladiis sufficeret ecclesia omnes infideles ad uiam reducere ueritatis. Primo, si papa sapientes et discretos, mortem sustinere paratos, apud saracenos, turcos et tartaros mitteret, qui infidelibus suos errores ostenderent et sanctae fidei catholicae ueritatem aperirent, ut ipsi infideles ad sacrum regenerationis lauacrum uenirent; deinde si resisterent, tunc papa contra ipsos procurare deberet gladium saecularem. Licitum et debitum est talem esse ordinationem, et qui in aliquo contra ordinationem est, phantasticus est et culpabilis, atque per consequens inordinatus.

Ait Petrus: Raimunde, Deus est omnipotens in omni tempore et ubique, et etiam primus est ordinator. Et Deo non oportet, ut papa, cardinales et reliqui illius sanctae congregationis patres constituant in Concilio talem ordinationem, quia, quando Deo placuerit, infideles ad uiam ueritatis reducet. Satis enim papae, cardinalibus et Concilii patribus esse uidebitur, ut christianos ordinent.

Ait Raimundus: Legitur (Luc. 12, 10), qui peccat in Spiritum sanctum, non remittitur peccatum; qui Spiritus est uniuersae bonitatis. Tu autem mihi hoc modo peccare uideris, qui non desideras maximum bonum publicm. Sed numquid tu scis papam et cardinales habere posse ad intrinsecam et extrinsecam ordinationem? Si uero ad intra christianos ordinent, bene quidem faciunt. Attamen si ab extra perditas oues non requirunt neque earum ordinationem reddituri. Et egomet ipsos accusabo, et me tunc excusabo, quia plures super re illa illis in Curia sermones feci, et super re eadem plures libros composui.

Ait clericus: Recordor, Raimunde, et frequenter audiui, plures principes ultra mare ad recuperandam Terram sanctam profectos, id frustra tentasse; quod si a Deo ordinatum fuisset, quod quaerebant, profecto effectus ostendisset.

Ait Raimundus: Possiblie est, Petre, eos magis propter se ipsos quam propter Deum ad recuperationem Terrae sanctae contendisse; quae quidem intentio diuinam non intrat ordinationem, quoniam in ea non est ordo. Quod si profecti sunt ordinatata intentione, sed aliquem defectum in pecunia, commeatibus et huiusmodi passi sunt, eis quoad intentionem non defuit ordo, et ideo meritum acquisiere; sed ordo defuit papae, cardinalibus et aliis christianis, qui sufficiens adiutorium non subministrauerunt.

Ait clericus: Raimunde, uideo complures praedicatores, ut fratres minores et alios religiosos, ad praedicandum saracenis, tartaris et aliis infidelibus se committere, sed paruus eorum adhuc, quem faciant, apparet fructus.

Ait Raimundus: Fratres, qui illuc tendnt, infidelium idiomata nesciunt, et ideo ad eos inordinate uadunt. Verumtamen si in terra christianorum eorum idiomata discerent, tunc ad eos ordinate possent profisci et multiplicem fructum facere. Deus autem semper adest illis, qui pro ipso bona ordinatione uigilant.

Ait clericus: Raimunde, non est alia ecclesia in mundo aeque bene ordinata ad seruiendum Deo, ut romana ecclesia. Et hoc potes uidere in ecclesiis, in quibus clerici ordinate celebrant, ordinate cantant et hujusmodi talia.

Ait Raimundus: Esto, ut dicis. Attamen quid est de quibusdam clericis, qui protinus extra aedem sacram cum magna pompa sunt equitantes et in pinguibus mensis comedentes, multas etiam et magnas beneficiorum prouisiones habentes? Pauperes autem Christi ad eorum portas clamant. Videturne tibi hic esse ordo consentaneus, quem habent clerici in ecclesia celebrandi et horas decantandi? Adhuc id a te quaero, si sit ordo unum bonum uirum scientificum unam paruam habere praebendam, et clericum illi prorsus oppositum multas habere magnas et, ut ipsi aiunt, pingues?

Ait clericus: Raimunde, phantasticus es, qui me talibus quaestionibus lacessis; et ideo de cetero tecum amplius conferre nolo.

Et abeuntes discesserunt ab inuicem clericus et Raimundus.

Ad gloriam et honorem Dei finitus est praesens liber a Raimundo anno 1311 incarnationis Domini nostri Iesu Christi.

24. Lo Concili (1311)
Catalan text: *Lo Concili.* In **Poesies**, p.106-134.

Lo Concili (1311)
Text as edited by Ramon d'Alòs-Moner in **Poesies**, p.106-107, lines 1-28.

I
Un concili vull començar
en mon coratge, e xantar

per ço que faça enamorar
tots cells qui ho poden far
      per Déu servir
e lo Sepulcre conquerir:
      molt ho desir!
En concili tan gran siats
e tan bellament ordenats
que Déus ne sia molt honrats
e mant hom ne sia salvats.
      E tot lo món
en llong e ample e en pregon
      n'haja aon.
En concili no façats for
per argent, castell ne per or;
temets-ho com seny sí que mor,
car si havets bo e gran cor,
      ah, què diran
juseu, sarraï, cristian,
      tartres e mant!
En concili no siats dubtós,
avar, ni trist, ne pererós;
tan forts siats complits d'amors,
de sospirs, llàgremes e plors,
      per bon amar,
que Déus vos faça acabar
      lo seu honrar.

VII

I have listed below some works discussing Llull's remarks on the Tartars/Mongols. These references were compiled in 2005 and some additions made in the years since, but lacking access to a library since retiring in 2014, I have not been able to examine more recent publications to find relevant materials.

Altaner (1928) Altaner, Berthold. "Glaubenszwang und Glaubensfreiheit in der Missionstheorie des Raymundus Lullus: ein Beitrag zur Geschichte des Toleranzgedankens" *Historisches Jahrbuch* 1928, 48. Bd. p.586-610.
Bonner (1980) Bonner, Anthony. "Notes de bibliografia i cronologia lul·lianes" *Estudios lulianos* 1980 v.24 p.71-86.
Borrás (1908) Borrás, J. "Lo que dice el B.to R. Lull de los mongoles o tártaros" *Bolletí de la Societat arqueológica luliana, Revista d'estudis histórichs,* v.12, Jan. 1908, p.7-10.
Cardelle de Hartmann (2000) Cardelle de Hartmann, Carmen. "Diálogo literario y polémica religiosa en la Edad Media (900-1400)" *Analecta Malacitana* no.6, May 2000. Available at: *AnMal electrónica,* www.anmal.uma.es/anmal/numero6/Cardelle.htm
Clausen (1955) Clausen, Agnes. *Lullus, muhammedanernes apostel.* København: G.E.C. Gads Forlag, 1955. See especially pages 54-68.
Colomer i Pous (1997) Colomer i Pous, Eusebi. *El pensament als països Catalans durant l'edat mitjana i el renaixement.* Barcelona : Publicacions de l'Abadia de Montserrat, 1997. See especially: "El diàleg interreligiós en Ramon Llull", p.113-179.
Euler(1990) Euler, Walter Andreas. *Unitas et pax: Religionsvergleich bei Raimundus Lullus und Nikolaus von Kues.* Würzburg: Echter; Altenberge: Telos Verlag, 1990.
Friedlein (2004) Friedlein, Roger. *Der Dialog bei Ramon Llull: Literarische Gestaltung als apologetische Strategie.* Tübingen: Max Niemeyer, 2004.
Garcías Palou (1981) Garcías Palou, Sebastian. *Ramón Llull y el Islam.* Palma de Mallorca, 1981. See especially chapter IX: "El viaje de Ramon Llull a Chipre y a Armenia."
Gayà (1997) Gayà, Jordi. "Ramon Llull en Oriente (1301): circunstancias de un viaje" *Studia lulliana* 1997 v.37, p.25-78.
Golubovich (1906) Golubovich, Girolamo. *Biblioteca bio-bibliografica della Terra Santa e dell'Oriente francescano. Tom 1: 1215-1300.* Quaracchi presso Firenze: Tipografia del

Collegio di S. Bonaventura, 1906. For the section on Llull see p.361-392.
Gottron (1912) Gottron, Adam. *Ramon Lulls Kreuzzugsideen.* Berlin und Leipzig: Dr. Walther Rothschild, 1912. (Abhandlungen zur mittleren und neueren Geschichte, Heft 39)
Hauf i Valls (1989) Hauf i Valls, Albert-Guillem. "Introducció" in Aitó de Gorigos. *La flor de les històries d'orient: versió del segle XIV.* Ed. by Albert-Guillem Hauf i Valls. Barcelona: Biblioteca Escriny de Textos Medievals Breus, Centre d'Estudis Medievals de Catalunya, 1989, p.5-71.
Hauf i Valls (1996) Hauf i Valls, Albert-Guillem. "Texto y contexto de *"La flor de las historias de Oriente"*: un programa de colaboración cristiano-mongólica" in *Juan Fernández de Heredia y su época: IV Curso sobre lengua y literatura en Aragón.* Zaragoza: Institución "Fernando el Católico", 1996. p.111-154.
Hillgarth (1971) *Ramon Lull and lullism in fourteenth-century France.* Oxford: Clarendon Press, 1971.
Kamar (1961) Kamar, E. "Projet de Raymond Lull *"De acquisitione Terrae Sanctae"*: introduction et édition critique du texte" *Studia orientalia christiana. Collectanea* v.6 p.3-131.
Nicolau (1979) Nicolau, Miguel. "Motivación misionera en las obras de Ramon Llull" in *Actas del II Congreso Internacional de Lulismo, Miramar, 19-24 octubre 1976* (Palma de Mallorca: Maioricensis Schola Lullistica, 1979) p.117-130.
Rodríguez Temperley (2001) Rodríguez Temperley, María Mercedes. "Narrar, informar, conquistar: los *Viajes* de Juan de Mandevilla en Aragón" *Studia neophilologica* 2001 v.73, p.184-196.
Schmieder (1994) Schmieder, Felicitas. *Europa und die Fremden: die Mongolen im Urteil des Abendlandes vom 13. bis in das 15. Jahrhundert.* Sigmaringen: Jan Thorbecke, 1994.
Schmieder (1998) Schmieder, Felicitas. "*Nota sectam maometicam atterendam a tartaris et christianis*: The Mongols as non-believing apocalyptic friends around the year 1260."

Journal of millennial studies Spring 1998, v.1, issue1. Available at: www.mille.org/journal.html

Schmieder (2000) Schmieder, Felicitas. *"Tartarus valde sapiens et eruditus in philosophia:* la langue des missionnaires en Asie" in *L'étranger au Moyen Âge: XXXe Congrès de la S.H.M.E.S. (Göttingen, juin 1999).* Paris: Publications de la Sorbonne, 2000, p.271-281.

Schmieder (2001) Schmieder, Felicitas. "Clash of civilizations in the medieval world: Christian strategies for diplomacy and conversion among the Mongols" *Annuario* (Istituto Romeno di cultura e ricerca umanistica), 2001, v.3. Available at: www.geocities.com/serban_marin/schmieder2001.html

Soper i Llopart (1992) Soper i Llopart, Albert. "El *Liber super Psalmum Quicumque* de Ramon Llull i l'opció pels tàrtars" *Studia lulliana* 1992 v.32 p.3-19.

Sugranyes de Franch (1954) Sugranyes de Franch, Ramon. *Raymond Lulle, docteur des missions: avec un choix de textes traduits et annotés.* Schöneck-Beckenried: Nouvelle Revue de Sciences Missionnaire, 1954. (Neue Zeitschrift für Missionswissenschaft, Supplementa V)

Urvoy (1980) Urvoy, Dominique. *Penser l'Islam: les présupposés islamiques de l'"Art" de Lull.* Paris: Vrin, 1980. See especially chapter 7 "Le problème mongol et la question du paganisme."

IX

The Mongols in Javanese Historiography and Literature[1]

When Khubilai sent his navy from Quanzhou through the southern seas in 1292 the final destination was Jawa and the reason given in the Chinese histories was that an earlier envoy named Meng Qi had been ill treated – branded in the face with a hot iron according to the *Tong jian gang mu* – and the expedition's purpose was to punish the offender: Kertanagara, the king of Singhasari. According to the *Tong jian gang mu*

> Upon his [Meng Qi's] return, the emperor, indignant that some puny barbarian king had dared brand so ignominiously one of his high officials, put together a flotilla with 30,000 men to avenge the insult and charged Yiheimishi and Shibi to lead it, with orders to bring him the head of the king of Jawa or to put him in chains and bring him on his feet before the throne to expiate the crime of

---

[1] Originally presented at the Eighth International Congress of Mongolists held in August 2002 and published in *Mongolica, an International Annual of Mongol Studies*, vol. 13(34), 2003, pages 283-291. That published version contained many typographical errors which have been corrected here.

> which he was guilty. (my translation from Mailla's expanded French version of the *Tong jian gang mu*)

Several brief accounts of that campaign are well known; the longest of them appears in the *Yuan shi*, where the main narrative is in Book 210 and other material is found in the biographies of the three generals in charge of the expedition (but not in the biography of Meng Qi). Wassaf and Rashid al-Din both wrote their accounts before the *Yuan shi* was compiled, but their versions are very brief and give a different outcome. Whereas the *Yuan shi* and the *Tong jian gang mu* both state that the army suffered heavy losses in the final battle, and that upon their return to China, Khubilai was angry at the results, Wassaf wrote otherwise:

> When they had landed on the elected coast they gained possession of the island ... through spreading the fear of the fury of their sword. ... His Majesty did not permit that certain death should exercise his power there, but put [Kertanagara's] son on the steps of the high throne. He bestowed on him a ceremonial dress of honor, and conferred on him much grace, and, against the payment of tribute and taxes in the shape of pearls and gold, he left the island in his hands. (Wassaf, from Spuler, 1988, p. 168-169)

There are other early records of the campaign of great interest to and long studied by Javanese historians and philologists, but they have remained unknown among Mongolists. Apart from the obvious linguistic reason – the texts are in medieval Javanese, two have never been translated into any language and the most important appeared in an English translation only in 1996 – these texts may have been dismissed by earlier scholars because the first of them to be published (in 1817) is a strange tale indeed. That work, a version of the *Kidung Panji-Wijayakrama*, was summarized in Groeneveldt's 1876 article "The expedition of the Mongols against Java in 1293, A.D." along with translations of the above mentioned portions of the *Yuan shi*. Of the Balinese manuscript which Raffles published in English translation in 1817, Groeneveldt says

> The Balinese account has been handed down through many generations, gradually losing in accuracy and becoming mixed with much of the fantastic and marvelous. (Groeneveldt, 1876, page 252)

Since nearly all subsequent accounts of this campaign have been based primarily or even solely on Groeneveldt's article or the *Yuan shi* directly, the summary which he provides of Raffles' text and his comments are enough to deter the serious historian, and the absence of the Javanese sources in subsequent histories of the Yuan era is understandable. It is also regrettable, and I think it is time to look again.

The full English version of the text which Raffles published in 1817 is dated 1543 and includes several references to the "King of Tatar whose name and title is Sri Laksemana" who is in Jawa visiting the Javanese king hamed Jaya Katong [Jayakatwang]. The following comments are found in Raffles' version:

> Jaya Katong, previous to the invasion of Browijaya, had promised his guest, the King of Tatar, whose name and title was Sri Laksemana, to give him his adopted daughter (wife to Browijaya) in marriage. This was however delayed. Several times did Laksemana press Jaya Katong to fulfil his promise, but he never received a positive answer.
> Laksemana therefore being informed that Browijaya of Majapahit had attacked Kediri, forthwith sent a letter to him, saying that he would cooperate with the people of Majapahit, provided Browijaya would be on good terms with him....

[Browijaya] invited the King of Tatar to visit him. On his arrival Browijaya received him with every attention, and made him a present of a beautiful virgin.

Laksemana remained for some time at Majapahit, during which Browijaya gave him two or three grand entertainments. He afterwards embarked on board of his own vessel and returned to his kingdom of Tatar. (Raffles, quoted from the 2nd edition of 1830, page 116)

The King of Tatar's letter is hardly a "letter of submission" as students of the Mongol empire have been accustomed to reading. Is there any other example in all the world's literature where a Mongol Khaan is treated in such a fashion, with invitations, parties and virgins? The Javanese apparently cultivated a very different opinion of the Mongols than did the Europeans. The difference appears in the earliest Javanese account of 1365, and persists through all those texts known to me, through the manuscript found by Raffles to the 1935 poem *Babad Majapait*. Only in 1992-1993 were new Javanese dramas published in which the Chinese version is adopted and the ancient Javanese version abandoned.

Raffles' manuscript was the first old Javanese text about the Mongols which was discovered by Europeans but it was not the last. By 1931 four other important texts of the 14th-16th centuries had been published. All of these texts were discovered and produced in Bali or Lombok but the language of the texts is middle Javanese. Why these stories survived in Bali and Lombok but not in Jawa is a matter beyond the scope of this paper, but a quick explanation would be that Bali was incorporated into the Majapahit empire in 1284 and the Hindu civilization which persisted in Bali and Lombok was favorable to the transmission of these texts while the spread of Islam throughout much of Jawa gave rise to other histories in which the Mongols were not mentioned.

In the present paper these texts will be described and compared with the Chinese accounts. In closing, I shall make a few remarks on modern interpretations appearing in histories of the ancient Javanese kingdoms of Singhasari and Majapahit and in the modern literatures of Jawa.

Deśavarṇana (also called *Nāgarakṛtāgama*)

The earliest mention of "Tatar"—the old Javanese word for "Mongol"—appears in the poem *Deśavarṇana* written by Mpu Prapañca in 1365. Canto 44 of the poem contains a description of the struggle between the kings of Kediri and Singhasari. Kadiri, a kingdom near to the kingdom of Singhasari in east Jawa just south of Madura, was ruled by Jayakatwang who, according to this text, attacked Singhasari and set himself up as ruler over all Jawa after the death of Kertanagara, the king of Singhasari. The heir to the throne of Singhasari, Prince Wijaya, fought against Jayakatwang. The outcome was that "Half with Tatar men he beat haji Jayakatwang, exterminated altogether" and the world which had been "terrified, in disaster and tumult" was set right and "the whole of Yawa-land (Java) turned mindful (of its duty), most humbly they entered into the Presence." (Pigeaud, 1960).

One sentence mentions the "Tatars": they appear nowhere else in the poem. That in itself poses interesting questions: why is nothing more said? The explanation which Pigeaud gave was that the *Deśavarṇana* (which means "Description of the country") was not a work of history but an account of Majapahit court life in the mid 14th century. That may suffice as an explanation for the brevity of the account, but another possibility comes to mind when the *Deśavarṇana* is read in conjunction with other later texts in which many pages are devoted to the Mongols. It may be that the significance of the arrival, defeat and departure of the Mongols as it is narrated in later works was developed in those later works, whereas for Mpu Prapañca the sole importance of the arrival of the Mongols was in the military aid which they gave Wijaya, enabling him to take his rightful place as rule over Jawa.

In the *Deśavarṇana* the Mongols appear as allies, not invaders; they help defeat a usurper and the king whom they assisted led the land of Jawa into an era of grace and glory. What the *Deśavarṇana* does not say is just as interesting: there are no laments, no tales of destruction and woe, no reference to invaders, no victory over the Mongols, no exultation over their defeat and departure, for neither the later battle of the Mongols against Wijaya nor their departure is mentioned.

Pararaton

The Pararaton was probably written in the 1480's shortly after the fall of Majapahit. It is a prose work of unknown authorship, considered by most scholars to be a work of history and is comparable to the Mongols' *Secret History*. It begins in the remote past with the mythical (or perhaps historical) ancestors of the eastern Javanese kingdoms and concludes with events immediately following the fall of the Majapahit empire in 1478. The Mongolian campaign to Jawa appears in the middle. In this text the Mongols are invited to come to Jawa by the Regent of Madura, Wiraraja, who claims to be a friend of the "Emperor of Tatar." Wijaya, the prince of Singhasari, having fled his enemies and living in exile, comes to Wiraraja and asks for his help. Wiraraja advises him to pretend to make peace with his enemy the usurper Jayakatwang, and when this is done and Wijaya has contacted those leaders and soldiers loyal to him, he writes to Wiraraja and asks him to join him in a war against Jayakatwang. Wiraraja replies to the messenger from Wijaya with the following plan:

> Tell your master that the Emperor of Tatar is a friend of mine. I will take the princess; you go back to Majapahit Kaki Panalasan! After your return I shall send a letter to Tatar, through the boat from Tatar which is here for trade. I have a boat too, and I will order it to get prepared to join them on their way to Tatar. I will invite the Tatar Emperor to attack Daha. If the king of Daha is defeated,

> the beautiful princess of Tumapel whose beauty has no equal all over the land of Java, will be offered to the Emperor of Tatar. That will be my trap for the Emperor of Tatar. Tell this to your master. Then I will join him in attacking Daha. (*Pararaton*, from Phalgunadi, p.111)

Not much of a friend, I would say, if he planned such a trap. Even so, the invitation is one of the most important differences between the Javanese texts and the Chinese histories. Whereas the Chinese texts attribute the sending of an army to Jawa to the branding of Khubilai's envoy Meng Qi, the *Deśavarṇana* offers no explanation for the Mongol presence in Jawa, and Raffles' Balinese manuscript has the "King of Tatar" writing to Wijaya telling him that he would join him in his war if only Wijaya would cooperate with him, the explanation in the *Pararaton* is more detailed and reappears in the later texts mentioned below. In fact, Meng Qi appears in none of the Javanese texts prior to the 20th century, a matter which I have discussed at length in an earlier book *Khubilai Khan and the Beautiful Princess of Tumapel* (revised edition of 2013, *Of Palm Wine, Women and War*).

The story continues in the *Pararaton* with the arrival of the Mongols, the defeat of Jayakatwang by the combined armies of Wijaya, Wiraraja and the Tatars (Mongols), after which Wijaya takes the princess (there are actually two princesses in this version) back to his capitol in Majapahit.

> Then the Tatar army came to Majapahit and demanded the princesses as promised by Wiraraja, who had said that the two princesses would be given to them after the fall of Daha. This issue bewildered all the ministers. Sora said: "Well I will fiercely attack the Tatar army if they come here!" (*Pararaton*, from Phalgunadi, p.113)

In Wiraraja's letter to Wijaya, only one princess was mentioned, but here both are stated to have been promised. The tale of each of the princesses is elaborated more fully in the

Kindung Panji Wijayakrama and the *Kidung Harsawijaya*, discussed below.

The story which follows is best told in the words of the *Pararaton* itself (from Phalgunadi's translation):

> In the evening when the sun had already set in the west, the Tatar army came to take the princesses. Wiraraja spoke: "Hey all of you in the Tatar army! Do not be in a hurry. The princesses are in a state of shock because they have undergone some shattering experiences at the time when Tumapel was defeated and particularly while Daha was being destroyed. They will really be frightened if they see all your pointed weapons. Tomorrow I will hand them over to you. They will be put in a box decorated with clothes. They will be brought and escorted to your boat. The reason to put them in the box is that they do not like to see the sharpness of the weapons. Moreover, whosoever from the Tatar army comes to take the princesses should be clean and have a comely bearing and he should not have too many companions. The princesses have clearly stated that if they see any weapon, they will jump into the sea as they reach the boat. So, all the risks, which you have taken in battle will go in vain if the princesses jump into the sea. Will it not be all futile then?"
>
> The Tatar army believed this while in truth they were being deceived. The commander of the Tatar army answered: "Your observations are quite correct."
>
> The Tatar army came hurriedly at the fixed time in great numbers to demand the princesses. Many of them did not bring arms. When they entered the gate, the guards closed and locked the gate from inside and outside. Sora tied his kris (sacred dagger) in his thigh and fiercely attacked the Tatars. The Tatar army suffered great losses. Rangga-Lawe attacked from outside the audience-hall. He chas-

ed away the Tatar army up to their camps. As the Tatars ran away to the Changu harbour, Rangga-Lawe still followed them. In the end they were all killed.

The *Pararaton* concludes the narrative of the Mongol battle with the statement that Jayakatwang's revolt happened in Shaka era 1197 (1275 A.D.), he was enthroned in Shaka year 1198 (1276 A.D.), and after having been captured, imprisoned and released by the Tatar king, he wrote a poem and died shortly thereafter.

The comment in the *Pararaton* about the Mongols coming to Majapahit unarmed is especially interesting in light of the comment found in Mailla's *Tong jian gang mu*, where it is stated that the Mongol generals were so convinced of the sincerity and allegiance of Wijaya that they sent only a very small escort with him to receive his submission and tribute. Not only the Chinese histories but the *Kidung Panji Wijayakrama* agree on the exact number sent as an escort; two officers and two hundred soldiers. In the *Pararaton*, the Mongols were not asking for submission – in none of the Javanese texts do the Mongols ask for submission or tribute – rather they want the princesses. It is easy to see that the princesses symbolize the land and people of Jawa in these later texts, but it is still important to note that in all these texts the Mongols are invited to Jawa with the promise of a princess, a promise which the *Pararaton* specifically describes as a trap, and when they come looking for the princesses they are only asking for fair play. This narrative development probably has its origin in Javanese attitudes rather than in Mongol practices, but is a matter which needs further explication.

Kidung Panji Wijayakrama

The first part of the *Kidung Rangga Lawe* is called *Kidung Panji Wijayakrama*. In this work as in the *Kidung Harsawijaya*, the fates of the princesses of Tumapel are described in much greater detail than in the *Pararaton*. The manuscript which Raffles found is considered to be a variation of the story, although it differs greatly from the version published by Berg in 1930. The chronogram, which appears in both Raffles' and Berg's versions is the same: shaka year 1465 (1543 A.D.). It is generally thought to be based on the *Pararaton*; some scholars have suggested that this work was written as early as 1334 and the *Pararaton* even at that early date was its source. On these matters of chronology and transmission history I am not competent to comment further.

The text itself is in Javanese verse, very romantic, and Berg's version–but not Raffles'–follows the same general story found in the *Pararaton*, from Kertanagara's expedition to Malayu with which it begins to the defeat of the Mongols with which it ends. The description of the Mongols is much longer than that found in the *Pararaton*, and many more details are given.

Kidung Harsawijaya

The only known manuscript[2] of this poem is from the 19th century but the language is much earlier; its original date of composition is unknown. the text departs from the other, earlier texts in many details, and the didactic intentions of the author are clearly the reason behind many of the changes and interpolations. For example, all of the kings are good kings and what happens to each one does not come as a surprise but is foretold and accepted as what must come to pass. Wijaya alone is still living at the end of the poem, the King of Tatar having been killed during his final battle against Wijaya. Berg (1930, my translation) summarized this final confrontation thus:

> In the palace at Majapahit the special troops were posted. They received orders not to attack immediately, but to wait to see if the Tatars would give signs of ill will. The Tatars meanwhile marched from Changgu toBubat. From there the Prime Minister, the Chamberlain and the Commander-in-Chief were sent to Majapahit.

---

[2] In a paper published in 2000 Robson noted Pigeaud's 1980 description of a second manuscript that I had not been aware of when this paper was written.

When Harsawijaya heard the Tatar war cries he became frightened: Majapahit was in big trouble now. He told Pusparasmi that the king of Tatar wanted her and asked her if she wouldn't rather marry the Tatar king. She rejected the proposal.

The Tatar soldiers with great fanfare entered Majapahit calling out their demand loudly: the delivery of the princess from Daha. The people of Majapahit remained calm at first, only attacking when the Tatars entered the walled area. The battle was fierce and in the end the Tatars were defeated. Those who fled were pursued, surrounded in Bubat and most of them killed. The Tatar Khan himself died according to the dharma in the shadow of a white Lotus.

That the princess from Daha—not Tumapel—was the center of attention is another difference most likely due to the author's desire to make the kings blameless: Wijaya did not offer his own wife as in the *Pararaton* and *Kidung Panji Wijayakrama*, but the enemy king's daughter. Having defeated Jayakatwang, the Mongols asked for fair play and the delivery of the princess of Daha, but she had committed suicide. Wijaya had taken both of the princesses of Tumapel as well as two princesses from Malayu, and when the King of Tatar learned that these four princesses were in Majapahit, he thought that he had been tricked. All the kings, including the king of Tatar, act fairly and honestly according to their knowledge and the promises made, but Wijaya alone survives and becomes king as had been predicted long ago.

The political result was that the "island" of Tatar became a subject of the Majapahit Empire, a result the opposite of that recorded by Wassaf, Rashid al-Din and the *Ming shi*.

That is a brief description of the early texts, but I hope sufficient to spark further interest. There is one other early text which mentions the Mongols—the *Kidung Sunda*—but it is of little interest, as it says only in passing that certain "ships are like the ones made in Tatar-land since his majesty Wijaya's war and the fall of Kediri." According to Zoetmulder's *Dictionary of Old Javanese*, this text and those discussed above are the only pre-20th century texts in which the word "tatar" appears independently or in compounds. In the 20th century, these texts have been the subject of great debate as well as serving as the basis of certain new literary works.

The most important—or at least influential—contributions to the study of the Mongols in Jawa have been made by C.C. Berg, G. Cœdès, N. Krom and D. Lombard. Berg (1965 and other papers) insisted that the war in Jawa was a result of a feud between the Javanese king Kertanagara of Singhasari and Khubilai, the former desirous of ousting Khubilai from all of southeast Asia and asserting his own control over this region. The war was brought with spiritual powers and much is made of Khubilai's conversion to Tibetan Buddhism.

Cœdès (1964), Krom (1931) and Lombard (1990) offered very different accounts of the war. For Krom, Meng Qi and the Chinese account were decisive, the Javanese material filling in the picture but not altering the explanation and narrative found in the *Yuan shi*. Lombard focused on the economic aspects of the war, an interpretation which has been favored by many, and combined with Berg's theories in the writings of Slametmuljana and Rossabi, among others. These matters have all been dealt with at greater length in my *Khubilai Khan and the beautiful princess of Tumapel*.

In 1935, approximately 400 years after the Mongols had been dropped from the Javanese traditions[3], a Sundanese archivist named Kadir Tisna Sujana wrote a historical poem in traditional 'tembang' style entitled *Babad Majapait*. This book, of no interest as a source for learning of the Mongol invasion of Jawa, is interesting nonetheless because it reintroduced the Mongols into modern Indonesian literatures. It was twice

---

[3] The Mongols do not appear in Islamic historiographical traditions in Jawa from the 16th century on.

reprinted and translated into Indonesian. The time of its composition—1935, just four years after the publication of the *Kidung Harsawijaya*—suggests that the parallel between the arrival of the Mongols to overthrow the usurper Jayakatwang and the Indonesian independence movement was recognized immediately upon the publication of the *kidungs*. The second printing of 1940 preceded by two years the arrival of the Japanese whose arrival came almost exactly 650 years after that of the Mongols.

On the 700th anniversary of the death of Kertanagara and the Mongol invasion of Jawa the Indonesian government produced a series of public performances in which the stories of Meng Qi and the Mongol army were turned into political instruments. The narrative in the performances of both the *Banjaran Singhasari* of 1992 and the *Banjaran Majapahit* of 1993 introduced Meng Qi as the reason for the Mongol campaign and eliminated all references to the princesses and Wiraraja's invitation. While the Mongol armies are not originally presented in a negative light and are in fact won over to Wijaya's side because of his promises of allegiance and sincerity, they are in the end described in negative terms, probably to justify the betrayal which followed. The early Javanese versions have been rejected and the new stories come closer to that version recorded in the *Yuan shi*.

References
I. Primary texts and translations
Babad Majapait:
    Kadir Tisna Sujana (1935). *Babad Madjapait.* Bale Poestaka.
Banjaran Majapahit. Surabaya: Dinas Pariwisata Daerah,
    Propinsi Dati I Jati, 1993.
Banjaran Singhasari. Surabaya: Dinas Pariwisata Daerah,
    Propinsi Dati I Jati, 1992.
Deśawarṇana:
    Prapañca, Mpu (1995). *Deśawarṇana*

(*Nāgarakṛtāgama*). Translated by Stuart Robson. Leiden: KITLV Press. (Verhandelingen van het Koninklijk instituut voor taal-, land- en volkenkunde ; 169)

Pigeaud, T.G.T. (1960). *Java in the 14th century: a study in cultural history : the Nagara-Kertagama by Rakawi Prapañca of Majapahit, 1365 A.D.* 3rd ed. The Hague: M. Nijhoff.

Kidung Harsawijaya:

Berg, C.C. (1931) *Kidung Harsa-Wijaya*. Tekst, inhoudsopgave en aanteekeningen door C.C. Berg. 's-Gravenhage: Martinus Nijhoff.

Kidung Panji Wijayakrama:

Berg, C.C. (1930) *Rangga Lawe: middeljavaansche historische roman: critisch uitgegeven..* Batavia: Kon. Bataviaasch Genoot-schap van Kunsten en Wetenschappen (*Bibliotheca Javanica*, 1)

Kidung Sunda:

Berg, C.C. (1927) *Kidung Sunda*. Inleiding, tekst, vertaling en aanteekeningen door C.C. Berg. 's-Gravenhage. (*Bijdragen tot de taal-, land- en volkenkunde van Nederlandsch-Indië*, deel 83)

Pararaton:

Brandes, J. (1897) *Pararaton (Ken Arok) of Het boek der koningen van Tumapel en van Majapahit*. Batavia (*Verhandelingen van het Bataviaasch Genootschap van Kunsten en Wetenschappen*, deel 49)

Phalgunadi, I Gusti Putu. (1996) *The Pararaton: a study of the southeast Asian chronicle*. New Delhi: Sundeep Prakashan. (Javanese text and English translation)

Tong jian gang mu:

御批資治通鑑綱目全書 : [一百九卷]. [北京] : 內府, 清康熙46年 [1708].

Mailla, Joseph-Anne-Marie de Moyriac de. (1777-1785) *Histoire générale de la Chine, ou Annales de cet empire, traduits du Tong-kien-kang-mou...* Paris. (French translation, with extensive interpolation)

Wassaf (تاريخ وصاف):

    Spuler, Bertold. (1988) *History of the Mongols based on eastern and western accounts of the thirteenth and fourteenth centuries.* Translated from the German by Helga and Stuart Drummond. New York: Dorset Press.

Yuan shi:

    Groeneveldt, W.P. (1876) "The expedition of the Mongols against Java in 1293, A.D." *The China review, or, Notes and queries on the Far East* v. 4, p. 246-254

II. Secondary literature

Bade, D.W. (2002). *Khubilai Khan and the beautiful princess of Tumapel: the Mongols between history and literature in Java.* Ulaanbaatar: Chuluunbat. Revised edition published in 2013 as: *Of Palm Wine, Women and War: The Mongolian Naval Expedition to Java in the 13th Century.* Singapore: ISEAS.

Berg, C.C. (1965) "The Javanese picture of the past" in Soedjatmoko et al. editors. *An introduction to Indonesian historiography.* Ithaca: Cornell University Press. p. 87-117

Cœdès, Georges (1964). *Les États Hindouisés d'Indochine et d'Indonésie.* 3d ed. Paris: Editions E. De Boccard.

Groeneveldt, W.P. (1876) "The expedition of the Mongols against Java in 1293, A.D." *The China review, or, Notes and queries on the Far East* v. 4, p. 246-254

Krom, N.J. (1931) *Hindoe-Javaansche geschiedenis.* 2. druk. 's-Gravenhage: M. Nijhoff.

Lombard, Denys. (1990) *Le carrefour javanais: essai d'histoire globale. Tome II: Les réseaux asiatiques.* Paris: Éditions de l'École des hautes études en sciences sociales.

Phalgunadi, I Gusti Putu. (1996) *The Pararaton: a study of the southeast Asian chronicle.* New Delhi: Sundeep Prakashan. (Javanese text, English translation and commentary)

Pigeaud, Theodore G.Th. (1960) *Java in the 14th century: a study in cultural history : the Nagara-Kertagama by Rakawi Prapañca of Majapahit, 1365 A.D.* 3rd ed. The Hague: M. Nijhoff.

Pigeaud, T.G.T. 1980. *Literature of Java: catalogue raisonné of Javanese manuscripts in the Library of the University of Leiden and other public collections in the Netherlands*, Vol. 4, Leiden: Leiden University Press. Supplement.

Raffles, Sir Thomas Stamford. (1817; 1830) *The history of Java.* 1st ed. London: Black, Parbury, and Allen, and John Murray, 1817. 2nd ed. London: John Murray.

Robson, Stuart. (2000) "The force of destiny, or the Kidung Harsa-Wijaya reread" *Indonesia and the Malay World*, 28:82, 243-253

Rossabi, Morris. (1988) *Khubilai Khan: his life and times.* Berkeley: University of California Press.

Slametmuljana. (1976) *A story of Majapahit.* Singapore: Singapore University Press.

Zoetmulder, Petrus Josephus (1982). *Old Javanese-English dictionary.* s-Gravenhage: M. Nijhoff.

X

(Spi)Ritual Warfare in Thirteenth Century Asia?
International Relations, the Balance of Powers and the Tantric Buddhism of Kertanagara and Khubilai Khan

Following up on Moens' (1924) remark that Kṛtanagara's Buddhism was similar to the Tantric Buddhism of Khubilai, C.C. Berg argued in a series of publications during the 1950s and 1960s that Kṛtanagara of Siṅhasāri adopted the particular form of Buddhism that he knew to be practised by Khubilai, great Khan of the Mongols, in order to acquire spiritual powers to aid him in an expected military engagement with the latter. Many others have argued that Khubilai adopted that particular form of Buddhism as an instrument of rule in order to justify his military conquest and reign over Tibet.

Is religion a mask for the will to power and its justification? Do the political-military situations of Kṛtanagara and Khubilai explain their adoption of Tantric Buddhism? Or are the relationships between religious and political practices not so simple and unidirectional? In this chapter I examine the connections between and proposed explanations for the Tantric Buddhism and political actions of Kṛtanagara and Khubilai in light of

Rosenstock-Huessy's theory of religion as life in the service of what one loves. If religion is understood thus, then both the religious and political practices of these two kings can be explained as following from their devotion to power: instead of politics explaining their (and our) religions, the gods they served explain their religion and their politics.

Kṛtanagara versus Khubilai

Moens (1924: 544) argued that the Buddhism ascribed to Kṛtanagara in the *Deśavarṇana* (formerly called *Nāgarakṛtāgama*) belonged to a *kālacakra* tradition of Tantric Buddhism,[1] and that Kṛtanagara's initiation into this form of Buddhism was much like Khubilai's consecration as Hevajra.[2] As a result of his consecration Khubilai would have become Mahāmitābha, which Moens regarded as the same as Mahākṣobhya, with which Kṛtanagara was associated by a statue in his image.[3] In a series of

---

[1] As observed by Griffiths (2014c), the emphasis on Kālacakra as the source of Tantric or Vajrayāna Buddhism in Indonesia is a rather stereotypical feature of early 20th-century scholarship (which has however been taken over uncritically in much later secondary literature) that seems to reflect the knowledge of the time on Tantric Buddhism, which heavily relied on sources from Tibet, where the Kālacakra indeed played an important role.

[2] Earlier Kern (1910a: 9) had noted that in Kṛtanagara's consecration as Jina, the term Jina—what European scholars referred to as Dhyāni-Buddha—was the same as that used in Tibet and Nepal, but Kern drew no conclusions from that connection. Nihom (1986: 485) stated that Moens had already suggested that Kṛtanagara was initiated in response to Khubilai's consecration, as it may be inferred by the following remarks (Moens 1924: 544): 'The most well-known of these rulers of China, Kublai Khan, contemporary of Kṛtanāgara, was consecrated as Jina through the Hevajrābhiṣeka' (*De meest bekende dezer keizers van China, Kublai Khan, tijdgenoot van Kṛtanāgara, werd tot Jina gewijd door de Hewajrābhiṣeka*), and 'The *iṣṭadewatā* of Kṛtanāgara, who thought of himself as Kublai's match, should not have been less demonic' (*De iṣṭadewatā van Kṛtanāgara, die zich Kublai's evenknie dacht, zal niet minder demonisch geweest zijn*). I have been unable to determine whether or not Moens was the first to suggest that Kṛtanagara imitated Khubilai.

[3] On the Simpang statue (now in Surabaya), see Kern 1910b and Poerbatjaraka 1922 for the earliest discussions, and Nihom 1986 for a post-Berg reinterpretation.

publications throughout the 1950s and 1960s, Berg[4] took Moens' association with Khubilai and went further with what he described in his last paper on the topic as a 'guess':

> Since Kĕrtanagara introduced a similar form of Buddhism in Java, we may guess that he followed Kubilai's example in order to acquire the same degree of power so as to be able to protect his country against Kubilai's raiders... (Berg 1965: 99)

Furthermore, Kṛtanagara's Amoghapāśa inscription of 1286 is understandable, Berg argued, only 'if interpreted as a symbolic invitation to join an alliance against Kubilai on the basis of Buddhism and connubium' (1965: 99). Describing Kṛtanagara as a pacifist, Berg (1956: 408) agreed with Krom that for Kṛtanagara it was fear of the Mongols that guided his foreign policy, not aggressive expansionist aims, and that the inscription expressed his desire to establish 'friendly relations with Champa and Malayu' (1956: 407).

Berg insisted that the texts that comprise the sources of our knowledge of Kṛtanagara's reign cannot be read on the basis of Western historiographical assumptions, but must be read within the cultural assumptions of the culture of origin. Such an exhortation is salutary, and perhaps it is primarily upon that basis that Berg captured his readers' attention. As summarized by Kwa (1970: 45), Berg also added that if we read these texts as their intended readers read them, then we find that they

---

[4] As this chapter is not a study of Berg's ideas but of the historiography related to Mongolian-Javanese relations in the 13th century, I shall make no attempt to present a survey of Berg's publications nor even present his ideas in his ownwords. I am in fact much more interested in how his ideas have been repeated and responded to than in his interpretations themselves. His principal publications relevant to the discussion are listed in the references for the reader's convenience (Berg 1950, 1951a, 1951b, 1953, 1956, 1962, 1965), but few of them will actually be discussed in what follows.

had a magical function: to legitimize and justify the contemporary political scene, to provide the reigning regime with a genealogy that justifies their being in power. The texts therefore had an optive, wish-fullfillment character, describing events that should have happened, not events that did happen.

That actually sounds very much like a reading made after Marxist historiography;[5] Zoetmulder (1974: 170), while crediting Berg with the indisputable merit of having shed light on the 'magical' aspect of Old Javanese literature, and the relation between the poem, its poet, and his kingly sponsor, also warned that 'it is doubtful whether the foundation is sufficiently sound to enable us to reconstruct a complete picture either of Old Javanese life and thought in general, or of the position of the poet within its framework'. Berg did declare that the *Deśavarṇana* was a priestly statement and 'therefore, an elaborate optative' (Berg 1965: 105). How Berg knew that he was reading texts in the way they were originally intended to be read is not clear, but it appears to be the case that his assumptions about the relationship between religion and politics underwrote his interpretations, not the assumptions that a 14th-century Buddhist (whether poet-priest, king, or ascetic) would have made (whatever those might have been). In any case, according to Berg's thesis, the proper interpretation of those texts concerning Kṛtanagara entailed that he strove to unite the Archipelago in a sacred confederacy through his supernatural powers obtained through Tantric rites, and that he did this in response to and in imitation of Khubilai.

From D.G.E. Hall (1955) to Kenneth Hall (2011), variants of this interpretation of the Kṛtanagara-Khubilai conflict, and in particular its religious dimension, have been repeated, criticized, misunderstood, misstated, and often accepted and asserted as fact. More significantly, narratives of Kṛtanagara's

---

[5] Not only post-Marxist, but according to Andries Teeuw, 'deconstructionist avant la lettre' (Teeuw 1991: 219).

adoption of Buddhism in imitation of Khubilai and against him—that is, as an act of pure realpolitik—have often been suggested without reference to Berg or any later scholarship, a disconcerting development about which Bosch was alarmed already in 1956.[6] As early as 1955, Hall wrote of Kṛtanagara that 'in imitation of Kublai's consecration as a Jina Buddha, he was in 1275 consecrated as a Bhairava Buddha, and strove to build up a sacred confederacy united by the power of Tantric Yoga to withstand the Mongols' (Hall 1955: 785), without providing any references to primary and secondary literature; and twenty-five years later when Mendis (1981: 316) wrote (also without references) of 'a "heavenly duel" between Kublai as the *avatar* of Buddhism against Kṛtanagara the *tantric power* of the Circle of Yoginis', he referred to this interpretation simply as 'the traditional Indonesian version'.[7] Mendis, however, was neither a careful reader nor a clear thinker, as he revealed in his reference to 'the legend that he [i.e., Khubilai] made himself a Djin Buddha to counteract Kṛtanagara' (ibid.: 319). Some scholars have even gone so far as to dismiss the 1293 invasion of Java as a myth, apparently having pushed Berg's reading to its most extreme conclusions.[8]

One may—and probably ought to—assume that Kṛtanagara was well informed about Khubilai's military campaigns throughout southeast and eastern Asia as well as his expansionist intentions, not only through the envoys sent from the Yuan

---

[6] Bosch 1956 remains the clearest refutation of Berg's early theories but Berg, rather than Bosch, informs most subsequent discussions.

[7] Although this reference to the 'traditional Indonesian version' made me suspicious, if O'Brien (2008) is right in her understanding of the *Sutasoma* as being based on the historical relations between Kṛtanagara and Khubilai, the *Sutasoma* may indeed represent the 'traditional' Javanese version. For O'Brien's reading of the *Sutasoma* and Kṛtanagara's relation to Khubilai, see below, as well as her essay in this volume. [i.e. the volume in which this paper was originally published. See Obrien (2016)]

[8] This appears to be the case with Michael Aung-Thwin (2011: 35), who recently remarked that the Mongols 'could not hold Java—if in fact that invasion were historical and not myth'.

court to Java but from merchants (both Arab and Chinese), refugees from southern China, and perhaps even refugees from the Muslim campaigns in northern India.[9] The *Yuan shi* records that Mongol envoys came to Java in 1279, 1280, 1281, and 1286 and that they came back without having obtained submission and royal hostages, and furthermore that a mission to Java in 1289 (?) resulted in the mistreatment of the Mongol envoy. These missions all occurred during Kṛtanagara's reign in Java and Khubilai's reign as Great Khan, and therefore indicate a prolonged diplomatic relationship between the two kings and resistance to Khubilai's demands on the part of Kṛtanagara. One can infer that in his interactions with the Mongol envoys Kṛtanagara both learned a great deal and developed his foreign policy accordingly. But exactly what he knew, how his knowledge directed his foreign policy, and how his religious practices related to his political decisions or to the religious practices of Khubilai are simply matters that are not on record.

The 20th- and 21st-century historiography of Kṛtanagara's domestic and foreign policy including his military campaigns has been oriented, guided, and often completely determined by the historians' assumptions about the nature of religion and its relation to politics, as much as by their assumptions about the writing of history and the interpretation of texts. Furthermore, Kṛtanagara's religion has been discussed in relation to the religion of Khubilai more often than not. That is to say, Kṛtanagara's religion has been seen as arising out of a relationship that was at once political and personal, but the personal dimension of his religious practices and beliefs (insofar as they can be determined) has been understood (in every case with which I am familiar) to be explicable in terms of the political conditions of his reign.

Why did Kṛtanagara embrace Tantric Buddhism? If he did so in imitation of Khubilai, then why was Khubilai initiated into Tantric Buddhism? If not in imitation of some other initiate,

---

[9] Reichle (2007: 102 ff.) discusses the possible influence of Newar art on the reliefs of Candi Jago, a suggestion she attributes already to Brandes (1904).

then why should one assume that Kṛtanagara's initiation was due to mimesis? What is the relation between politics and religion in the lives and reigns of these two kings? If their religion follows from mimesis, of what relevance is politics? If political conditions explain their religious actions and orientations, of what relevance is mimesis? In what follows I shall look at how scholars have understood and written about first Khubilai's and then Kṛtanagara's adoption of Tantric Buddhism, and then look at the relations between religion, politics, and power. The religious and political worlds of Khubilai and Kṛtanagara will be reassessed in light of that discussion, and also in light of the related ideologies adopted by dynasties from other locales of maritime Asia in the 11th to 14th century.

Khubilai's religion

> All known sources, Chinese, Mongol, and Tibetan, agree that Khubilai was given a consecration (*abhiṣeka*) in 1253. It was an initiation to the rites of dGes-pa rdo-rje (Sans. Hevajra), a tutelary deity specially worshipped in the Sa-skya monasteries and whose cult is closely linked with that of Mahākāla, a protector and defender of the faith who is, like Hevajra, represented in a terrifying aspect. It seems that rites connected with Hevajra and Mahākāla became customary for every enthronement of a Yüan emperor, a fact which is also mentioned in the Chinese sources. The terrible Mahākāla was invoked when the Sino-Mongol armies went into battle. (Franke 1981: 308)

As a point of departure in an examination of Khubilai's religion, we note that Franke's statement reveals one of the problems the reader of histories encounters: while Franke confidently asserted in 1981 that 'all known sources' agree on 1253 as the date of Khubilai's consecration, we find Lokesh Chandra stating in 1995 (1995c: 156, without any references or argument) that Khubilai was initiated twice—first in 1264 and again in 1269—as a prelude to aggression, and an even more recent historian asserting with equal confidence that his consecration took place only once in 1263, citing a number of Tibetan sources to back up his claim (Davidson 2005: 14, 379, n. 27). Seyfort Ruegg (1995: 40) agreed with Franke that the consecration occurred in 1253, but that was only the first consecration, which was followed by a second consecration in 1258 (ibid.: 42) and a third one for which he gave no date (ibid.: 49). This dispute does not matter in the discussion that follows, for my concern here is only with the nature of Khubilai's religious orientation, not in specific dates, but it does illustrate how easy it is to build narratives—and counter-narratives—in the absence of first-hand knowledge that circumscribes the historian's situation.

Moses (1977) situated Mongolian Buddhism in the context of the earlier history of Buddhism in Central Asia. He noted that the earliest Buddhist remains in Mongolia are Kitan, and went on to claim that the Kitan adopted Buddhism like their predecessors the To-pa Wei and Uygur since it provided 'a prop for the barbarian ruling class. Without such a prop the barbarians had no way other than force and terror to enlist the loyalty and support of the Chinese masses' (ibid.: 37). Yet this Buddhism-as-state-policy was not adopted by the Kitan in their relations with the 'outer barbarians', and 'religion played no part in control of the dissident tribes' (ibid.: 37). It was after they had conquered a sedentary civilization that

> the need arose for a sustaining state religion.... The need to cloak their ruler in symbols which would attract an essentially alien population is obvious. So, too, is the need to present the barbarian ruler as a protector of faiths and a divine figure. Only in this way could a conquest chieftain capture the loyalty or fear of a conquered population, and counter the traditional state philosophy of a ruling class. (Moses 1977: 40).

The Mongols, Moses claimed, followed those earlier traditions. At the beginning of Khubilai's reign, 'co-optation of popular Buddhism seemed one way of appealing to the mass in their own language' (ibid.: 66-67), but Khubilai's Buddhism was shaped by Turco-Mongol Buddhism rather than a Chinese form. According to a Tibetan account (often characterized as legendary), Tibetan Buddhism reached the Mongol court through Sakya Paṇḍita, who met with Godan (second son of Ögödei Khan, in charge of Gansu) in AD 1246 after the election of Güyük as Great Khan (ibid.: 76). 'Out of gratitude, and most likely out of political need, the two became allies' (ibid.: 77). According to that account, 'Phags-pa was at that meeting in 1246. By 1255 he had become Godan's advisor in both spiritual and political matters, and after 1260 he was recommended to Khubilai. Moses argued that Khubilai was already oriented towards Buddhism and that 'the usual assertion that Qubilai was converted by 'Phags-pa is misleading. Qubilai was already Buddhist and already familiar with western Buddhism' (ibid.: 77). Rossabi's understanding of Khubilai's Buddhism differed significantly from Moses', but both wrote of the relationship between Khubilai's Buddhism and his politics in the same terms. Khubilai, Rossabi wrote, won over the Buddhists by 'appearing to be attracted to their religion' (Rossabi 1988: 145). Tibetan Buddhism, he argued

> was the ideal vehicle for his political purposes. It could offer ideological justification for the Mongol ruler's accession to power. Its emphasis on magic... appealed to Khubilai, but its most attractive feature was its involvement in politics.... The Tibetan 'Phags-pa lama of the Sa-skya sect proved a useful figure to support Khubilai's aspiration to be perceived as the rightful ruler of China. ... As soon as Khubilai took power, he began to woo the 'Phags-pa with honors and titles. (Rossabi 1988: 143)

If we compare the accounts of Mongolists like Moses and Rossabi with accounts by scholars of Tibetan and Tantric history, we see clearly how different perspectives lead to significantly different narratives. Scholar of Tantrism Ying Chua (2003: 45) claimed that 'Phags-pa's role in Khubilai's court was 'as spiritual master of Kublai' and that this 'was the pivotal force of their relations'. Having first converted Khubilai's wife Chabi and initiated her into Hevajra and Mahākāla, he then brought Khubilai 'under his religious influence, conceivably assisted by Chabi's encouragement' (ibid.: 45). Khubilai 'took Mahākāla as his personal deity (yidam) and tutelary' (ibid.) with full awareness of Mahākāla's powerful and militant character.

On the face of it, this description of the relation between 'Phags-pa and Khubilai seems significantly different from both Moses' and Rossabi's description, for instead of Khubilai 'coopting' or 'appearing to be interested' in Buddhism, here we find 'Phags-pa to be the guiding figure, gradually bringing the Mongol court under his influence rather than the Mongol Khan bringing the Tibetan(s) under his influence. Chua proceeds to portray the Buddhists providing spiritual aid for Khubilai's military campaigns, and providing him with 'sacred authority to rule':

> Phagpa directed Anige, the imperial art director (see below), to create an image of Mahakala for use in a ritual to aid the Khan in his battles against the Southern Song. Even during Kublai's lifetime, Phagpa and other Tibetan Buddhists recognized him as an emanation or incarnation of the Bodhisattva Manjushri, as well as a Universal Emperor, or Chakravartin, a Buddhist title denoting a benevolent, virtuous ruler who promotes the well-being, education, and diverse religious paths of all his people.... The identification of Kublai with Manjushri is particularly significant in view of Manjushri's role, since at least Tang dynasty, as China's Bodhisattva, residing in his sacred abode on Mount Wutai in Shanxi province. This

association thus provided Kublai with the religious sanction he needed to secure his sacred authority to rule China. (Chua 2003: 45-46)

Thus, to Chua, the adoption of an esoteric Tibetan sect would serve to legitimate Khubilai in the eyes of his Chinese subjects. The desire to explain religion in terms of its functioning as a political legitimation has led Ronald Davidson, a historian of Tantric Buddhism in India and Tibet, to provide yet another perspective. Grounding his account in a narrative of the development of the Sakya sect within Tibetan Buddhism, Davidson (2005: 374) argued that members of the Khön clan 'domesticated the wild image of Virūpa, making the Lamdré, one of the most esoteric systems of siddha practice'. The Sakya monks, 'skillful in the world, spiritually mature, with magical and administrative ability, possessed of internal divinities and external alliances—powerful in every sense of the word', prepared the form of Buddhism that 'became a great part of the ground from which the seeds for the association of Sakya patriarchs with Khubilai Khan would eventually be grown' (ibid.). Davidson noted that some scholars (he cites Franke 1981 and Heissig 1980) have interpreted 'Phags-pa's involvement in Mongolian affairs as a sign that he was the one who 'legitimated Khubilai as a "universal monarch" (*cakravartin*), or divine bodhisattva', but that few have asked 'what was there about Sakya Paṇḍita and Pakpa that caused the Mongols to require their presence in the first place' (Davidson 2005: 7).[10] In David-

---

[10] Davidson does not mention that some of those who have asked the question have regarded the Mongol invitations to Tibetan monks as demands rather than invitations, and the Tibetans' presence at court more a matter of hostages than spiritual advisors. While Wylie (1977: 113), citing *The Golden Annals of Lamaism*, declared that the 'invitation to 'Phags-pa was an ultimatum accompanied by the threat of military action', and Heissig (1980: 24) flatly stated that the Tibetan monks were taken specifically as hostages, Petech wrote more cautiously of Köden's (Godan in Moses' transcription above) invitation to the Sakya Paṇḍita that 'a refusal was out of the question'

son's view, the Sakya Paṇḍita fascinated the Mongols with his abilities, 'yogic systems, magical rites, monastic decorum, clan connections, intellectual acumen, administrative ability, medicine, logic, language', and in fact in their dealings with Tibetans throughout the years the Mongols always selected those with the most skills and abilities. Davidson (ibid.: 375-76) also argued that the Sakya monks, as neoconservatives, were good Buddhists who

> did not elect to mandate their vision through the force of law, even when given the opportunity by their Mongol lords. They would be magnanimous rulers: having achieved victory, they could afford to grant religious freedom to those at the margins. In this, they were similar to other Buddhists who were satisfied that eventually all the world would see the truth.

Davidson pointed out that the common manner of understanding the role of these Tibetans in Mongolian Buddhist affairs 'reflects the predisposition of those authors to assess this role principally through the filters of Chinese political documents' (ibid.: 8).[11] He observed that 'Phags-pa's Buddhism 'was

---

(Petech 1983: 181) and referred to the young 'Phags-pa as 'practically a hostage' (ibid.: 185).

[11] Franke (1981: 297) noted this matter and his comments are worth being quoted in full here: "Chinese history was written by Chinese intellectuals, and the majority of these were not active Buddhists. A negative bias in all official and most private sources as far as the attitude towards Buddhism is concerned must therefore be expected. The picture changes as soon as one turns to Tibetan sources. These are exclusively Buddhist-Lamaist and concerned only with the propagation of the faith. Activities of Tibetan lamas in Yüan China, which appeared to the Chinese as arrogant and insolent and at the best as foreign extravaganzas, may be viewed in Tibetan sources as selfless missionary efforts aimed at influencing Mongol rulers and propagating the doctrine of the Buddha throughout the whole empire... At the risk of oversimplification it could be said that the respective sources reflect the genuine antagonism between state and religion, and that the aim of the Tibetan lamas was precisely to bridge the gulf between religion and state by creating a theocratic theory of secular rule."

perhaps the least accommodating to actual shamanic practice' (ibid.) and that none of the arguments about the usefulness of Buddhism to the Mongols could be applied to Hülegü's adoption of Buddhism, since 'no muslim population has ever perceived the Buddhist religion as legitimate' (ibid.: 9). Far from legitimating Mongol rule, Buddhism in the Il-Khanate and arguably also at Khubilai's court problematized Mongol rule, for 'esoteric Buddhism also tended to reinforce a social agenda that militated against long term political unity' (ibid.: 10).

Jagchid (1988) was one of those who did ask why the Mongols adopted Buddhism, and in particular he asked why Khubilai chose 'Tibetan Buddhism as his personal faith' (ibid.: 89). Of course this way of asking the question—framing it as a matter of personal faith—if taken seriously almost requires setting aside politics as the main factor, and it is no surprise that Jagchid answers his own question the way he does:

> Political reasons aside, the cultural similarity between the Mongols and Tibetans and their common distance from the Chinese may have been the main factors which caused Khubilai to make this historic decision. (ibid.)

Clearly, this is a pretty weak response to such an important question, and no more preferable than offering stark political motives as the deciding matter in his 'faith'. Heissig, while not asking the question of why the Mongols chose Tibetan Buddhism, offered an answer anyway, and did so as though the question did not even need to be asked. For Heissig (1980: 24), 'the first conversion of the Mongols to Lamaism did not go very deep' and 'the first contacts of the Mongols with the Lamaist church in Tibet were primarily political in nature'. It was not due to any spiritual need that 'Phags-pa arrived at the Mongol court, but because Khubilai 'wanted to hold a representative of the *Sa skya pa*' as a hostage (ibid.). The subsequent conversion to Buddhism of the Mongols at the court and the ruling class was a result of 'Phags-pa's 'adroitness in arousing the interest of the ruling class in his religion ... the influence of Tibetan medicine as practiced by the Tibetan monks, which proved more convincing to the Mongols... and on the greater magical effectiveness of Tantric magic' (ibid.). In a conclusion similar to Jagchid's, Heissig blandly states that Tibetan Buddhism 'fitted in especially well with the political dynamism of the Mongols and with their militant nature' (ibid.: 25).

'Phags-pa himself wrote of Khubilai's adoption of Buddhism in a passage quoted in a Buddhist chronicle from the Yuan era and written in Chinese, the *Fozu lidai tongzai* (佛祖歷代通載). In this passage he states simply that Khubilai 'subjugated many countries and territories and became powerful by extending his frontiers. He adopted the teachings and the Law of the Buddha and civilized his people according to the Law. Therefore the teachings of the Buddha flourished twice as much as before' (quoted in Franke 1981: 306), the only connection between the expansions of the religious and political realms being that the latter facilitated the former—not the other way around.

How seriously should such an interpretation be taken? Franke notes that the Mongol rulers appear here as the legitimate successors of the Buddhist universal emperors, not the Chinese dynasty, and Khubilai's son Zhen Jin (真金) is addressed in this work as 'Bodhisattva Imperial Prince', this being 'one of the many instances of Buddhist sacralization conferred upon the family of Chinggis Khan by the Tibetan lamas' (Franke 1981: 307). Here the sacralization is made in the context of a Buddhist history—not a Chinese or Mongolian or even Tibetan history—but Franke immediately follows this note with a remark which puts the whole matter under the aegis of the political once more: 'Because of its inherent supranational character, Buddhist sacralization was acceptable to the Mongols. It provided them with a sacral kingship that legitimized their domination over China and the world' (ibid.: 307).

Petech (1983) provided an account of the many Tibetan Buddhist lamas who had contacts with the Mongol court, from

Chinggis Khan to Khubilai and the patronage of Tibetan sects by the Mongol royal family. The history is varied and extensive: miracle workers (such as Karma Pakshi), learned monks and interreligious disputations (some of which were presided over by the not yet khan Khubilai), and negotiations regarding Mongol policy towards Tibet are all well documented prior to Khubilai's patronage of 'Phags-pa. Regarding this latter monk and the role he was to play at the Mongol court, Petech asks: 'Why did Khubilai select the young Sa-skya hierarch?' (Petech 1983: 184). Like most writers on this matter, Petech offers a political explanation: 'He was the religious chief who offered the best guarantees of intelligent subservience to the aims of the new ruler of China' (ibid.: 185). While Petech mentions 'Phags-pa's initiation of Khubilai into Buddhism, he has nothing more to say about Khubilai's religious life, and indeed in a later work Buddhism plays almost no role at all in Khubilai's relations with Tibetan Buddhists: Khubilai selected 'Phags-pa 'as his advisor and tool in Tibetan matters' (Petech 1990: 16) and that is all there was to the relationship.

In a counter-narrative to all those who offer the 'Buddhist explanation'—that Buddhism simply legitimated the Mongol rulers—Elverskog argued that it was the rites related to the cult of Chinggis Khan alone that provided the Mongol rulers with their political legitimacy in the early imperial period. Although Franke (1981: 308) stated that Tantric rites were a part of every Yuan enthronement, Elverskog argued that there was a dual legitimation involving both Buddhist rites and rites pertaining to the cult of Chinggis. If Elverskog is correct, Khubilai could not have derived his legitimacy from his adoption of Tantric Buddhism unless the results of his initiation were such as to indicate the blessings of heaven (according to the cult of Chinggis).

There is of course one clearly documented link between Khubilai's political-military policies and the Buddhists within the Mongol Empire, namely that representatives of all religions were required to pray to their gods for the Khan's good fortune and blessing, and this included prayers for military campaigns.

'Phags-pa not only performed rituals for the success of the khan's armies, but as noted above, engaged artists as well for the making of religious articles for the performance of those rituals. Atwood (2004: 249) argued that Mongol policy towards all religions from the time of Chinggis Khan onwards was based on one simple assumption: that prayer benefited the ruler. In a similar fashion, Jagchid claimed that 'if foreign priests, monks, or *khoja*s communicated with Heaven and prayed for the khan, they also would be honored as *boes*, for the more prayers for the life of the khan and the tranquility of the people the better' (Jagchid 1979: 7). Yet the study of state policy regarding religion is not at all the same as studying Khubilai's religious beliefs, practices, and orientation. Atwood's remark that 'of all the khans, Qubilai Khan (r. 1260-94) tried hardest to curtail religious privileges' (Atwood 2004: 251) is a clear reminder of the difference between understanding Khubilai's religion and understanding his religious policy; everything is much simpler if one tries only to understand state policy.

Apart from Davidson's account, historians have been nearly unanimous in seeing and understanding Khubilai's religion as primarily or even solely a matter of political expediency. It is as though Khubilai, because he was a powerful member of the ruling class, could have no experience of or interest in religion except as a tool of state policy. Davidson's narrative, the questions he asks, and the criticisms he offers suggest that Khubilai's Buddhism has never been adequately discussed for the simple reason that it has never been taken seriously. Theoretical orientations and unstated assumptions have determined the discussions of Khubilai's Buddhism so completely as to have rendered religion invisible in the relevant historiography: in the historiography of Khubilai's Buddhism, there is hardly anything but realpolitik.

In fact, it is even a bit worse than that. In many discussions there is simply a restatement of what some earlier writer had written, without any critical engagement and often without understanding or restating either the complexity of the issues involved or the sources from whence knowledge has been obtained. To make matters worse, the Mongols are often portrayed as barbarians—simple-minded, rural-dwelling nomads of yesteryear—fascinated by the magic and miracles of charlatans, shamans, and miracle workers, envious and in awe of the baubles of urban civilization and its religions. It is therefore this predisposition that explains their religious life and orientation. When it comes to religion among the Mongols, attitudes that would not be countenanced in discussions of other social practices abound in the writings of Sinologists, Mongolists, and Tibetologists.

Kṛtanagara's religion
If the historiography of Khubilai's Buddhism leaves a lot to be desired, so does that relating to Kṛtanagara's Buddhism.

The sources for learning of Kṛtanagara are few but varied. He himself left a number of inscriptions, and there are later inscriptions mentioning him. There are lengthy passages in the *Deśavarṇana* of 1365 and in the 16th(?)-century *Pararaton* as well as in the later *kiduṅ*.[12] Since the *Deśavarṇana* was written by a Buddhist and the *Pararaton* by a 'somewhat anti-Buddhist' (O'Brien 2008: 237), interpreting what they have to say about Kṛtanagara's religion is fraught with problems. The inscriptions, on the other hand, are brief but accompanied by statuary, and although each aids in the interpretation of the other, their interpretation is no easier than understanding the longer poems and prose works, as the literature on these inscriptions clearly demonstrates.

In the Jaka Dolog inscription there are four verses in Sanskrit that tell of Kṛtanagara; interpreting what they have to say about that king involves translation, and on that there has been no consensus. Nihom (1986: 487) suggested translating them thus:

---

[12] The dating of the *Pararaton* and the *kiduṅ*s is irrelevant to the discussion here.

Just as the Indra of the kings of the earth is the sage, the master of the four continents, (so) he is the son of Śrī Jayawardhanī (and) born of the essence of Śrī Hariwarddhana. (10) Endowed with the complete truth, he is the teacher of the doctrine of the Dharma. Actively engaged in the ritual actions which redeem the fallen, he is the best of those who know the lawbooks. (11)

Named Jñānaśiwabajra, he is fully conversant with the gnosis of enlightenment. One who has the limbs (of the *ṣaḍaṅgayoga*) purified by the rays of Insight, he is adorned with the jewel which is mind. (12)

With devotion having erected this (image) conformable to the nature of Mahākṣobhya, in the cemetery named Wurara he had previously had consecrated himself. (13)

Nihom's conclusion was that they reveal a great deal about Kṛtanagara's Buddhism, that 'there is good reason to suppose that a cult of Hevajra was practised by the royal house', and that 'the consecration of Kṛtanagara was indeed in all probability a consequence, in syncopation or reaction, to the tantric consecrations of Kublai Khan' (Nihom 1986: 497). The big surprise in this conclusion is that Nihom mentions nothing at all about Khubilai or the Mongols between his reference to Moens' suggestion in his first paragraph and this closing remark.

Lokesh Chandra agreed with Nihom that the Jaka Dolog inscription informs us of Kṛtanagara's Buddhism, but what Nihom learned from the inscription was not exactly what Lokesh Chandra learned. Among other differences, Lokesh Chandra argued that Kṛtanagara's Buddhism was of the *Guhyasamājatantra* tradition. He did agree with Nihom on several other matters, namely that 'Kṛtanagara had performed consecrations and he had been purified by the luminosity of knowledge ... which made him ever more dedicated to Dharma. National stabilization was achieved through cosmic powers'

(Lokesh Chandra 1995c: 154).[13] Lokesh Chandra also agreed that his initiation imitated Khubilai's:

> Kublai Khan got initiated into *Hevajra* in 1264 and again in 1269, as a prelude to further conquests. To stem the Mongol threat of aggression, Kṛtanagara imitated Kublai Khan's dedication and tried to develop magical might by taking the empowerment of Akṣobhya. The *Hevajra* pertains to Mother Tantras and Akṣobhya to Father Tantras. To supersede Kublai Khan who had been initiated into Mother Tantras, he got empowered into the more virile and powerful Father Tantras represented by *Guhyasamāja* (Wayman 1973: 234-35). The first empowerment referred to in the inscription could have taken place in 1281, when Kṛtanagara had been invited to come in person to the imperial court and to pay homage to the Mongol Emperor (Lokesh Chandra 1995c: 156-57).

Lokesh Chandra takes the old argument one step further, suggesting that the re-dedication of the statue followed upon Kṛtanagara's mistreatment of the envoy sent by Khubilai to Java in 1289 (Meng Qi, according to the undated notice in the *Yuan shi*):

> To avert any serious eventuality the King re-dedicated the same image, which had warded off for eight years the calamitous situation, with more esoteric rites to gain supernatural powers to preempt the aggression. (ibid.: 157)

Another inscription mentioning Kṛtanagara is the Amoghapāśa inscription, an inscription in two parts. The longer part

---

[13] Lokesh Chandra earlier in the article attributed unification of the island realm to Kṛtanagara's father Viṣṇuvardhana (to whom the statue was dedicated).

on the back in praise of Amoghapāśa/Ādityavarman was added upon the reconsecration of the statue in the time of Ādityavarman (r. 1347-76), a reconsecration that ritually asserted his independence from Java (Kozok and Reijn 2010: 136). The inscription on the base (which was not altered or removed for the reconsecration) records that the statue was sent by *mahārājādhirāja* Kṛtanagara as a gift to the people of Malayu in 1286. The inscription contains no further information on Kṛtanagara or his relations with Malayu except that he hoped that they would enjoy this and the other fourteen statues that he had sent. Both the *Deśavarṇana* ('the King gave the order to move against the land of Malayu' in Robson's translation [1995: 54]) and the *Pararaton* ('he sent an expedition to attack Malayu' [Phalgunadi 1996: 99]) present Kṛtanagara's expedition to Malayu as a military action, and an eventually successful conquest (as his gift of statues also indicates). Nevertheless Sedyawati (2004: 721) concurred with Berg in thinking that the Amoghapāśa inscription indicated 'a religious diplomatic expedition rather than a military one' and made no mention of Khubilai or a campaign to gather allies against him.

The *Deśavarṇana* contains the lengthiest description of Kṛtanagara and was written by the Buddhist Mpu Prapañca. In that poem Kṛtanagara is in one passage (Canto 43: 2) called Jñānabajreśvara, 'the king whose weapon is knowledge' (Berg 1965: 97). The land of Malayu was defeated 'through his divine incarnation' (Canto 41.5), as would later be the case with Bali too. Likewise the other regions sought protection at the feet of the King:

> The whole territories of Pahang and of Malayu bowed humbly before him;
> The whole of Gurun and of Bakulapura also took refuge before him,
> Not to mention Sunda and Madura, for the whole of Java was unquestioningly devoted to him. (Robson 1995: 55)

After this description of conquests and lands under his dominion (unless we accept that those lands did indeed seek his protection instead of being conquered), the text continues with a description of his religious character in Canto 42.3 and the whole of Canto 43:

> Canto 42
> 3. Nevertheless the King was not negligent, was free of intoxication, and was more and more energetic in his policy,
> For he had realized how difficult it is to protect the world in the age of Kali.
> This is why he held fast to esoteric doctrines and observances, and was firmly committed to the sect of the Buddhists,
> In order to imitate the kings of old, and to guarantee the continued prosperity of the world. (Robson 1995: 55)

Here we do have an explicit reference to imitation, but it is not in imitation of Khubilai that Kṛtanagara was 'committed to the sect of the Buddhists' but rather 'the kings of old'. In Canto 43 Prapañca declares that 'only the divine being who concentrates on the six supernatural faculties of the Buddha could protect the world as god-king' and it was for that reason that 'the King was firmly devoted to the Śākhya Lion, And attentively adhering to the Five Commandments he was inaugurated and duly consecrated' (Robson 1995: 55). Having been consecrated as a Jina, 'the King studied the scriptures on reasoning, analysis and so on till he was completely accomplished' (ibid.). At this point in his description of Kṛtanagara the author then mentions his esoteric rites:

> Canto 43
> 3. But as he grew somewhat older he held to all sorts of esoteric rites;

Mainly of course it was the Subhūti Tantra the essence of which he guarded and cherished in his heart.

He applied himself to worship, yoga and meditation for the stability of the whole world....

4. He had mastered completely the sixfold stategy against enemies, was learned in the scriptures and expert in the works containing teaching on reality;

He was very virtuous, firm in his Buddhist observances and very energetic in the rites for application of magic. (Robson 1995: 55-56)

As an example of Buddhist hagiography it is unremarkable that he saw it as his duty to 'protect the world in the age of Kali' and engaged in religious practices 'for the stability of the whole world', but these same practices (whatever they were) were perhaps regarded quite differently by the non-Buddhist author of the *Pararaton*. In that text Kṛtanagara's consecration as Bhaṭṭāra Śiva-Buddha is mentioned (Phalgunadi 1996: 99), but the unknown author later relates that when he was attacked by Jaya-katon, 'King Kṛtanagara Bhaṭṭāra Śiva-Buddha was then merrily absorbed in enjoying palm wine' (ibid.). The author again notes that Kṛtanagara was drinking palm wine when he narrates the circumstances of his death, but gives no further indication as to the nature of that drinking session, nor does he describe it as either religious or irreligious. Many scholars writing of this passage have concluded that the drinking was part of a Tantric Hevajra ritual and therefore probably accompanied by orgies and other transgressive practices. When Fic (2003: 86) declared that 'Kṛtanagara was assassinated while performing a Tantrik rite', we should understand that the hypothesis vigorously argued by earlier historians has become a simple and unquestioned truth. More carefully, Hall (2011: 320) noted that although Kṛtanagara was known as Śiva-Buddha, 'neither his inscriptions nor the long *Nāgarakĕrtāgama* passage dealing with his reign show unambiguous evidence of Śaivism' but clearly indicate Tantric Buddhism of the Vajrayāna variety. The ceremonies associated with that variety of Buddhism—such as the *gaṇacakra* mentioned in *Deśavarṇana* 43.3—remain, however, unclear (ibid.).[14]

The *kiduṅ* offer pointed critiques of Kṛtanagara. He is described as a bad king 'like a hot sun beating down mercilessly upon all' in the *Raṅga Lave* (Berg 1930: 35), living a gay and carefree life even as war broke out and his killers bore down upon him (1930: 36-39). His religious life is evident only in his title Śiva-Buddha. The *Kiduṅ Harṣavijaya* offers a bit more, but not much. Kṛtanagara is described in less than flattering terms: he pays no attention to his ministers, who leave his service one after the other or are exiled. He declares his intention to become an ascetic (a *bhagavan*) but changes his mind after being encouraged to subject Malayu to his rule and take the princesses of Malayu, Dara-Petak, and Dara-Jiṅga as wives for his nephew Harṣavijaya.[15] After he learns of Jayakatoṅ's attack upon the capitol, he wants to close the palace gates but his former prime minister and Virakṛti reprimand him for his cowardice, reminding him that 'a king who died in the women's quarters would end up in hell' (Berg 1931: 77). He therefore goes out to do battle and, fighting alone, is killed; his death is marked by natural phenomena.

---

[14] Unclear, that is, at least to Hall and all those still looking for the *Subhūti-tantra* (on which, see Kandahjaya's contribution, this volume, pp. 98-99). For Lukas (2004), the associated ceremonies were known: 'In this Bhairavist (Tantric) tradition attempts are made to come into power in a Rimbaud-like *dereglement systematique des sens*—drunkenness, sexual orgies and ritual murder.... The Bhairava-rituals—during which, among other things, a sexual intercourse between the Lord of the ring (*mandala*) and the *yogini*s—were sufficient to give rise to the consolidation of the ruler's power (*sakti*): The *yogini*s were therefore chiefly considered to be representatives of magic power'.

[15] Christie (1964: 58) claimed that in 'the *Kidung Harṣa-wijaya* Krtanagara became *bhagavan* (as did Vikramavardhane [sic] later), a statement which seems to have implied an attempt to increase the royal *kesekten* (cf. Skt. *sakti*) by spiritual exercises and *tapa*. While this is not affirmed in the *Nagarakrtagama* or the inscriptions, it is consistent with these sources'.

In these *kiduṅ*s, apart from the narrative concerning his desire to retire and become an ascetic, little is revealed about his religious life and practices. The reproach about dying in the women's quarters clearly indicates that the author of the *Kiduṅ Harṣavijaya* could not have considered whatever Kṛtanagara was doing at the end of his life to have been responsible religious behaviour, whether or not Tantric rituals were involved.

Surveying all of these sources for the religious life and foreign policies of Kṛtanagara, there seems to be not one shred of evidence to connect his Buddhism directly with Khubilai, nor his campaign to Malayu with a threat from the North, however plausible both explanations may appear to be. Nevertheless, from Berg in the 1950s to the present, Kṛtanagara's Buddhism and his foreign policy have been repeatedly linked to and presumed to be explained by Khubilai's Buddhism and foreign policy. What is most striking about that literature is that explaining Kṛtanagara's Buddhism in terms of realpolitik and mimesis appears to be the only option ever considered by most historians, primarily because of the historians' own assumptions about the relations between religion and politics. This is all the more striking when we consider O'Brien (2008), in which such 'obvious' explanations are set aside in the interest of inquiring into the self-understanding of an early author. Having observed that in the historiography concerning the worlds of Khubilai and Kṛtanagara the relation between religion and politics has been much discussed and everywhere explained but rarely questioned, it seems necessary to proceed by questioning that relationship.

Powers, religious and political
Benedict Anderson (1990: 23) offered as one of the distinguishing features of the Javanese understanding of power that 'power does not raise the question of legitimacy'. As he described it, it 'would be meaningless to claim the right to rule on the basis of differential sources of power.... Power is neither legitimate nor illegitimate. Power is' (ibid.). This of course raises significant

questions about any attempt to 'see' in Javanese religion the legitimation of a political regime, and Anderson (ibid.: 26) noted this in reference to ceremonies of state:

> This obsession with ceremony has commonly been interpreted either as simple love of ideologizing; as manipulative sleight-of-hand, concealing political and economic realities from the population; or as a way of formally integrating conflicting groups and interests.... Such judgments are doubtless partly valid... but it would be unreasonable to deny that the importance attached to ceremonies may also have a more traditional basis, certainly in the minds of the spectators and probably, if to a lesser degree, in the minds of the leaders themselves.

Thus, according to Anderson, in Java religious rituals and ceremonies are means of acquiring power, and neither masks nor justifications for the exercise of power. Yet Anderson misses a crucial point: if 'power is', then we are dealing with a metaphysical presupposition which both precedes and informs social structures, political action, and theological disputation, and not with ideological constructions elaborated on the basis of a pre-existing situation.

In his study of the historiography of Mongol-Manchu relations, Elverskog (2006) noticed that state-supported Buddhism was everywhere understood to be 'a form of Dharmic agitprop that secured the support of the Qing dynasty's Buddhist subjects' (ibid.: 3). The assumption he found throughout was that the Manchus secured the loyalty of their Mongol subjects by 'ritually confirming their rule through the symbols, myths and history of Buddhist political authority' (ibid.). He noted that the Jesuit Amiot described the relationship this way already in the late 18th century, as did the Qianlong emperor in his 'Proclamation on Lamas'. Elverskog (ibid.: 3-4) observed that this interpretation has been especially favoured by Mongols:

Ever since then, virtually every source touching upon the Mongols, Buddhism and the Qing dynasty has echoed the same refrain... they all agree: the Manchus used Buddhism to rule the Mongols.... The 'Buddhist explanation' assumes that by promoting the Dharma the Manchus were able to ensure the loyalty of their Mongol subjects.

Whereas 'Buddhist history often reads like a laundry list of famous Asian rulers who promoted the faith' (ibid.: 9), Elverskog found 'conceptualizations of community, state formation, political authority and religion' informing one another (ibid.: 11). He suggested that the theoretical concerns of historians who arrive after the fact 'potentially distort our understanding of the past' (ibid.: 15).

Elverskog turned the terms of the discussion upside down. Given that Nurhaci (the Jurchen leader to whom the Khorchin Mongols gave allegiance in 1626 and whose descendants established the Qing dynasty of China) was 'praised as a divine ruler who saves the Khorchins', Elverskog questioned whether we should think of this as a conquest or a submission, for 'using such terms not only shapes but also defines our interpretation' (ibid.: 16).[16] He suggested instead that:

> In large measure the Mongols hoped that the Manchu state could restore order among the fractious Mongol groups. Rather than seeing the Mongols as inherently anti-Qing, we need to recognize that many Mongols actually welcomed the rise of the Manchu state within the parameters of the *ulus/törö* framework. (ibid.: 30)

The *ulus/törö* framework he mentioned was the Mongolian system of state organizing and mediating among independent local authorities. Elverskog argued that what was at stake

---

[16] This is precisely what is at stake for the interpretation of Mpu Prapañca's remark quoted above that the regions under Kṛtanagara's dominion 'sought protection at the feet of the King'.

for the Mongol groups was not their independent existence 'but the absence of a proper mediating authority' (ibid.). The question that remains is why Nurhaci and the later Manchu rulers were described in religious terms ('divine ruler' etc.). Contrary to traditional historiography, it appears that the desire for peace among the various Mongol groups justified their unification with the Manchu state, which possessed the requisite political power to end the internecine warfare and effect a peace. Elverskog suggested that 'most often, actual military, political and economic success is ipso facto evidence of God's grace, while failure is proof of having lost favor. Yet ... for the Mongols, God was a dynamic force that demanded prayer in order to secure blessings and continued favor' (ibid.: 48). Political power (as well as its acceptance) depended upon the ritually secured blessing of God. At least some Mongols understood that the Manchus possessed the political power as the blessing of God, which the Mongols no longer possessed.

Bourdieu (1991: 20) argued that 'religious specialists must always conceal that their struggles have political interests at stake'. It seems to be clear in the case of both Kṛtanagara and Khubilai that Tantric Buddhist practices were inextricably involved in their orientations and actions as rulers, but that political interests were nowhere concealed. In spite of the near unanimous agreement of three centuries of historians, I propose to argue in a manner similar to Elverskog that the religious aspects of the political crises in the 13th century were not simply produced to legitimate or conceal political conditions, but were in fact a way of understanding the situation and at the same time the beliefs which produced the situation; the political significance of Kṛtanagara's and Khubilai's religious engagements arose from those engagements rather than determining them. In short, Kṛtanagara and Khubilai responded to the powers that moved and shook the world of their time—including the actions of both of these kings—on the basis of their beliefs about the world in which they found themselves, and for both of these kings their beliefs and actions were oriented (we might say disoriented) by Tantric Buddhism.

Tantric buddhism and the love of kings

To argue—as many have—that Kṛtanagara's adoption of Tantric Buddhism was in imitation of or in response to Khubilai's initiation requires the assumption that Tantric Buddhism offered effective power—spiritual, political, and military power—and that neither Kṛtanagara nor Khubilai ever questioned that. Without that operative assumption, mimesis makes no sense. If indeed Kṛtanagara and Khubilai understood their situation as one of (spi)ritual warfare in which Tantric Buddhism offered the greatest potency in action, we may acknowledge the political conditions as prompting the question of power and its attainment but not as explaining the adoption of Tantric Buddhism, much less the belief in its efficacy. And if both kings believed in the efficacy of Tantric Buddhism, there is no need to assume any act of mimesis. If we re-examine Kṛtanagara's and Khubilai's Buddhism with the understanding that it cannot be explained by their political situation, we are left with the question: 'Why Tantric Buddhism?'

In Bade (2013) I argued that Mongol expansion in the 13th century was driven by traditional Mongol beliefs about the means for achieving social peace, namely social unity.[17] During the reign of Chinggis, the belief in one truth, one world, and one ruler to ensure peace and justice through his own actions which expressed both the order of God and the order of the world had come to be the foundation of that social unity, a matter explicitly recorded in later Mongol rulers' correspondence with the papal

---

[17] That work, as the present chapter, was greatly influenced by my readings of the works of Eugen Rosenstock-Huessy, in particular his *Out of Revolution* (Rosenstock-Huessy 1993). While he wrote very little on Buddhism, his *Soziologie* (Rosenstock-Huessy 1956-58) contains a few remarks and a great deal of his thought about religion. Although the secondary literature on him is not extensive, three recent works are relevant: Cristaudo 2008 on power, Cristaudo 2012 on religion and politics, and Leutzsch 2009 on globalization and international relations.

authorities. These Mongol notions can be found in the *Secret History* (*Mongγol-un niγuca tobčiyan*) and other documents of the 13th century, and provided the foundation for the religious and political worlds into which Khubilai was born. In Khubilai's youth the Mongols came into contact with Buddhism while campaigning in the south, and sometime during the reign of Ögedei (1229-41) two Kashmiri monks, Otochi and Namo, arrived at the Mongol court (Jagchid and Hyer 1979: 178). In the years that followed Khubilai was introduced to Tantric Buddhism and eventually consecrated in (one or more) Hevajra ceremonies (see discussion above). Why did he embrace this form of Buddhism?

The *Secret History* records that Alan Gua, the mythical ancestor of the Mongols, taught her sons that power is achieved through unity, and that through unity her sons could become lords of the earth and lords of the air. By the time of Khubilai, the question had become how to produce and maintain that unity on the scale of an empire. For this task, Mongolian mythology and traditions provided no answer. 'Phags-pa proposed an answer involving Tantric practices and all the evidence indicates that Khubilai embraced that religious-ritual path to acquiring the power his position required.[18] In doing so he also embraced the religio-political doctrine of the *cakravartin*, 'a just and virtuous world-monarch' initiating 'a universal, world-wide empire of enduring tranquility' and 'who should put an end to the perpetual struggle of the contending states' (Zimmer 1952: 128). The Tantric initiate 'strives after the attainment of supreme insight, however he may conceive this. And one concomitant of this supreme insight is supernatural power' (Pott 1966: 105).

---

[18] Pott (1966: 68ff.) provided a discussion of the ceremony he assumed accompanied Khubilai's consecration, and even suggests that a set of bronze statues discovered and photographed in the 1920s (and disappearing again shortly thereafter, its fate remaining unknown) was originally produced for use 'at Khubilai's Hevajravaśitā'. Sharrock (2006: 63) suggested as an alternative interpretation that 'the bronzes may have been created for a performance of the *cakrasaṁvara-tantra*'.

Davidson (2002: 168) argued that Esoteric Buddhism was 'accepted and supported by the monarchs on the Indian borderlands, for they understood that Buddhist institutions had provided them with exactly the right combination of political and religious authority'. Those rulers of foreign lands—among whom both Kṛtanagara and Khubilai should be counted—received training, rituals, spells, and medicine, all of which 'could be used in service to the authenticity of the monarch and his state' (ibid.). Davidson understood the relation of foreign monarchs to Esoteric Buddhism on the basis of his understanding of its origins in Indian feudal society:

> Thus institutional esoterism sought to sacralize observable reality, employing the techniques that had always been successful. Here, the Buddha was depicted as a king with a crown, clothed in all the ornaments of royalty. Here, the monks received the ritual coronation and became divine in the process. Here, they envisioned the spiritual state filled with Buddhas and bodhisattvas, with worldly beings and families of divinities. Here, they acted as agents for the Dharma, for the law. They performed the ceremonies that—in their minds—would bring peace where there was war, wealth where there was poverty, control where there was chaos, and destruction to the enemies of religion. (Davidson 2002: 168)

In his view, monks and *siddha*s sought to bring the real into line with their spiritual vision through their involvement 'with real courts of local lords' (ibid.: 334). Yet the rituals they devised for coronation 'yielded dominion within a maṇḍala of vassal figures and conferred control over self and others in a world where hierarchy was not the primary model of social relations, it was the only model' (ibid.).

Once again it appears that the religious is both determined and explained by the social and political conditions within which it appears. The *siddha*s (at least some of them) produced their distinctive doctrines and ways of life 'in a desperate move to make sense of the world that continued to unravel as the gods seemingly supported the capricious conduct of men with swords, power, and wealth' (ibid.: 335). And in every case their goal was 'the appropriation of power' and in their scriptures they 'maintained various versions of the imperial model of dominion over the gods, the sorcerers, and other religious groups' (ibid.: 335). Yet Davidson argued that for Buddhists, 'the fundamental reason they could engage the world in this way is that they believed in the transformation of personality' (ibid.: 164). The rituals of coronation and 'the public persona of the overlord is, among other things, an attempt to impress it with a consensual sense of responsibility' (ibid.). Whence this belief? Two pages later Davidson offered a hint:

> How often can a monk visualize himself as King of the World, erotic and powerful, without being captured by the fantasy of his own vision? When the new scriptures explicitly proclaim that the individual can become all-powerful in this one life, what perspective can be expected of a semiliterate monk from a small village that has just been burned and had its wells poisoned by the local warlord in a dispute over tribute?... They would surely ask whether there were not some way to harness the power of Vajrapāṇi, the General of Secrets, to overcome these armies and to rectify the barbaric displays of inhumanity. In the process they would, as the *Mahākālantantra* teaches, try to use magic and visualization to engage in battle with the forces of evil and obtain success to rule the state. (ibid.: 166)

Davidson offers quite a contrasting response to Tantric teachings depending upon whether he is dealing with a 'semiliterate monk from a small village' (who responds by being carried away with his own fantasies) or the kings of foreign lands (who 'understood that Buddhist institutions had provided them with exactly the right combination of political and religious authority'). Is it not kings and emperors who are more given to megalomania and fantastic dreams about their own divinity? If we rewrite the paragraph quoted above, substituting Khubilai or Kṛtanagara for monk, we have a new way to approach the relationship between political reality and religious belief, not only in the 13th century but in our own time as well.

The widespread adoption of Tantric Buddhism at courts throughout Asia in the 13th and 14th centuries does not indicate the clever appropriation of religion as a 'prop for the barbarian ruling class' (Moses, as quoted above) nor as a means of legitimating their rule any more than it indicates the attraction of religious medicine, magic, and miracles, or the superiority of urban civilization to those rulers. If Tantric Buddhism arose in response to that world characterized by 'the capricious conduct of men with swords, power, and wealth' (ibid.: 335)—and this does seem to be the case—it did not arise as an attempt to justify or legitimate those conditions but to challenge and to change them. It was a response to political and social conditions, and judging by its spread throughout Asia, it was a particularly powerful response. The consequences of the adoption of Tantric Buddhism, both for the Buddhist monks and laity as well as for the kings and nobility who embraced it, were perhaps not what those who fashioned it would have desired, predicted, or even imagined, but they seem fairly clear in hindsight.

Tantric Buddhism, with its imagination of a just and universal world ruler bringing about a state of affairs on earth that would mirror the heavenly state of affairs—the world as it ought to be—was not just a fantasy world of escape for monks and a useful mask hiding ugly realities for kings; it was a powerful motivating force that shaped political and social conditions throughout Asia. For some, the Buddhist rulers brought peace and political stability; for others, the Buddhist rulers brought war, destruction, and death. Whether Kṛtanagara was described as a wise king ushering in an era of expanding peace and prosperity, as a foolish and belligerent king, or as a rebellious local official threatening the peace and stability of the empire depended upon the point of view of the authors who wrote about him. For Mpu Prapañca, Kṛtanagara's Tantric Buddhism provided the realm with a period of peace that was interrupted by his assassination, an act which plunged the world into a period of social disorder and evil. For the authors of the *Pararaton* and the *kiduṅ*, Kṛtanagara's Tantric rituals (or more precisely, those of his behaviours that later historians have assumed were Tantric rituals) were his downfall. For the Chinese chroniclers, Kṛtanagara threatened world peace by resisting and even insulting the envoy of the ruler of heaven, but his religious practices were never mentioned. And at the other end, the Tibetan 'Phags-pa credited Khubilai with the expansion of Buddhism and world order as *cakravartin*.

As a technique for obtaining power and control over the world, Tantric Buddhism—and especially its rituals—came to occupy the same place in 13th- and 14th-century Asian societies that science and technology occupies in our own time. The advocates of scientific method, like the advocates of Tantric Buddhism, have claimed that this method alone leads to knowledge and that knowledge is power. In his theological treatise *Meditationes sacrae* (1597), the early advocate of scientific method Francis Bacon wrote *ipsa scientia potestas est* ('knowledge itself is power') and in the 1651 edition of *Leviathan* (written by Bacon's secretary, the young Thomas Hobbes) we find the phrase *scientia potentia est* for the first time.[19] The order in

---

[19] In *Novum Organum*, the later work in which the foundation of modern scientific method was first outlined, Bacon (1872 I: 222) wrote: 'Now, the empire of man, over things, has its foundation exclusively in the arts and sciences; for it is only by an obedience to her laws, that Nature can be commanded' (*Hominis autem imperium in res, in solis artibus et scientiis ponitur. Naturae enim non imperatur, nisi parendo*). The spiritual practices of Tantric Buddhism that are supposed to bring the initiate to absolute knowledge—to God—are precisely those which are to rid the initiate of all attachment, desires, and the perspective of separation, just as in Baconian science it is necessary to know Nature's laws—reality as it is rather than as we desire it to be—in order to have the knowledge that would allow us to act effectively

which these phrases appeared in England reflects the priority of the ideology over its political expression. Political orientations and political actions are always preceded and oriented by beliefs about the way the world is, about who we are, and about how we ought to respond to the world in which we find ourselves.

The parallels between 13th- and 14th-century Tantric Buddhism and technoscience in our time as a means—the only effective means—of controlling and remaking the world according to our own desires and demands do not end with the identification of knowledge and power. Either the ruling class become initiates or the initiates become the ruling class, for in both cases it is the possession of power that is sought and the service of power that is actually realized. In the time of Kṛtanagara and Khubilai, as in our time, lives put into the service of power lead to war and global disorder, while those actors themselves proclaim that their way offers the sole effective means to a world of peace and justice. I stress the difference between effective and legitimate, for it is not the legitimacy of the regime (the service of any particular power) that matters but efficacy. For the mediaeval Mongol and Javanese kings as for the scientist and politician of today, what is achieved is its own justification because it has been achieved. The Tantric conception of knowledge as something to be obtained by particular methods and techniques is identical to the modern scientific conception of knowledge, and in both cases the acquisition of knowledge is the acquisition

---

upon Her (gender is important here!). This is why knowledge alone confers true and effective power. But the initiate or scientist who desires knowledge in order to obtain power to rule over the world of man and nature is acting on the basis of desires that reflect the absence of that knowledge, and this perverts the entire enterprise. Were we to know the mind of God we would be lovers suffering for all creation, not tyrants dreaming of controlling her. As Davidson (2002: 161) noted, the ritual system of Tantric Buddhism 'sacralized the political metaphor', imagining the Buddha in the image of the kings of India. In similar fashion for Bacon and the science he founded, God is conceived according to the Renaissance European ruler, as an all-powerful being imposing its will on all, and that both reveals Bacon's failures as a theologian and predicts the future trajectory of science.

of power as such, natural and supernatural. With the acquisition of complete and perfect knowledge through science, we shall become God:

> If we do discover a complete theory, it should in time be understandable in broad principle by everyone, not just a few scientists. Then we shall all, philosophers, scientists, and just ordinary people, be able to take part in the discussion of the question of why it is that we and the universe exist. If we find the answer to that, it would be the ultimate triumph of human reason—for then we would know the mind of God. (Hawking 1998: 191)

The desire for power and the means of obtaining it does not arise from political conditions, but from our being born into the world and the necessity of negotiating our lives within that world. Living involves struggles in the realms of bodily existence, desires and frustrations, social relations, and natural environment. All questions of acting involve the exercise of power as they always entail consequences and corresponding actions in the world around us. We may act out of habit and instinct or we may set our minds to learning about the world and adjusting our thoughts and actions in accordance with what we learn. The development of Tantric Buddhism and modern science were both responses to the world in a particular time and place, and both were/are oriented by the idea that knowledge is power, total knowledge being total power.

Kṛtanagara and Khubilai both lived in a time of war and social crisis, and if we are to believe the histories that have been written, it seems that war and social crisis were in great part due to their own actions. They each lived in a world in which it was widely believed that only a single king could rule, however there may be many lesser rulers within his realm, a polity conceived as containing 'core zones of authority and buffer client states' (Davidson 2002: 337). They both sought to rule as divine rulers with complete knowledge and complete power.

Their social position set each of them certain problems of action, and in seeking to act within that world, they sought a means for securing their own effectiveness. Tantric Buddhism supplied the most advanced and effective science known in their world and time. Were they living today, both would seek out the services of physicists and psychologists, just as Hitler secured the services of Heisenberg, Elizabeth Hecker, and Johannes Heinrich Schultz, while Roosevelt accepted the services of Oppenheimer, Leo Szilard, Erik Erikson, and Jerome Bruner (among many others on both sides).[20]

When their two worlds came together, as they did during the diplomatic missions sent by Khubilai to Kṛtanagara, submission or war loomed as the only two options. Both Kṛtanagara's refusals to meet Khubilai's demands and Khubilai's repeated missions indicate that neither king was willing to submit to the other, since both were intent on being the one king within the realm; war was inevitable. Because the Mongol offers of peace via submission did not allow refusal we may assume that peace negotiations were not really ever at stake—only proper submission to Khubilai. We may assume the same for Kṛtanagara since no peace was ever concluded and in 1289 (?) an envoy from Khubilai was sent back to the Mongol court with an unambiguous refusal of Khubilai's offer. Political and military actions both follow from the idea, the belief in, and the commitment to realizing heaven on earth through becoming God. War was therefore spiritual before it was ritual and physical.

What distinguishes this approach to the relation between religion and politics, what makes this analysis something other than realpolitik, is that by putting what one loves and serves at the root of human action—in other words, religion—the love of power (and realpolitik) becomes a love that can be overridden or contested by other loves. Those counter-loves may be proposed by religious teaching or by encounter. Tantric Buddhism can thus be seen on the one hand as a response to political condi-

---

[20] The physicists enlisted are well known; for psychologists and the Third Reich, see Cocks 1997; for the Americans, see Hoffman 1992.

tions, and on the other as creating those very conditions; in both cases, its existence produces the conditions for its use and manipulation by any actors in any contested political realm.

If Tantric Buddhism is understood as a response to, and a creator of, social and political conditions, then the involvement of actors other than kings and rulers is important and perhaps crucial. The political role of 'Phags-pa's Buddhism and that of other monks has often been investigated, as has the role of Buddhism in the policies of kings and rulers, although almost always from a perspective giving priority to the political. The importance of other agents—such as women—in determining the political and social conditions of Java and Mongolia has been given far less attention than it deserves. Both Worsley (1991) and O'Brien (2008) have stressed the importance of women in the Javanese conception of kingship, in particular the role of the queen in relation to the king and the nation. They have also noted Kṛtanagara's association with Tantric rites which bring together male and female. Others have noted the involvement of Chabi in getting Khubilai to pursue initiation with 'Phags-pa, as well as attributing to her the idea of dividing Khubilai's and 'Phags-pa's realms between the earthly and the spiritual.[21] If indeed these two kings loved power, they also seem to have loved their queens. Could it be that Tantric Buddhism was introduced to the courts in both Java and Mongolia not only because the kings believed that it would bring them power but more importantly because the women they loved realized that power was too dangerous to leave in the hands of men alone? A focus on the legitimating function of religion has kept the historians' attention away from its guiding and constraining functions (its role in demanding, initiating, and directing as well as inhibiting change), and has led them to misunderstand or ignore the involvement of other agents (e.g., monks, women) situated differently than a king, perhaps acting upon assumptions other than realpolitik, and probably driven by other desires.

---

[21] Seyfort Ruegg (1991: 448) cites the Mongolian historian 'Jig-med-rig-pa'i-rdo-rje as making this claim in his *Hor Chos'byung* of 1918.

In a recent study of a 14th-century Old Javanese *kakavin*, Mpu Tantular's *Sutasoma*, O'Brien (2008) offered one of the most interesting variations on the Kṛtanagara-Khubilai war yet published. She has argued that Candi Jago made 'a very clear and eloquent statement about the status of Javanese kingship and the Singhasari dynasty' and that Kṛtanagara had the monument made 'as a statement to the world, perhaps even more so, as a warning to Khubilai' (O'Brien 2008: 245). In her book on the *Sutasoma* she argued that the author attempted 'literally to prove the royal divinity of Kṛtanagara and, given that his great-grandson, Rājasanagara, was also practising a similar if not the same system of Buddhist mysticism, then he too was Wairocana in mortal embodiment' (O'Brien 2008: 245). According to her, the *Sutasoma* was an allegory that utilized a story known to its readers—the life of Kṛtanagara and the Mongol attempt to conquer Java—presented as a Buddhist tale to argue that Kṛtanagara had been a Buddha from birth. In her reading we are presented with a 14th-century interpretation of the spiritual meaning of the war in Java and the kings involved. It is a reading that is radically different from Berg's readings of the *kiduṅ*, the *Deśavarṇana*, and the *Pararaton* because she has not tried to unmask the political realities falsified by the texts, but instead set out to understand what the story meant and how it may have a historical analogue that its original readership (or audience) would (or at least might) have known and understood.

O'Brien's hypothesis is that in the protagonists of the *Sutasoma* we can see the historical figures of Kṛtanagara (= Sutasoma himself), Khubilai (= Poruṣāda), Bajradevī (= Candravatī), Viṣṇuvardhana (= Mahāketu), Mahākāla (as himself), Ken Aṅrok (= Agrakumāra), and even Chinggis Khan (= Śūciloma). Prince Sutasoma must confront evil, yet violence is forbidden to him. In the final showdown with Poruṣāda (for which she would have us read Khubilai), she would like to see an analogy for the Kṛtanagara-Khubilai conflict, but of course the analogy could not extend to the actual historical invasion for by that time Kṛtanagara was dead. In the climax, Sutasoma/Kṛtanagara defeats both Poruṣāda and Mahākāla through his 'Buddha-Mind, the weapon of Absolute Knowledge' (O'Brien 2008). The story thus read offers us the meaning of the Kṛtanagara-Khubilai relationship and the tensions of international relations in late 13th-century Asia as it was perhaps understood in 14th-century Java, and not as a 21st-century historian would write it. If O'Brien is on the right track here, then for Mpu Tantular and his readers, there was indeed (spi)ritual warfare—as well as a naval campaign and land battles—for the 14th-century Javanese, and perhaps for Kṛtanagara and Khubilai as well.

In such a reading, the politico-military world of Kṛtanagara and Khubilai is nowhere legitimated by religious practices of any sort but understood entirely in terms of 'the spirit of the times', which was a spirit of war and conflicting territorial claims as a Buddhist saw it. Instead of Berg's optative, we have a poet's record of the resolution of a great crisis, the aversion of social collapse, and the establishment of peace. For the readers or hearers of that story, there were not only historical parallels to be drawn relating to the time of Kṛtanagara and Khubilai, but contemporary parallels as well, and, perhaps most importantly, lessons for the future. Mpu Tantular's *Sutasoma* was, in similar fashion to his *Arjunavijaya* in Worsley's analysis, a story for the future rather than a dead statement about the past. No history worth reading can be otherwise.

Conclusion

Were the politico-military actions of Kṛtanagara and Khubilai legitimated or supported by their religious practices? Were their politico-military successes proof of the genuineness of their religious practices or indications of the superficiality and concealing function of the latter? The possibility of asking these questions challenges the assumption that the political and the religious dimensions of human action may be investigated and understood separately. Following Humphrey and Ujeed (2013: 23) I would insist that while 'Buddhism ... cannot be explained by given social practices, [it] is nevertheless inflected by them—

and vice versa'. The long history of philosophical and practical efforts to find a workable relationship between the religious and the political dimensions of social life suggests that their separation always leads to making a totalitarian religion out of politics or a totalitarian politics out of religion.

Instead of always and only seeing religion as concealing political and economic realities, as a fiction maintained to ground and legitimize existing power structures and a ruling class, we may see religion as the expression of a judgement concerning the past and a will towards a desired future. Humphrey and Ujeed offer an excellent case of this when they argued that the genealogy compiled by Mergen Gegen 'was little concerned with the preoccupations anthropologists have usually assigned to it, property and legitimate succession, but instead it created a framework through time for a moral world' (ibid.: 91). The past being judged may be seen as a golden age, a time of previous peace to be re-established; it may also be seen as a chaotic period of violence from which the new powers will extricate us. This is precisely how Lokesh Chandra (1995c: 152) understood the description of Viṣṇuvardhana in the Jaka Dolog inscription. 'The internecine assassinations were absolved by virtue of ushering in an era of peace and prosperity, kindness to the people (kṛpālu), and fervent devotion and dedication to Dharma', Lokesh Chandra wrote, and 'the past acts of coming to power had been blood-stained and their expiation was to ensure the continuance of his dynasty by political, social and religious achievements' (ibid.). The making of peace was an achievement, the conquest of chaos and the establishment of social security.

Historiography is always and necessarily an attempt to interpret and 'divine' the meaning of events, and consequently belongs in the realm of the spiritual and the religious. It is never possible to argue about 'what happened' without making assumptions about the meaning of artefacts, the meaning of texts, the meaning of words, and the meaning of actions: whether an initiation into Tantric Buddhism is described as a religious experience or a political strategy will be determined in large part by how the historian understands religion, politics, and the relation between them. A historian who understands religion as a strategy for concealing political truths will produce a history like those encountered above in the historiography of the religious life of Khubilai and Kṛtanagara. A historian who does not make that reduction may not provide a better understanding, but the possibility of a more complex and perhaps better interpretation of the past at least remains open.

References

Anderson, Benedict (1990 [1972]). "The idea of power in Javanese culture." In his: *Language and Power: Exploring Political Cultures in Indonesia*. Ithaca and London: Cornell University Press. p. 17-77. Originally published in 1972 in: C. Holt (ed.), *Culture and Politics in Indonesia*. Ithaca, N.Y.: Cornell University Press, p. 1-69.

Atwood, Christopher P. (2004). "Validation by holiness or sovereignty: religious toleration as political theology in the Mongol world empire of the Thirteenth Century" *The International History Review*, Vol. 26, No. 2 (Jun., 2004), p. 237-256.

Aung-Thwin, Michael A. (2011). "A new/old look at "classical" and "post-classical" Southeast Asia/Burma." In: Michael Arthur Aung-Thwin and Kenneth R. Hall (eds.), *New Perspectives on the history and Historiography of Southeast Asia: Continuing Expolorations*. London and New York: Routledge, p. 25-55.

Bacon, Francis (1597). *Meditationes Sacrae*. Londini: Excusum impensis Humfredi Hooper.

Bacon, Francis (1872). *The Works of Francis Bacon* (collected and edited by James Spedding et al.) New edition. London: Longmans.

Bade, David (2013). *Of Palm Wine, Women and War: The Mongolian Naval Expedition to Java in the 13th Century*. Singapore: ISEAS.

Berg, C.C. (1930). *Rangga Lawe: middeljavaansche historische roman : critisch uitgegeven*. Batavia: Batavia's genootschap, Weltevreden: Albrecht & Co. (Bibliotheca Javanica ; 1)

Berg, C.C. (1931). *Kidung Harṣa-Wijaya: tekst, inhoudsopgave en aanteeekeningen*. 's-Gravenhage: Martinus Nijhoff.

Berg, C.C. (1950). "De geschiedenis van pril Majapahit I. Het mysterie van de vier dochters van Krtanagara" *Indonesië* 4de jaargang p. 481-420

Berg, C.C. (1951a). "De geschiedenis van pril Majapahit II. Achtergrond en oplossing der pril-Majapahitse conflicten" *Indonesië* 5de jaargang p. 193-233

Berg, C.C. (1951b). "De Sadeng-oorlog en de mythe van Groot-Majapahit" *Indonesië* 5de jaargang p.385-422.

Berg, C.C. (1953). *Herkomst, vorm en functie der Middeljavaanse rijksdelingstheorie*. Amsterdam: N.V. Noord-Hollandsche Uitgeverij. (Verhandelingen der Koninklijke Nederlandse Akademievan Wetenschappen, Afd. Letterkunde, Nieuwe reeks, deel LIX, no. 1)

Berg, C.C. (1956). "Krtanagara's maleise affaire" *Indonesië* 9de jaargang p. 386-417.

Berg, C.C. (1962). *Het rijk van de vijfvoudige Buddha*. Amsterdam: N.V. Noord-Hollandische Uitgevers Maatschappij. (Verhandelingen der Koninklijke Nederlandse Akademie van Wetenschappen, Afd. Letterkunde. Nieuwe reeks ; Deel LXIX, no. 1)

Berg, C.C. (1965). "The Javanese picture of the past" In: Soedjatmoko et al. (editors), *An Introduction to Indonesian Historiography*. Ithaca: Cornell University Press. p.87-117.

Bosch, F.D.K. (1956). "C.C. Berg and ancient Javanese history" *Bijdragen tot de Taal-, Land- en Volkenkunde* 112 no: 1, p. 1-24

Bourdieu, Pierre (1991). "Genesis and structure of the religious field" *Comparative Social Research* 13 p.1-44.

Brandes, Jan Laurens Andries (1904). *Archeologisch onderzoek op Java en Madura. I: Beschrijving van de ruïne bij de desa Toempang, genaamd Tjandi Djago, in de residentie Pasoeroean.* 's Gravenhage: Martinus Nijhoff; Batavia: Albrecht & Co.

Chandra, Lokesh (in collaboration with Mrs. Sudarshana Devi Singhai) (1995). "The Jaka Dolog inscription of King Kṛtanagara." In his: *Cultural Horizons of India: Studies in Tantra and Buddhism, Art and Archaeology, Language and Literature.* New Delhi: International Academy of IndianCulture and Aditya Prakashan. Volume 4, p. 148-166.

Christie, Anthony (1964). "The political use of imported religion: an historical example from Java" *Archives de sociologie des religions*, 9e Année, No. 17 (Jan. - Jun., 1964), pp. 53-62.

Chua, Ying (2003). "Tantra in China" In: John C. Huntington et al. *The Circle of Bliss: Buddhist Meditational Art.* (Chicago: Serindia ; Columbus: Columbus Museum of Art) p. 45-50.

Cocks, Geoffrey (1997). *Psychotherapy in the Third Reich: The Göring Institute* (2nd ed., rev. & exp.). New Brunswick, New Jersey: Transaction Publishers.

Cristaudo, Wayne (2009). *Power, Love and Evil: Contribution to a Philosophy of the Damaged.* Amsterdam/New York: Rodopi.

Cristaudo, Wayne (2012). *Religion, Redemption, and Revolution: The New Speech Thinking of Franz Rosenzweig and Eugen Rosenstock-Huessy.* Toronto: University of Toronto Press.

Davidson, Ronald M. (2002). *Indian Esoteric Buddhism: a Social History of the Tantric Movement.* New York: Columbia University Press.

Davidson, Ronald M. (2005). *Tibetan Renaissance: Tantric Buddhism in the Rebirth of Tibetan Culture.* New York: Columbia University Press.

Elverskog, Johan (2006). *Our Great Qing: The Mongols, Buddhism and the State in Late Imperial China.* Honolulu: University of Hawai'i Press.

Fic, Victor M. (2003). *From Majapahit and Sukuh to Megawati Sukarnoputri: Continuity and Change in Pluralism of Religion, Culture and Politics of Indonesia from the XV to the XXI Century.* New Delhi: Abhinav Publications.

Franke, Herbert (1981). "Tibetans in Yüan China" In: John D. Langlois, Jr. (ed.), *China under Mongol Rule.* Princeton: Princeton University Press. p. 296-328.

Griffiths, A. (2014). "Inscriptions of Sumatra, III: The Padang Lawas Corpus studied along with inscriptions from Sorik Merapi (North Sumatra) and Maura Takus (Riau)" in D. Perret (ed.), *History of Padang Lawas, North Sumatra. II: Societies of Padang Lawas (9th c.-13th c.),* pp. 211-262. Paris: Association Archipel.

Hall, D.G.E. (1955). "China and South-East Asia -- yesterday and today. Part I" *Far Eastern Economic Review* v. XVIII no. 25 (June 23, 1955) p.784-785. Reprinted (with Part II) as "China and South-East Asia" in *The University of Hong Kong History Society Annual,* 1960 p.6-11.

Hall, Kenneth R. (2011). *History of Early Southeast Asia: Maritime Trade and Societal Development, 100-1500.* Lanham, Maryland: Rowman & Littlefield.

Hawking, Stephen (1998). *A Brief History of Time.* Updated and expanded tenth anniversary ed. New York: Bantam Books.

Heissig, Walther (1980). *The Religions of Mongolia.* Translated from the German edition by Geoffrey Samuel. London and Henley: Routledge & Kegan Paul.

Hobbes, Thomas (1651). *Leviathan, Or, The Matter, Form, and Power of a Common-Wealth Ecclesiastical and Civil.* London :Printed for Andrew Crooke.

Hoffman, L. E. (1992). "American psychologists and wartime research on Germany, 1941–1945" *American Psychologist,* 47(2), p.264–273.

Humphrey, Caroline and Ujeed, Hürelbaatar (2013). *A Monastery in Time: The Making of Mongolian Buddhism.* Chicago: University of Chicago Press.

Jagchid, Sechin (1979). "The Mongol Khans and Chinese Buddhism and Taoism" *The Journal of The International Association of Buddhist Studies* v. 2 nr. 1 p. 7-28.

Jagchid, Sechin (1988). "Why the Mongolian Khans adopted Tibetan Buddhism as their faith" In his: *Essays in Mongolian Studies.* Provo, Utah: David M. Kennedy Center for International Studies, Brigham Young University. (Monograph series ; v. 3). Originally published in: *Proceedings of the 3d East Asian Altaistic Conference,* Taipei, 1969, p. 108-128.

Jagchic, Sechin and Paul Hyer (1979). *Mongolia's Culture and Society.* Boulder: Westview.

Kern, Hendrik (1910). "De Sanskrit-inscriptie van 't Mahākṣobhya-beeld te Simpang" *Tijdschrift voor Indische Taal-, Land- en Volkenkunde* LII p.99-108.

Kern, Hendrik (1910a). "Geschiedkundige gegevens in 't gedicht Nāgarakṛĕtāgama" *Bijdragen tot de Taal-, Land- en Volkenkunde van Nederlandsch-Indië,* Deel 63,1ste/2de Afl., [7e Volgreeks, 9e Deel], p. 1-32.

Kozok, Uli, and Eric van Reijn (2010). "Adityawarman: three incriptions of the Sumatran king of all supreme kings. Translated and annotated from H. Kern and F.D.K. Bosch", *Indonesia and the Malay World,* Vol. 38, Issue 110, p. 135-158.

Kwa, Chong Guan (1970). "The historical roots of Indonesian irredentism" *Asian Studies,* Vol. VIII, No. 1, pp. 38–52.

Leutzsch, A. (2009). *Geschichte der Globalisierung als globalisierte Geschichte: die historische Konstruktion der Weltgesellschaft bei Rosenstock-Huessy und Braudel.* Frankfurt/New York: Campus Verlag.

Lukas, Helmut (2003). *Theories of Indianization: Exemplified by Selected Case Studies from Indonesia (Insular Southeast Asia) Südostasien.* (Working Papers, Band 1),

Wien: Kommission für Sozialanthropologie, Österreichische Akademie der Wissenschaften. Accessed 20 February 2014 at: http://www.oeaw.ac.at/sozant/files/working_papers/suedostasien/soa001.pdf

Mendis, Vernon L.B. (1981). *Currents of Asian History*. Colombo: Lake House Investments Ltd, Publishers.

Moens, J.L. (1924). "Het Boeddhisme op Java en Sumatra in zijn laatste bloeiperiode" *Tijdschrift van het Bataviaasch Genootschap van Kunsten en Wetenschappen*, 64, pp.521-579.

Moses, Larry William (1977). *The Political Role of Mongol Buddhism*. Bloomington, Indiana: Asian Studies Research Institute, Indiana University. (Indiana University Uralic Altaic Series ; vol. 133)

Nihom, Max (1986). "The identification and original site of a cult statue on East Java: the Jaka Dolog" *Journal of the American Oriental Society* v. 106 nr. 3 p .485-499 + 501.

O'Brien, Kate (2008). *Sutasoma: the Ancient Tale of a Buddha-Prince from 14th century Java by the Poet Mpu Tantular. A translation in English and study*. Bangkok: Orchid

O'Brien, Kate (2016). "The tale of Sudhana and Manoharā on Candi Jago: an interpretation of a series of narrative bas-reliefs on a 13th-century East Javanese monument" in Andrea Acri (ed.), *Esoteric Buddhism in Mediaeval Maritime Asia: Networks of Masters, Texts, Icons*. Singapore: ISEAS Press, pp.275-319.

Petech, Luciano (1983). "Tibetan relations with Sung China and with the Mongols" In: Morris Rossabi (ed.), *China Among Equals: the Middle Kingdom and its Neighbors, 10th-14th Centuries.* Berkeley: University of California Press. p. 173-203.

Petech, Luciano (1990). *Central Tibet and the Mongols: the Yüan-Sa-Skya Pperiod of Tibetan History*. Rome: Istituto italiano per il medio ed estremo Oriente. (Serie Orientale Roma ; vol. LXV)

Phalgunadi, I Gusti Putu (1996). *The Pararaton: a Study of the Southeast Asian Chronicle*. New Delhi: Sundeep Prakashan.

Poerbatjaraka (1922). "De inscriptie van het Mahākṣobhya-beeld te Simpang" *Bijdragen tot de Taal-, Land-, en Volkenkunde* LXXVIII p.426-462.

Pott, P.H. (1966). *Yoga and Yantra: Their Interrelation and Their Significance for Indian Archaeology*. The Hague: Nijhoff.

Prapañca, Mpu (1995). *Deśawarṇana (Nāgarakṛtāgama)*. Translated by Stuart Robson. Leiden: KITLV Press. (Verhandelingen van het Koninklijk instituut voor taal-, land- en volkenkunde ; 169)

Reichl, Natasha (2007). *Violence and Serenity: Late Buddhist Sculpture from Indonesia*. Honolulu: University of Hawai'i Press.

Rosenstock-Huessy, Eugen (1956-1958). *Soziologie: Band I: Die Übermacht der Räume; Band II: Die Vollzahl der Zeiten*. Stuttgart: Kohlhammer.

Rosenstock-Huessy, Eugen (1993 [1938]). *Out of Revolution: Autobiography of Western Man*. Providence, RI/Oxford: Berg.

Rossabi, Morris (1988). *Khubilai Khan: His Life and Times*. Berkeley: University of California Press.

Sedyawati, Edi (2004). "Kertenagara (r. 1268-1292). Harboring ambitions beyond Java" In: Keat Gin Ooi (ed.), *Southeast Asia: A Historical Encyclopedia, from Angkor Wat to East Timor*. Santa Barbara, California: ABC-CLIO. p. 720-722.

Seyfort Ruegg, D. (1995). *Ordre spirituel et ordre temorel dans la pensée bouddhique d el'Inde et du Tibet: quatre conférences au Collège de France*. Paris: Collège de France, Institut de civilisation indienne.

Sharrock, P.D. (2006). "Hevajra at Bantéay Chmàr" *The Journal of the Walters Art Museum* v.64-65, p.49-64.

Teeuw, Andries (1991). "The text" In: J.J. Ras and S.O. Robson (eds.), *Variation, transformation and meaning : studies on Indonesian literatures in honour of A. Teeuw*. Leiden : KITLV Press. (Verhandelingen van het Koninklijk Instituut voor Taal-, Land- en Volkenkunde 144) p. 211-229.

Worsley, Peter (1991). "Mpu Tantular's kakawin Arjunawijaya and conceptions of kingship in fourteenth century Java" In *Variation, transformation and meaning : studies on Indonesian literatures in honour of A. Teeuw*. Leiden : KITLV Press. (Verhandelingen van het Koninklijk Instituut voor Taal-, Land- en Volkenkunde 144) p.163-190.

Wylie, Turrell V. (1977). "The first Mongol conquest of Tibet reinterpreted" *Harvard Journal of Asiatic Studies,* Vol. 37, No. 1, p. 103-133.

Zimmer, H. (1952). *Philosophies of India*. London: Routledge & Kegan Paul.

Zoetmulder, P.J. (1974). *Kalangwan: a summary of Old Javanese literature*. The Hague: Nijhoff.

XI

China as a Sea Power, 1127–1368[1]

My first thought upon learning of the publication of this volume is that I wish I had been able to read it before publishing my own study of the Yuan naval campaign to Jawa. After having read Lo's book, I can now definitely state that I would have had to rewrite and rethink certain sections of my book in light of Lo's research. Lo's book was the most comprehensive treatment of China's pre-Ming maritime history in a European language at the time of its composition in 1957, and from then until 2012 when it was finally published, the only book to rival his "preliminary survey" has been *La marine chinoise du Xe siècle au XIVe siècle* by Jacques Dars (1992). José Din Ta-San and Francisco F. Olesa Muñido's 1965 monograph *El poder naval chino, desde sus orígines hasta la caída de la dinastía Ming (siglos VI a. de

---

[1] Review of Lo Jung-Pang (ed. Bruce A. Elleman): *China as a Sea Power, 1127–1368. A Preliminary Survey of the Maritime Expansion and Naval Exploits of the Chinese People during the Southern Song and Yuan Periods.* xxx, 378 pp. Singapore: NUS Press, 2012; Hong Kong: Hong Kong University Press, 2012.

J.C. - XVII d. de J.C.) covers a similar time span but lacks the depth of Lo's research and interpretation.

Lo's greatest strength is his familiarity with Chinese sources; his greatest weaknesses are the ways in which he occasionally uses those sources: uncritically and without discussion of conflicting accounts in other sources. His strengths and failures are both evident in his brief discussion of Khubilai's campaign to Java. Lo draws upon sources that I have never seen cited in any other publication about that campaign, and his account offers some surprises. His discussion of the spread of anti-Mongol sentiment throughout Southeast Asia by Chinese who fled before the Mongols—including remnants of the Southern Song army and navy—combined with his note about the Cham king Indravarman's request for aid from Java add much to the complexity of the story of the Yuan campaign to Java. On the other hand—and this is partly Elleman's fault—it is sometimes impossible to know from whence Lo took his material. We are told a story, with an occasional footnote, but the story is not simply taken from the Chinese sources: it is interpreted and represented, and where the sources disagree, those disagreements are not mentioned. Even when he cites a source, the citation is sometimes difficult to decipher. For example, footnote 55 on page 221 offers "GCWL, ch. 41, p. 16" and nothing else. Since the book contains no list of abbreviations and that abbreviation is nowhere spelled out, the reader is left wondering. There are earlier references to Su Tianzhuo, *Guochao Wenlei* (1342), (SBCK) and to Su Tianzhuo, *Guochao Wenlei* (SBBY), and I have assumed that these all refer to the 1342 compilation *Guochao Wenlei* (國朝文類) also known as the *Yuan wenlei* (元文類), but neither Lo nor Ellemann offer more definite bibliographical information, and the "Selected bibliography" includes neither Su Tianzhuo nor any reference to a GCWL, SBBY, SBCK or *Guochao Wenlei*. Yet in spite of the irritating absence of clear and complete references and more footnotes to indicate exactly what are the sources of his Lo's narrative, just learning that the *Guochao Wenlei* includes material that has not appeared in any previous discussion of the Java campaign was an important find for this reader.

While Lo's utilization of previously undiscussed sources for Song-Yuan maritime history is a strong point, his underutilization of non-Chinese sources is a problem, especially when it comes to interpretation of the Chinese discussion of foreign lands and peoples. It may be that he did not have access to Niwa Tomosaburo's monograph on Yuan relations with Java (中国・ジャバ交渉史 - *Chūgoku Jyaba kōshōshi*) as it had only been published in 1953, but Lo used no non-Chinese sources for that campaign when there had been a spate of publications in Dutch between 1894 and 1957 as well as discussions in more general histories written in Dutch, English and French. It is also more than surprising that a monograph on Yuan China should rely so completely on Chinese sources: of the immense literature in European languages on the Mongols and Yuan China, Lo cites a single biography of Chinggis Khan (Martin, 1950) and Howorth's *History of the Mongols* from 1876—nothing else. In his accounts of the campaigns to Japan and Korea, Lo does refer to both Japanese and Korean works, though they are few, but in his accounts of the campaigns to Annam and Champa, he relies almost entirely on Chinese sources, citing Vietnamese sources only as they are cited or quoted in secondary literature in Japanese.

This sino-centric approach to the history of China is not that surprising in a work written in the 1950's, but it is no less problematic for that. In the many passages detailing the composition of soldiers, sailors, commanders and crew, we repeatedly find a multi-ethnic navy drawn from all over the Yuan territory, yet Lo comes very close to stating that the Yuan conquest of the Southern Song was a civil war rather than a conquest by a non-Han people:

> This merely emphasizes the fact that the Yuan navy was patterned after the Song navy, used captured Song ships and crew, and exploited Song maritime experience and

> technology. Its guiding geniuses were Han Chinese, from Zhang Song who built boats for Chinggis Qan in 1218, ... to Zhang Hongfan, whose victory at Yaishan climaxed the rise of the Yuan navy. Without the assistance of the Han Chinese, the Mongols would have had a difficult task in building a navy and in their conquest of South China. In retrospect, the Yuan navy was essentially the Song navy. (p. 246)

The impression that Lo's narrative gives—at least to a Mongolist—is that he proceeds from Song to Ming as though the Mongols were simply incorporated into Chinese history rather than radically altering it. He takes great pains to argue that it was the threat from the Jin and the Yuan from the north that turned the Song leadership southward towards the sea and the development of its navy, but his maritime history of the Yuan is set out as a history of the Han navy. We are informed that the "guiding geniuses" of the Yuan navy were "Han Chinese" and the entire narrative of the Yuan conquest of the Southern Song is a narrative of a civil war. Far from understanding the Yuan adoption of the Song navy as consistent with their practice elsewhere of incorporating enemy soldiers and technologies into their military strategy, Lo would apparently like us to believe that Han Chinese defeated the Southern Song and the Mongols were actually – subservient? – to Han military—or at least naval—superiority. In Lo's interpretation, the Mongols could not have conquered China: only the Song navy could do that.

Perhaps this reviewer's interest in Mongolian affairs reads too much into Lo's conclusions, but passing from the Song navy to the Ming navy as though the Mongols were involved only peripherally is a bit much. It is especially jarring when the main thesis Lo wishes to develop is that Chinese naval power waxed and waned according to "cycles of cohesion and division, strength and weakness, prosperity and impoverishment, and expansion and contraction" (p. 343). In his conclusion Lo states clearly that it was the Mongols who "reunited China by force" (p. 342), but you would hardly get that understanding from the narrative that precedes the conclusion.

In spite of my rather serious reservations about Lo's attitude towards sources and his use (and non-use) of them, the book is a wonderful addition to an all too sparse literature. I truly regret not having had the opportunity to read it many years ago, and expect to turn to it again as I turn my own attention to the Mongol campaigns in mainland Southeast Asia. For anyone interested in the Yuan campaigns from Korea to Java, it is a very good book to begin with, and for anyone interested in the history of overseas communities of Chinese, the book also has much to offer.

XII

Eurasian Influences on Yuan China[1]

The impact of Chinggis Khan and the Mongols on thirteenth century Eurasia has long been the main preoccupation of both popular and scholarly writers on the Mongols. Until recently, that impact has been described in almost entirely negative terms, the Mongols often having been characterized as 'barbarians.' Coinciding with recent political changes in Eurasia and especially in Mongolia, a new historiography has attempted to present a more positive history of the Mongols, to the point of deifying Chinggis Khan. The contributors to *Eurasian Influences on Yuan China* have sought to look at the thirteenth century Mongol world from a very different perspective, namely the Mongol influence and lasting effects on Chinese customs, practices and institutions, and the influence of foreigners (non-Mongols) on China (nota bene: not on the Mongols) during the Yuan period.

The majority of papers in this volume deal with Western Asian influences on China, and thus on the introduction of

---

[1] Review of: Rossabi, Morris (ed.). *Eurasian Influences on Yuan China*. Singapore: Institute of Southeast Asian Studies, 2013. (Nalanda-Sriwijaya Series)

Islamic science and civilization into China. One paper focuses on the contributions to Korean civilization of members of a fourteenth century Uighur family at the Yuan court that emigrated to Korea in 1358; European influences on China are mentioned only in the context of the transmission of Greek geography, medicine and astronomy to China through Western Asian intermediaries.

In his paper "Whose secret intent?" George Lane describes some Persian responses to Mongol rule in which the Mongols are welcomed as the bringers of justice. In Mustawfi's Zafarnamah the Chief Justice of Qazvin, having appealed to Möngke to destroy the Ismaili menace, declares "He who comes over the river Amu Darya finds the Qa'an's justice" (p. 24) and it is that justice that he wishes the Mongols to establish in Qazvin. Mongol camps in Iran and Azerbaijan were places where conquered and conquerors, "the Muslims of Eastern Turkestan and their Mongol saviors" developed peaceful contacts and "social intercourse at various levels, including trade, the provision of skills, and the exchange of expertise and information" (p. 16-17). These camps "provided shelter to learned men" and artisans. The incorporation of Iran into the Mongol empire was followed by a stream of "those who sought to ally themselves with the new power" (p. 21) as well as "others who looked east with thoughts of fame and fortune" (p. 22). These emigrants, merchants, scholars, artisans and servants of the government who made their way to China brought their culture, arts and sciences with them. Yet the influence of the Yuan Muslim communities was limited and not long-lasting Chaffee claims in the next paper in the volume, because of their "alien, semi-colonial character" (p. 54).

Whether Chaffee is correct in his assessment of the Muslim influences on Yuan China, it is in his paper "Cultural transmission by sea: maritime trade routes in Yuan China" that one of the volume's chief defects appears most clearly: an almost total absence of theoretical discussion. The absence is most noticeable in Chaffee's remarks on the Mongol encouragement of trade:

> Lest we imagine the Mongols to be precursors to Adam Smith, we should remember that they were warriors and empire-builders first and foremost. They were adept at adapting to local circumstances, at utilising peoples, technologies, and trade to their own ends. But those ends led to a hybridisation of practices, in which commerce involved politics and patronage in addition to considerations of purely economic exchange. (p. 43)

Perhaps I am missing something, but I cannot imagine such a thing as "a purely economic exchange," and certainly not in the long history of China up until and including today. Far from leading to a hybridisation of practices, it would appear that in China (and throughout Asia) there was a long evolution of tribute-trade relations in which local politics and international relations were involved in all aspects of commerce (see e.g. Hamashita Takeshi, "The tribute trade system and modern Asia" in *Memoirs of the Research Department of the Toyo Bunko*, no. 46 (1988), p.7-25).

Another instance of the absence of theoretical questions appears in Rossabi's paper "Notes on Mongol influences on the Ming Dynasty". Rossabi notes the presence of Mongol dress in Ming ceramic funerary figures portraying Imperial Guards but asks

> The clothing worn by the Imperial Guards may have symbolic significance, but could wearing of such garb be superficial and not particularly important? Although various military honour guards in other civilisations have worn decorative costumes, which employed foreign motifs, did this truly reflect substantial influence or was it a concerted effort to co-opt or even to link them to the other's glorious heritage? (p. 208)

No less than Chaffee's remark on "purely economic exchange" Rossabi's remarks on the semiology of clothing and dress—especially when that involves imperial military uniforms!—suggest that he has never thought about the matter at all.

Interreligious relations are not dismissed as superficial nor as "not particularly important" in Ma Juan's paper "The conflicts between Islam and Confucianism and their influence in the Yuan Dynasty" but when the author remarks that

> Islam, as a minority religion, readily adjusted to Confucianism in order to survive... "The Muslim minority was, in part, strengthened by its relations with Confucianism ... Conflict created solidarity ... enhanced its cohesion, and contributed to its identity. ... The community persisted into the Ming and later dynasties through a combination of conflict and cooperation. (p. 68)

what have we learned? It seems to this review that we have learned nothing at all.

The major theoretical issues that I had hoped this volume would address are actually brought out into the open only in Hyunhee Park's paper "Cross-cultural exchange and geographic knowledge of the world in Yuan China." In this paper the main topic is on the introduction of Islamic geographic knowledge into China as that is evident in the only extant Yuan era map of the world, but the discussion of the use of grids in maps complicates the history.

> Although tables of longitudinal and latitudinal coordinates had existed in Islamic geography before this time, the production of grid maps constituted a new development. Jonathan Bloom argues that the grid concept was probably transmitted from China to the Islamic world for use in architectural planning. ... Needham called the style of the grid map a "Mongol style." ... It seems highly

likely, then, that these Muslim scholars in the Yuan court adapted their new concept of longitude and latitude coordinates to the construction of world maps. Whichever is more accurate, the possibility of such complicated mutual influences is intriguing. (p. 141-142)

The production of the map was (according to Hyunhee Park) probably originally undertaken by order of the Mongol emperor Khubilai Khan (died 1294) and completed in 14th century Yuan China. It reveals that its makers had both Chinese and Islamic geographic knowledge, but how to tease out what is Chinese, what is Islamic and what is Mongol?

Economics and clothing are not the main issues discussed in the volume, but these as well as religion, language, art, astronomy, architecture, cartography, geography and medicine are all presented as pre-existing objects (whether knowledge, practices, or material objects) that are transmitted or transferred from one civilization to another. We have cross-cultural exchange and influences, but the peoples, the knowledge and the civilizations are presented as though they are side-by-side rather than mixed up at the core. Lane remarks that "It was these rudimentary contacts [in the military camps of Iran and Azerbaijan] which also underpinned the emergence of a Mongol empire built on cultural and commercial exchange" (p. 17) but Iran remains Iran and the Mongols remain invaders—even though the latter are invited to rule Iran and establish justice there. If it was the contacts that "underpinned the emergence" of the empire, how does this affect the way we think of influence? exchange? cross-cultural? foreign?

Perhaps the very focus of the conference upon which the volume was based—foreign influences on China—led the contributors to focus on the foreign, but all of the papers (and not just Park's) should lead readers to question what we mean by foreign and by influence in discussions of ethnic groups, cultures, nations and civilizations. A very simple example: by whom, when, how and why might this book—a record of a workshop at Binghamton University in 2009, attended by scholars at institutions in London, Binghamton, Nanjing, Würzburg, Harvard, Yale, Munich, New York, Beijing and Philadelphia, published in Singapore, with bibliographical references to and discussions of works in Chinese, English, French, German, Japanese and Persian—be described as a foreign influence? If the objection is raised that this is an example of modern globalisation, then what is Eurasia, and what were the Mongol empire and Yuan China? I do not have an answer to that question, but I had hoped that the matters discussed at the conference and reflected in this volume would have asked some deeper questions about what it is we are studying when we claim to be studying "influences" whether "Eurasian" or "foreign." At least in my own case it seems that everything that comes to me from the past (whether 1354, 2009 or yesterday) and from anywhere outside my skin is both foreign and an influence, but that to speak of the time and "skin" of a continent, a people, a nation, a culture, a civilization, a religion or a language calls for a deeper understanding of any and all of these than is evident anywhere in the volume.

XIII

Mongolian Studies and Socialist Cooperation: the East European Scientific Expeditions to Mongolia

Abstract

Funding for Mongolian studies in the United States throughout the 1960s and 1970s was largely the result of the Cold War mentality, and the same is true for Mongolian studies in eastern Europe, although there "socialist cooperation" was the rationale given for this sudden increase in interest in Mongolia. Cold war fears and the rhetoric of socialist cooperation were the two public faces of societies isolated from each other politically, yet nevertheless in need of a larger world and knowledge of it. With the United States government's support for the study of its communist enemies, Mongolian studies benefited, but study and research in the MPR was almost impossible. The desire to strengthen socialist unity served similary as a motivation for Mongolian studies in eastern Europe, but in contrast to the situation in the United States, there was massive governmental support for study and research in Mongolia. In this paper I describe several of the scientific expeditions organized in eastern Europe from the 1950's through the 1980's.

1. The Situation Before Cooperation

Between the first and second world wars Mongolia was largely closed to American and European researchers, including those in that part of Eastern Europe that lay west of the Soviet Union.[1] Research on Mongolia in both the United States and in Eastern Europe was largely library based during that period: neither the United States nor any Eastern European state other than the Soviet Union had diplomatic relations with Mongolia at that time. There were a few exceptions, notably the American Museum of Natural History expeditions and a small number of other East European scholars during the 1920s and 1930s (see e.g. Nielipiński, 1936). Ligeti was unable to visit Mongolia for political reasons, but he did manage to conduct research on Mongolian languages in Inner Mongolia from 1928 to 1931 and in Afghanistan during 1936-1937 (Sárközi and Birtalan, 1997). A few socialists such as Bohumír Šmeral (Myšková, 1959) from Czechoslovakia visited Mongolia during the late 20's and early 30's, but socialist cooperation was still only a theory in the minds of European and American socialists, and where it had been put into practice—in the Soviet Union and the People's Republic of Mongolia—it appears from our present vantage point to have had little to do with cooperation and much to do with exploitation.

The Second World War changed many things, and among all that happened as a result of those changes were the two matters that I wish to discuss here. With the rise of the Cold War an active policy of cooperation among socialist states was introduced–and enforced–among the eastern European nations,

---

[1] This is a revised version of the paper presented at the PIAC/Mongolia Society conference in 2011. I have limited the scope of this article to expeditions involving Poland, Czechoslovakia and Hungary for reasons of economy (to deal with Soviet based expeditions would have made this far too large a project), for reasons of availability of material—the sections on Bulgaria and Germany in the first volume of the *International Bibliography on Mongolian Studies* (Schwarz and Bira, 1997) contain no references to any such expeditions—and most importantly for reasons of my own background, interest and knowledge. While East German-Mongolian relations is a topic I know not at all and I do not think I will live long enough to investigate Soviet-Mongolian relations in depth, I do hope to investigate Mongolia's relations with the Balkan states in the future.

and as part of that policy programs for foreign study, cultural, scientific and technical exchange were instituted. Unlike their American counterparts and their own situation during and immediately preceding that war, East European scholars were now able to pursue research in Mongolia.[2]

2. An Arranged Marriage: Mongolia, Eastern Europe and the CMEA

Albania opened diplomatic relations with Mongolia in 1949, Bulgaria, Czechoslovakia, the German Democratic Republic, Hungary, Poland and Romania all established diplomatic relations with Mongolia in 1950,[3] and Yugoslavia established relations in 1956.[4] Yet although the Council for Mutual Economic

---

[2] Although it was possible for East European researchers to study in Mongolia, the conditions of research were apparently severely constrained by the governments involved, a fact noted in passing by Sárközi in her introductory remarks to a narrative of the expeditions of 1989 and subsequent years: "A Mongóliában 1989-90-ben lezajlott rendszerváltás után lehetővé vált, hogy kutatók, még külföldről érkezett kutatók is, szabadon utazhassanak az országban, s találkozhassanak a vidéken élő emberekkel, ami korábban tilos és teljesen elképzelhetetlen volt." [The political changes of 1989-1990 in Mongolia made it possible for researchers, including researchers from abroad, to travel more freely in the country and meet the people living in the coutryside—something that had earlier been forbidden and completely inconceivable.] (Sárközi, 2008)

[3] Information from the Mongolian Ministry of Foreign Affairs' website: http://www.mfat.gov.mn/index.php?option=com_content&view=article&id=70&Itemid=83&lang=en viewed 22 October 2012. The date for the establishment of relations with Germany given in this source is 1974, i.e. relations with the Federal Republic of Germany. Relations between the German Democratic Republic and Mongolia were established on 13 April 1950 according to Ingrid Muth in *Die DDR-Aussenpolitik 1949-1972* (Berlin, Ch. Links Verlag, 2000), p. 234.

[4] "Nineteen agreements, concluded between the Governments of SFR Yugoslavia and Mongolia, continue in force between them. They include the Trade and Payments Agreement; Agreement on Cultural Cooperation; Agreement on Scientific and Technological Cooperation; Agreement Establishing the Intergovernmental Committee for Economic and Scientific and Technical

Assistance (hereafter: CMEA) had already been established in 1949, it was not until 1962 that Mongolia became a member of that group. Mongolia was embraced by the CMEA later than some had wanted for the simple reason that some of the governments of the Eastern European socialist nations did not want to be forced into accepting Mongolia as a trading partner.[5] This matter was rarely mentioned by East European scholars writing during the socialist era but has recently become a focus of some attention.[6] To a child of the peasantry as I am, there is something bizarre in calling an arranged marriage followed by a shot-

---

Cooperation, etc." Republic of Serbia Ministry of Foreign Affairs, http://www.mfa.gov.rs/Policy/Bilaterala/Mongolia/basic_e.html viewed 22 October 2012.

[5] "Soviet-initiated Comecon support for the Council's three least-developed members—Cuba, Mongolia, and Vietnam—has clearly benefited them, but the burden on the six East European Comecon members has been most unwelcome." (Goodrich, 1992)

[6] For example Juríková, drawing on archival materials in Mongolia, wrote an idyllic history of Czechoslovak-Mongolian economic relations from 1956 through 1980 which due to its having been "founded on the principles of Marxism-Leninism" demonstrates the "truth of Lenin's teachings and the possibility of a feudal society's direct transition to socialism" (Juríková, 1987: 734). Searching for information on this period in the Mongolian National Archives during a visit in 2001, I found nothing of interest except one item in the inventory, and that folder, I was told, could not be located. Szalontai, however, was able to find enough in the Hungarian National Archives to suggest a rewriting of the period immediately prior to Mongolia's admission into the CMEA. In a brief but fascinating essay he described the situation thus: "In September 1960 the Communist diplomats accredited to the Mongolian People's Republic joined forces to lodge a formal complaint against their ill-treatment at the hands of various Mongolian cadres. The Soviets, though generally satisfied, found the officials of the diplomat's shop very uncooperative. The Hungarians pointed out that the leaders of the mass organizations consistently ignored their requests for meetings. The Czechoslovak embassy was so laxly guarded that an unknown local managed to enter the ambassador's bedroom to ask for directions. The Poles noted that the officials of the telephone exchange deliberately hindered them in contacting Warsaw. Even an otherwise reserved North Vietnamese diplomat complained bitterly about the recurrent shortages of electricity and water." (Szalontai, 2004, p. 18)

gun wedding "cooperation", but it is nevertheless true that the results of shotgun weddings do not usually result in gunshot wounds or funerals, but rather in two people getting to know each other; and in the case of arranged marriages—if the fiddler on the roof is to be believed—some even come to love each other.

In June 1962 after a period of participating in the CMEA as an observer and shortly after it had been admitted into the United Nations in October of 1961 (http://www.un-mongolia.mn/web/), Mongolia officially became a member of the CMEA (Adler-Karlsson, 1963, p.141). One year later in July 1963 Tsedenbal wrote to Cyrankiewicz, the Polish Premier, applying for admission to the Warsaw Pact—perhaps with Soviet support (Mastny and Byrne, 2005, p.152-153)—but after objections from Polish and Romanian politicians the application was rejected (Mastny and Byrne, 2005, p.154-156; Kádár, 1963).[7] Despite the rejection of its Warsaw Pact application, several treaties of mutual economic assistance and cooperation in a variety of areas were signed shortly thereafter between Mongolian and other CMEA member states, and a period of intensive scientific exchange between Mongolia and Poland, Czechoslovakia, East Germany and Hungary followed. Scientific expeditions to Mongolia (including joint expeditions and international expeditions) became regular features of the five year plans of Mongolia, Czechoslovakia, East Germany, Hungary and Poland. The Mongolian Academy of Sciences—established in 1961—and the Czechoslovak Academy of Sciences signed their first agreement on cooperation in November 1962, just 4 months after Mongolia joined the CMEA (Grollová, 1992). However, cultural, scientific and technical exchanges between Mongolia and the socialist

---

[7] Kádár János (1963) offered the following account of the deliberations regarding Mongolia's membership in the Warsaw Pact: "It is quite possible that after Mongolia's admission we'll get all the disadvantages but none of the advantages. This was the reason why the meeting decided not to discuss the question."

nations of Eastern Europe as well as trade relations actually began well before Mongolia was admitted into the CMEA.

3. Technical Exchanges and Scientific Expeditions

Already in 1954 Poland and Mongolia had signed agreements on cooperation in the area of radio communication (Poland and Mongolia, 1954), and in 1956 Romania and Mongolia signed an agreement concerning cultural co-operation (Romania and Mongolian People's Republic, 1956). Also in 1956 a team of Czech doctors visited Mongolia and an agreement on health matters in Mongolia was signed (Podepsání, 1956). The following year a group of Mongolian doctors visited Czechoslovakia and another agreement was signed (Podepsání, 1957). During 1957-1958 a Hungarian linguistic and ethnographic research expedition was undertaken at the invitation of the Mongolian Scientific Committee of Higher Education (Kara, Kőhalmi and Róna-Tas, 1958). In 1958 the Polish and Mongolian governments signed a treaty concerning cultural cooperation (Poland and Mongolia, 1958), the first Hungarian archaeological expedition with Gábori Miklos took place (Gábori, 1962 and 1963) and the first cooperative expedition undertaken by the Czech Academy of Sciences got underway. The Czechoslovak-Mongolian archeological expedition under the direction of N. Ser-Odzhav and Lumír Jisl conducted excavations in the complex of Kültegin monuments. The Czech archeologists were accompanied by "a physician and anthropologist (E. Vlček), a technical assistant, a surveyor, a photographer, a driver and an administrative worker, and on the Mongolian side archaeologists Perlé and Navan and ethnographer Badamkhatam. Twenty-five students of Choibalsan University, Ulanbator, worked at the locality investigated" (Vlček, 1959, p. 133). A full report of the medical and anthropological portion of the expedition was published in Vlček (1965). The next year (1959) the first Polish physical anthropologists to arrive in Mongolia since Lubicz-

Grochowski and Połczyński in 1933 (Nielipiński, 1936) worked in Mongolia from August through November (Michalski, 1960).

More archaeological expeditions followed in the early 1960s. Beginning in 1961 joint Hungarian-Mongolian teams of archaeologists worked in Mongolia (Gábori, 1962 and 1963; Erdélyi 1962, 1963 and 1966; Erdélyi, Dorjsüren and Navan, 1967). According to Maenchen-Helfen in his brief review of archaeological expeditions to Mongolia, the expedition had bad luck:

> A Mongol-Hungarian expedition in 1961 had bad luck. The kurgans excavated in the Noin Ula moun-tains had been so thoroughly robbed that only very few things were found: a fragment of embroidered silk, a few horse bits of the usual type, corroded iron knives, and arrow-heads. However, one skull was so well preserved that it could be measured. Like the Hsiung-nu skull examined by Debets, it belongs to the Baikal type of the North Asiatic Mongoloids. (Maenchen-Helfen, 1964-1965, p.369)

At least one later account, however, described the expeditions as trouble free, without mentioning the results of the 1961 trip:

> [T]he four archaeological expeditions sent between 1961 and 1964 to Mongolia under the direction of István Erdélyi encountered no difficulties. The Mongolian expedition of 1961 investigated pit mounds of the Hiung-nu period (1st century BC) at Noin-Ula while that in 1962 studied burials dating from the 10th-5th centuries BC between the rivers of Orchon and Selenga. Work in 1963 was conducted at an AD 7th century pit-grave with a stone superstructure in the valley of the river Huniy, where graves of the Hiung-nu period were also unearthed. Works continued at the latter cemetery in the last, 1964, season. (Török (2000), p. 29-30)

Regardless of luck good or bad, the expeditions did not stop, and they continued regularly through the end of socialist cooperation and beyond (Erdélyi 1963, 1966, 1993; Erdélyi and Ferenczy 1963; Erdélyi and Cewendordz, 1993). A Polish-Mongolian archaeological expedition in 1962 was more fortunate than the Hungarian expedition of 1961: during that expedition Edward Tryjarski discovered three fragments of Ongin inscriptions (Tryjarski, 1965).

By 1961 Polish geologists were working in Mongolia and Polish architects had helped design Ulaanbaatar's city plan and architectural future (Szober, 1965). That same year an agreement between the Polish and Mongolian academies of sciences was signed. The Polish palaeontologist Zofia Kielan-Jaworowska described the origins of that agreement in the following words:

> The idea of organizing the Polish-Mongolian Palaeontological Expeditions to Mongolia was born in the Palaeozoological Institute of the Polish Academy of Sciences, during the Assembly of the representatives of the Academies of Sciences of the People's Democracies, held in Warsaw in March, 1961. The instigator of this project was Professor ROMAN KOZLOWSKI, doyen of Polish palaeontologists. Professor Kozlowski's project was well received by the authorities of both Academies. In September of 1961, an official delegation of the Polish Academy of Sciences, with Professor KOZLOWSKI as a member, went to Ulan Bator, to sign an agreement on scientific co-operation between the two Academies. (Kielan-Jaworowska and Dovchin (1968), p. 8)

It was also in 1961 that the first publication of the results of the Mongolian Expeditions of the Institute of Zoology of the Polish Academy of Sciences appeared (Jaczewski, 1961), although the author of that paper had published a paper on Mongolian fauna already in 1960 (Jaczewski, 1960). Mongolian-East German biological expeditions began in 1962 and between 1963 and 1968 a series of six international zoological expeditions under the leadership of the Hungarian entomologist Kaszab Zoltán took place. According to the Coleoptera Collection Brief History on the Hungarian Natural History Museum (Museum Magyar Természettudományi Múzeum) website, Kaszab

> brought back about half million animal specimens, including 200,000 beetles. The results were published in scientific journals in a series (Ergebnisse der zoologischen Forschungen von Dr. Z. Kaszab in der Mongolei), which comprised over 500 papers. There are 200 scientists among the authors, from 20 countries. The number of printed pages is nearly 8000. Of the tens of thousands of animal species reported from Mongolia, 1600 were formerly unknown to the scientific world and 1900 species which had been known from other parts of Central Asia previously, had for the first time been found in Mongolia by Zoltán Kaszab. http://www.mttm.hu/en/department_of_zoology/collection/coleoptera_collection

Other biological expeditions included the Mongol-Czech ichthyoparasitological expedition of 1966 (for Communication no. 1 of the expedition see Ergens and Dulmaa (1967); Kocian (1999) erroneously dates the first expedition in 1969[8]), a Mong-

---

[8] In his history of the Zoological Department of Bratislava University Kocian briefly described the Slovak participation in the Czechoslovak-Mongolian biological expeditions: "Významným obdobím pre zviditeľnenie vedeckej práce katedry boli tiež sedemdesiate a osemdesiate roky, kedy niektorí členovia pracoviska sa v spolupráci s Mongolskou štátnou univerzitou v Ulan-Bátare, Irkutskou štátnou univerzitou, ale aj s pracovníkmi univerzít v Moskve, Katoviciach a Halle, pravidelne zúčastňovali viactýždenných zoologických expedíc do Mongolska. Bol to výskum zameraný na prebádanie prírodných zdrojov tohto štátu a naši pracovníci skúmali hlavne ektoparazity, ich hostiteľov a pôdnu faunu. Prvou lastovičkou – pionierom toho, na naše pomery ojedineleho projektu bol vlastne prof. Hensel, ktorý už v r. 1969 bol na I. československo-mongolskej ichtyologickej expedícii spolu s dr.

olian-Czechoslovakian entomological-botanical expedition in 1965 and 1966 (for the first report of the expedition, see Dlabola 1967), two Polish expeditions in cooperation with the Mongolian Ministry of Forestry in 1979 to study argali sheep and Siberian ibex (Dzięciołowski et al. 1980), the Mongol-Czechoslovak Zoological University Expeditions during the 1980's and the Slovak-Mongolian biological expeditions in the 1970-1980's (Kocian, 1999). Martin-Luther-Universität Halle-Wittenberg issued a number of publications in the 1980s that were the result of a research program on the biological resources of Mongolia, a program which involved scientists from other eastern European countries.[9]

Pivničkom z KU v Prahe. Od 1974 začala druhá etapa na omnoho širšej báze a zo všetkých vtedajších zoologických pracovísk fakulty v Mongolsku pracovali Cyprich, Dúha, Halgoš, Jedlička, Kiefer, Krumpál, Majzlan a Országh. Celkove bolo zorganizovaných 8 expedícií. Výsledky sa prezentovali aj na pravidelných konferenciách v Ulanbátare, Irkutsku, Moskve, Halle a dvakrát (1978 a 1984) aj v Bratislave, z ktorých vyšli aj samostatné zborníky. [The 1970s and 1980s were an important period for the visibility of the scientific work of the department. During that period some members worked in cooperation with the Mongolian State University in Ulaanbaatar and Irkutsk State University, and together with staff from the universities in Moscow, Katowice and Halle regularly attended zoological expeditions to Mongolia. These were undertaken to explore the natural resources of this country and our colleagues studied mainly ectoparasites and their hosts and soil fauna. The earliest pioneer of our Mongolian projects was actually prof. Hensel who already in 1969 participated in the First Czechoslovak-Mongolian Ichthyological expedition with dr. Cellar from Charles University in Prague. The second phase of a much broader-based research project involved all the zoological faculty in Mongolia: Cyprich, Dúha, Halgoš, Jedlička, Kiefer, Krumpál, Majzlan a Országh. A total of eight expeditions were organized. The results were presented at regular conferences in Ulaanbaatar, Irkutsk, Moscow, Halle and twice (1978 and 1984) in Bratislava, which were published in separate volumes.] (Kocian, 1999)

[9] For more information, see the program "International Symposium in Halle/ Saale, 25-29 March 2012 "Biodiversity Research in Mongolia" 50 Years of Mongolian-German Biological Expeditions: an Anniversary (1962-2012)" http://greif.uni-greifswald.de/floragreif/floragreif-content/misc/ Programm-Mongoleisymposium.pdf (accessed 7 Nov. 2012). A select bibliography is

The Kaszab expeditions involved the most countries, the most scholars and led to more publications than any of the other expeditions of the 1950-1980s but they did not catch public attention like the palaeontological expeditions undertaken by the Polish Academy of Sciences beginning in 1963 and continuing annually through 1971 (excepting 1966) under the leadership of Zofia Kielan-Jaworowska. Her accounts of those expeditions are available in a series of books and articles most of which are available in English (Kielan-Jaworowska, 1969; Kielan-Jaworowska and Dovchin, 1968; Kielan-Jaworowska and Barsbold, 1972). She records one incident that is especially interesting in the context of this paper. Michon Scott summarized the incident thus:

> Amid the tensions of the Cold War, it must have been difficult to write a book with international appeal, but Kielan-Jaworowska managed with tact—giving credit where it was due to both her Soviet and American predecessors—and humor. She included a report from a colleague who recounted that one evening the Mongolian hosts serenaded the Poles with beautiful songs, then insisted their guests reciprocate. "It turned out that singing was not exactly our forte, and the only songs we could execute passably in chorus were Christmas carols," her colleague explained. "When requested to translate the words, we got out of the difficulty by claiming they were old revolutionary songs." Michon Scott at http://www.strangescience.net/zofia.htm

The expeditions led by Kielan-Jaworowska have subsequently been described as spectacular in terms of the amount and quality of the fossils that they brought to Mongolian and Polish institutions, but there is another reason to regard the expeditions as spectacular. If we consider that the Mongolian government did

---

also available at: http://greif.uni-greifswald.de/floragreif/?cat=20 (accessed 7 Nov. 2012).

not permit American scientists to collect fossils in Mongolia from the late 1920s to the late 1980s (Lyon, 2001), that the planned Soviet-Mongolian expeditions of the early 1940s failed to materialize because of the Second World War, that the Sino-Soviet expeditions of 1957-1959 were interrupted by political hostilities between the two coordinating nations, and that there were no further expeditions until Mongolia invited the American Museum of Natural History to return once again in 1990, the Polish expeditions are demonstrably one of very few examples of successful socialist cooperation in paleontology. Furthermore, the specimens taken during the Polish expeditions were divided between Mongolian and Polish institutions in such a way as to ensure that unique specimens all remained in Mongolia:

> When each expedition was completed, the paleontological collections gathered by subsequent expeditions were provisionally divided in Ulan Bator between the Polish and the Mongolian partners, and a significant portion was then dispatched to Warsaw by train. Based on later agreements between the academies of both countries, the majority of the dinosaur specimens, especially the holotypes, were to be returned to Mongolia upon completion of the scientific studies. And that is what indeed happened. Only remains of taxa that were represented by more than one specimen in the collections remained in Poland. (Kielan-Jaworowska, 2010: 14)

This was in stark contrast to the fate of specimens and political-military conditions in the earlier expeditions of Andrews and the American Museum of Natural History in the 1920s, Hedin and the Sino-Swedish expeditions of the 1930s, and the Soviet-Mongolian expeditions of 1948-1949. Of the Soviet-Mongolian expeditions Kielan-Jaworowska noted "All of these skeletons, except for one that was returned to Mongolia, were housed in Moscow." (ibid.)

Veterinary cooperation as part of the CMEA plan began about 1965 with reports being published regularly in Polish journals betweem 1965 and 1975 (Gostyński (1965), Laskowski (1967), Dzieciuchowicz (1972), Trzcianka (1974), Ignatowicz (1975)) with a history of the program during 1976-1980 published in 1984 (Badyoczek, 1984). Reports on East German (Splisteser, 1975) and Czech (Černovský and Ševčík, 1965; Vašák, 1968) veterinary expeditions were also published during the same period.

Polish-Mongolian cooperation in the area of medicine and public health began about the same time as veterinary cooperation: in 1965 the Polish journal of public health *Służba zdrowia* published an article on a medical expedition to Mongolia (Łepkowski, 1965) and the same journal published a report by a Mongolian doctor on Mongolian-CMEA cooperation in matters of public health in 1987 (Cerennadmid, 1987). Czechoslovak-Mongolian cooperation in matters of public health dates back to the visit of a group of doctors in 1956 and continued right up to the end of socialist cooperation in Czechoslovakia (Kolář, 1987). One of the main activities of that cooperative program was the training of Mongolian doctors, 51 of whom studied in Czechoslovakia between 1961 and 1974 (Rödling, 1974). Mongolian-Czechoslovak university cooperation began as largely the exchange of technicians, but particularly in the case of cooperation in public health and medicine, the education and training of Mongolians became a significant aspect of Czech-Mongolian relations, with a large impact on Mongolian studies and public awareness of Mongolia among Czech citizens. According to Grollová (1992, p. 286)

> Czechoslovak colleges and universities as well as secondary schools have provided education for Mongolian architects, creative artists, teachers, ethnographers... The number of mongolian students who graduated from Czechoslovak colleges and universities has amounted to as many as 300 and hundreds more secondary school

students and qualified workers have been invited to Czechoslovakia for training and other specialized stays in Czechoslovak enterprizes. ... Some of them work as interpreters and translators of Czech and Slovak literature.

The same situation existed in Poland where between 1960 and 2012 over 200 Mongolian students have studied in Polish institutions (http://hcpmongolia.com/eng/index.php?moduls=115), and in Hungary:

> In 1956 ... B. Rinchen became the first Mongolian student to take his PhD at ELTE BTK. Since that time, altogether over 400 Mongolians have completed their training in various Hungarian institutes of higher education. (Szandtner, 2010)

Almost all of the east European scientific expeditions to Mongolia included Mongolian participants, and were thus instrumental in furthering Mongolian studies not only in eastern Europe but in Mongolia as well.

While the Hungarian ethnographic expeditions that took place in 1957-1958 were not repeated until the early 1990s, Polish ethnographic expeditions only began in 1965, but they continued throughout the socialist period in Poland, with publications arising from that research still appearing through the 1990's (e.g. Potkanski and Szynkiewicz, 1993). Early results of the Polish ethnographic expeditions were published in a series of three volumes—*Współczesna Mongolia* in 1968, *Studia mongolskie* in 1969, and *Z badań nad społeczeństwem i kulturą Mongolii* in 1973—while later publications appeared regularly in the journals *Etnografia polska* and *Ethnologia polona*, papers in the former written in Polish and in the latter in English. Of particular importance are the numerous works by Kabzińska-Stawarz on Mongolian games and sport (esp. Kabzińska-Stawarz, 1991), Sławoj Szynkiewicz's books and papers on family, kinship and social structure (e.g. Szynkiewicz, 1981;

Potkanski and Szynkiewicz, 1993) and Jerzy Wasilewski on Mongolian cosmology, conceptions of space, yurts and shamanism (e.g. Wasilewski, 1979). During the final years of socialist cooperation the Polish-Mongolian agreement on cultural and scientific cooperation for the years 1986-1990 led to a joint Polish-Mongolian project for photogrammetric documentation of Janraisig Temple (Wanot, 1990).[10]

Other major areas of scientific cooperation were in geology and physical geography. The first Polish Geological Expeditions to Mongolia took place from 1961 to 1965 (Don and Dumicz, 1984), and in 1968 Janusz K. Kozłowski, Jerzy Lefeld and Huhnbaatar undertook a Polish-Mongolian geological/archaeological expedition to study the Stone Age in the Gobi (Kozłowski, 1972). Czech geologists began planning an expedition to Mongolia in 1963 with the first expedition taking place in 1964 (Krauter, 1963); twenty five years later Krauter (1989) published an article celebrating 25 years of Czechoslovak-Mongolian geological cooperation. Hungarian geophysical expeditions to Mongolia began in 1957 and continued through 1990 (Erdős, undated). In 1974 a series of international geological expeditions involving Hungarian, Polish and Czech scientists (among others) was initiated, and continued through the last of the five year plans untill the demise of the CMEA in 1991 (Bjamba, 1979; Werner, 1982). Also in 1974 the first Mongolian-Polish Geographical Expedition to the Khangai Mountains took place and work continued through 1980 (Klimek, 1984). The results of those expeditions were published between 1975 and 1985 in about 150 books and articles.

Narratives of several of the scientific expeditions were published as monographs for the general reader. Hungarian

---

[10] Wanot (1990) reports on this joint project, but gives no information beyond the two organizing bodies, the State Ateliers for Conservation of Cultural Property in Warsaw and the State Enterprise for Conservation of Cultural Property in Ulanbaatar. At the time of revising this paper (October 2012) I had found no further publications or other information sources relating to this project.

ethnologist Diószegi Vilmos (1960) published an account of his 1957-1958 expedition among the Soyot and Buriat (among other peoples) of the Soviet Union, which although not arising out of Hungarian-Mongolian cooperation was still an example of socialist cooperation in the area of Mongolian studies. One year later Róna-Tas András (1961) published a popular account of his participation in the 1957-1958 Hungarian linguistic and ethnological expedition to Mongolia. Several histories and personal narratives of the geological, geographical and paleontological expeditions were published, the most well known of those being Zofia Kielan-Jaworowska's account of the paleontological expeditions, translated into English as *Hunting for Dinosaurs*. Another account of those expeditions is Maciej Kuczyński's *Zwrotnik dinozaura*, as well as the same author's *Wyprawa po dinozaury*, a work written for young readers. Edmund Rutkowski published an account of the Polish geological expeditions entitled *Trzy dni geologa w Mongolii* [A geologist's three days in Mongolia]. In 2002 Benjamín Tinák—a Slovak doctor with the 1966 Czechoslovak Geological Expedition to Mongolia—published *Zo sveta,* a collection which includes articles originally published in 1967 narrating his experiences in Mongolia. Erdős László Szakmány has posted a multipart history of the Hungarian geophysical expeditions on his website with an extensive collection of photographs and videos to accompany it (http://mongolia.gportal.hu/). Members of the Polish ethnographical expeditions also wrote a few books that were not just for an academic readership. Stanisław Godziński's monograph on lamaist legends and myths and Iwona Kabzińska-Stawarz's *Games of Mongolian Shepherds* could be read and enjoyed by a wider audience. Jerzy Wasilewski's *Podróże do piekieł: rzecz o szamańskich misteriach* [Journeys to hell: concerning shamanic mysteries] went through two editions in Poland. Numerous articles appeared in the popular press from the very beginning, including press reports about the expeditions, personal accounts by the participants and essays by journalists along for the ride. A conference devoted to all areas of Polish-Mongolian relations including the scientific expeditions took place in 1981 and the published proceedings of the conference contain several articles describing the expeditions as well as bibliographies of each and a list of Warsaw University Masters' theses written on Mongolian topics from 1958 to 1981 (see Kojło, 1984).

4. Mongolian Studies as International Relations

Mongolian studies in Eastern Europe comprises much more than those fields represented by the scientific expeditions (for history and bibliography of Polish mongolistics, see Bade, 1992 and 1997, Szynkiewicz, 1986 and Bareja-Starzyńska, 2007; for Czechoslovakia, see Grollová, 1992 and Bade, 1997a; and for Hungary, see Birtalan, 1997). Studies of Mongolian languages, literatures, religious life, politics, law, economics and many other topics were pursued throughout Eastern Europe under socialism, especially in Czechoslovakia, East Germany, Hungary and Poland, but I have focused on the history of Mongolian-East European scientific expeditions since they were a part of the history of Mongolian studies that is both unlike the western European and American experience of that era and rarely noted by American or west European mongolists.[11]

A fair amount of the published research that came out of the expeditions is available in English, French, German or Russian in specialized journals. Yet as important as the scientific literature is as science, the more popular literature also played an important role on the international level. Jerzy Wasilewski's *Podróże do piekieł: rzecz o szamańskich misteriach* for example

---

[11] As one good example, the instructions given to country coordinators of the *International Bibliography on Mongolian Studies* (Schwarz and Bira, 1997) included a list of topics to be included and how to arrange them. In that list only the humanities and social sciences are represented, effectively excluding most of the literature related to any of the joint expeditions other than the linguistic, archaeological and ethnographical expeditions. No study of socialist cooperation can afford to exclude the many other expeditions briefly noted above.

led me to a personal story of Polish-Mongolian cooperation. When I mentioned this book to a Polish-American student back in 1991, she mentioned that her mother had known some of the people who had participated in the geological expeditions. The next day the student approached me with a request: her mother would like to borrow the book and read it.

That response to a casual comment about things Mongolian is quite different from the kind of response I have often heard from Americans to whom I happen to mention Mongolia. Although the situation has changed greatly during the past 20 years, the response I used to get from Americans was usually along the lines of "Now just where is Mongolia?" Once when inquiring of a librarian at a major American research library if the library had any bibliographies on Mongolia in the reference collection and if so where might I find them, I was referred to the Africana Library. The point I wish to make with these personal anecdotes is that socialist cooperation may not have been cooperation like we would like cooperation to be, it may not have brought about the kinds of lasting economic or social advantages for one or the other sides of the relationship desired, but the very simple fact that people from Eastern Europe could study and engage in research in Mongolia with Mongolians and that Mongolian students and scholars could go to Eastern Europe and study and do research side by side with Europeans opened up the possibility that the two peoples could in fact learn to cooperate and embrace each other without the coerciveness and restrictions of a government program. One significant aspect of the history of Mongolian-East European relations is that scholarly and cultural relations were established soon after the socialist regimes took power in Eastern Europe, nearly a full decade prior to the acceptance of Mongolia as a full partner in the CMEA. Physicians, archaeologists, paleontologists and anthropologists led the way in welcoming Mongolia into the international community, and since the end of socialist cooperation Polish and Czech scholars have been instrumental in maintaining relations with Mongolia: mongolists Jiří Šíma and Ivana

Grollová became ambassadors to Mongolia from the Czech Republic, and the linguist Stanisław Godziński the Polish ambassador to Mongolia.

I would like to close with another anecdote told by the Polish anthropologist Agata Bareja-Starzyńska during her visit to the University of Chicago a few years ago. She told of studying the old Mongolian script and literatures in Mongolia during the early 1980s when their study was officially not permitted. The students kept the proper texts next to the unacceptable texts and in the event that an unexpected visitor entered the classroom they would simply place the proper text over the improper one. The old genereration of Mongolian scholars passed on an even older tradition of learning to a younger generation of Europeans who wanted to learn and were thus complicit in their teacher's deception. That young Polish scholar then returned to Poland where she now translates Mongolian literature and teaches Mongolian philology and civilization to a still younger generation.

In her history of the Polish anthropological expeditions Zofia Sokolewicz concluded her history with the following remarks:

> The expeditions were thus never independent of politics. They were supposed to prove the existence of cooperation and friendship between communist countries, to channel aid towards developing countries, and to prove that one was committed to opening up towards the world. ... Overall one can conclude that, despite their many limitations, these anthropological expeditions really did facilitate international cooperation. The Mongolian expedition brought Poles into contact with Mongolists and Altaists from all over the world. The same applies to research on Carpathian pastoralism and to the other studies mentioned here. Each of them offered a window on the world. (Sokolewcz, 2005: 300).

The personal relationships that were fostered between Mongolian and European scholars under programs of socialist cooperation did not in fact foster *socialist cooperation* for that seems to have died some time ago, but one of the legacies of socialist cooperation does seem to have been that it fostered another kind of cooperation, the kind of cooperation that the Mongolia Society under very different circumstances has also sought to encourage for the past 50 years. Grollová made precisely this point in her description of Mongolian studies under late socialist cooperation:

> In the 1970's and the 1980's the loudly proclaimed fraternal relations between the two countries began to change into mere formal shaking of hands and inefficient ideologically motivated plans of co-operation. Real experts in and friends of Mongolia however, grew outside conference halls and comfortable offices. They included particularly people who had worked in rough Mongolian steppe for many months and got personally acquainted with Mongolian people and their living conditions. (Grollová, 1992, p.286)

It is this familiarity with real Mongolians rather than ideological constructions that Grollová suggested will be a great advantage for Czech mongolists in the near future. Genuine cooperation, like good science and scholarship, does not follow an ideology whether socialist or capitalist but on the contrary undermines ideologies, leaving them behind for historians to argue about.

References

Adler-Karlsson, Gunnar (1963). "The Council for Mutual Economic Assistance" *Economics of planning*, v.3 nr.3 (December 1963) p.141-148.

Bade, David (1992). *Polsko-Mongolska polka: bibliografia prac polaków oraz prac wydanych w Polsce*. Thesis, MLS, University of Illinois at Urbana-Champaign.

Bade, David (1997). "Poland" In: *International bibliography on Mongolian studies*. Ulaanbaatar: The Secretariat of the International Association for Mongol Studies, 1997. v. 1 (=*Mongolica*, v.8), p.253-364.

Bade, David (1997a). *Ještě jedna Československá bibliografie Mongolska*. Chicago: The author.

Badyoczek, Andrzej (1984). "Współpraca polsko-mongolska w dziedzinie weterynarii w latach 1976-1980" In: Kojło, Stefan, editor (1984). *Polska-Mongolia: przemiany rewolucyjne w Mongolii i problemy współpracy polsko-mongolskiej*. Warszawa: Instytut Krajów Socjalistycznych PAN, p. 175-183.

Bareja-Starzyńska, Agata (2007) "Mongolian studies in Poland" Гуманитарные исследования Внутренней Азии no.1 p.95-100.

Birtalan Ágnes (1997). "Hungary" *International bibliography on Mongolian studies*. Ulaanbaatar: The Secretariat of the international Association for Mongol Studies, v. 1 (*Mongolica*, v.8(29)), p. 191-222.

Bjamba, Żambyn (1979). "Činnost Mezinárodní geologické expedice v Mongolsku" *Geologický průzkum* r.21 č.10 p.302-304.

Cerennadmid, Cz. (1987). "Korzystna współpraca" *Służba zdrowia* nr.11 p.4.

Černovský, Jan and Ševčík, Bohumil (1965). "Poznatky z diagnostických akcí v Mongolsku" *Veterinářství* r.15 č. 6 p.249-252.

Curtis, Glenn E. (1992). *Czechoslovakia: a country study*. Washington DC: Federal Research Division of the Library of Congress.

Diószegi Vilmos (1960). *Sámánok nyomában Szibéria földjén. Egy néprajzi kutatóút története*. Budapest: Magvető Könyvkiadó. In English: *Tracing shamans in Siberia. The story of an ethnographical research expedition*. Translated from Hungarian by Anita Rajkay Babó. Oosterhout: Anthropological Publications, 1968.

Dlabola, Jiří (1967). "Ergebnisse der 1. mongolisch-tschechoslowakishen entomologisch-botanischen Expedition in der Mongoliei Nr. 1: Reisebericht, Lokalitätenübersicht und Beschreibungen neuer Zikadenarten (Homopt. Auchenorrhyncha)" *Acta faunistica entomologica Musei nationalis Pragae* sv. 1 p. 1-34.

Don, Jerzy and Dumicz, Marian (1984). "Polish geological investigations in western Mongolia: a symnoptic review" *Prace geologiczno-mineralogiczne* nr. 9 p. 167-188 (Acta Universitatis Wratislaviensis, nr. 529)

Dynowski, Witold (1968). *Współczesna Mongolia*. Wrocław: Zakład Narodowy im. Ossolińskich.

Dynowski, Witold and Maria Frankowska, editors (1973). *Z badań nad spółeczeństwem i kulturą Mongolii*. Wrocław: Zakład Narodowy im. Ossolińskich.

Dzięciołowski, Ryszard; Krupka, Jerzy; Bajandelger; Dziedzic, Roman (1980). "Argali and Siberian Ibex populations in the Khuhsyrh Reserve in Mongllian Altai" *Acta theriologica* v.25 fasc. 16 p.213-219.

Dzieciuchowicz, Mieczysław (1972). "Mongolia przykładem współpracy weterynaryjnej w ramach RWPG" *Życie weterynaryjne* v.47 nr.9 p.261-265.

Erdélyi, István (1962). "Jelentés a mongol-magyar expedíció 1961. évi munkálatairól." *Akadémiai Értesítő* v.89 p.93-100.

Erdélyi István (1963). "A mongol-magyar régészeti expedíció 1961-1963. évi eredményei" *Magyar Tudomány* v. 60 p. 647-651.

Erdélyi István (1966). "Az 1964. évi mongol-magyar régészeti expedíció eredményei" *A Magyar Tudományos Akadémia II. Osztályának Közleményei,* v. 15 p. 123-128.

Erdélyi, István (1993). "Az 1990 évi mongóliai közös mongolmagyar ásatás eredményei (előzetes jelentés)" *Keletkutatás tavasz,* p.62-65.

Erdélyi István and Ferenczy L. (1963). "Jelentés a magyar-mongol expedíció 1962. évi eredményeir" *Archaeológiai Értesítő* v. 90 p. 120-126.

Erdélyi, István and D. Cewendorz (1993). "A mongol-magyar közös régészeti kutatások újabb eredményei (1986-1989)," *Akadémiai Értesítő* v.120 p.63-69.

Erdélyi István, C. Dorjsüren, and D. Navan (1967). "Results of the Mongolian-Hungarian archaelogical expeditions 1961-1964" *Acta archaeologica academiae scientiarum hungaricae* v. 19 p. 335-370

Erdős László Szakmány. *Expedíció története.* Viewed 10 October 2012 at: http://mongolia.gportal.hu/

Ergens, R.; Dulmaa, A. (1968). "Monogenoidea from fishes of the genus Oreoleuciscus (Cyprinidae) from Mongolia. Communication no. 1" *Folia parasitologica* r.17 č. 1 p.1-11.

Gábori, Miklos (1962). "Compte rendu de mon voyage en Mongolie en 1961" *Archaeológiai Értesítő* v. 89, p.101-106.

Gábori, Miklos (1963). "New data on Paleolithic finds in Mongolia" *Asian Perspectives* v.7 nr.1/2 (summer/winter 1963) p.105-112.

Goodrich, Malinda K. (1992). "Appendix B. The Council for Mutual Economic Assistance" In: Glenn E. Curtis (ed.), *Czechoslovakia: a country study.* Washington DC: Federal Research Division of the Library of Congress.

Gostyński, Aleksander (1965). "Notatki z pobytu w Mongolii" *Życie weterynaryjne* v.42 nr.3 p.81-85.

Grollová, Ivana (1992). "The past and the future of Mongolian Studies in Czechoslovakia" *Archiv orientální* v.60 nr.3 p. 285-290.

Ignatowicz, Jan (1975). "Czar i prawa stepu: z zagranicznej weterynarii" *Życie weterynaryjne* v.50 nr.1 p.28-29.

Jaczewski, Tadeusz (1960). "Corixidae /Heteroptera/ from the Mongolian People's Republic and some adjacent regions" *Fragmenta faunistica* t. 8 nr.20 p.305-314.

Jaczewski, Tadeusz (1961). "Further notes on aquatic Heteroptera of the Mongolian People's Republic and some adjacent regions" *Fragmenta faunistica* t. 9 nr.1 p. 1-9.

Juríková, Eva (1987). "Československo-mongolská hospodárska spolupráca v rokoch 1956-1980" *Historický časopis* r. 35, č. 5, p. 716-735.

Kabzińska-Stawarz, Iwona (1991). *Games of Mongolian shepherds*. Warsaw: Institute of The History of Material Culture, Polish Academy of Sciences.

Kádár János (1963). "Excerpts of Report to the Hungarian Politburo on the PCC Meeting by the First Secretary of the MSzMP (János Kádár) 31 July 1963" Viewed online 18 October 2012 at: http://www.php.isn.ethz.ch/collections/colltopic.cfm?lng=en&id=17907&navinfo=14465

Kara György, Uray Kőhalmi Katalin and Róna-Tas András (1958). "Jelentés mongóliai tanulmányutunkról" *Magyar Tudományos Akadémia I. Osztályának Közleményei* v.12, p.469-514.

Kara György, Uray Kőhalmi Katalin and Róna-Tas András (1958a). "Nyelvészeti és néprajzi tanulmányúton Mongóliában" *Magyar Tudomány*, 305–328.

Kielan-Jaworowska, Zofia (1969). *Polowanie na Dinozaury*. Warszawa: Wydawnictwa Geologiczne. English translation: *Hunting for dinosaurs*. Cambridge, Mass.: MIT Press, 1969.

Kielan-Jaworowska, Zofia (2010). *Zofia Kielan-Jaworowska - Autobiography*. Available on the Polyglot Paleontologist cite hosted by the Smithsonian National Museum of Natural History. www.paleoglot.org/files/ZKJ%20autobio2.doc (accessed 7 Nov. 2012)

Kielan-Jaworowska, Zofia & Naydin Dovchin (1968), "Narrative of the Polish-Mongolian Palaeontological Expeditions 1963-1965" *Palaeontologia Polonica*, No. 19, p.7-30 + IV plates

Kielan-Jaworowska, Zofia & Rinchen Barsbold (1972). "Narra-tive of the Polish-Mongolian Palaeontological Expeditions 1967-1971" *Palaeontologia Polonica,* No. 27, p.5-13 + II plates.

Klimek, Kazimierz (1984). "Polskie badania fizyczno-geograficzne w Mongolii w latach 1974-1980" In: Kojło, Stefan, editor (1984). *Polska-Mongolia: przemiany rewolucyjne w Mongolii i problemy współpracy polsko-mongolskiej.* Warszawa: Instytut Krajów Socjalistycznych PAN, p. 201-225.

Kocian, Ľudovít (1999). "Šesťdesiat rokov Katedry zoológie Prírodovedeckej fakulty Univerzity Komenského v Bratislave" *Správy Slovenskej zoologickej spoločnosti,* 17, p. 27–52. Viewed online 17 October 2012 at: http://zoology.fns.uniba.sk/v2005/sk_historia.htm#full

Kojło, Stefan, editor (1984). *Polska-Mongolia: przemiany rewolucyjne w Mongolii i problemy współpracy polsko-mongolskiej.* Warszawa: Instytut Krajów Socjalistycznych PAN.

Kolář, Václav (1987). "Vědeckotechnická spolupráce ve službách obyvatelstvu v rámci RVHP" *Národní výbory* r. 36 č. 5 p. 8.

Kozłowski, Janusz K. (1972). "Research on the Stone age in South Mongolia in 1968" *Archaeologia polona,* v. XIII, p.231-261.

Krauter, Mojmír (1963). "K zahájení prací československých geologů v Mongolské lidové republice" *Geologický průzkum* r.5 č.10 p.318.

Krauter, Mojmír (1989). "25. výročí čs.mongolské spolupráce v oblasti geologie" *Geologický průzkum* r.31 č.3 p.93-94.

Kuczyński, Maciej (1977). *Zwrotnik dinozaura.* Warszawa: Iskry.

Laskowski, Ryszard (1967). "Pół roku w kraju kumysem płynącym" *Życie weterynaryjne* v.42 nr.3 p.81-85.

Łepkowski, Marek (1965). "Wyprawa do Mongolii" *Służba zdrowia* nr. 46 p. 8.

Lyon, Gabrielle (2001). "Timeline of expeditions in Outer and Inner Mongolia." On the website of the *Dinosaur Expedition 2001: Chinese-American Dinosaur Expedition.* http://www.projectexploration.org/mongolia/timeline.htm

Maenchen-Helfen, Otto (1964-1965). Review of: Umehara Sueji, *Mōko Noin Ura hakken no ibutsu. (Studies of Noin-Ula Finds in North Mongolia)* Tokyo, The Toyo Bunko, 1960; and S.I.Rudenko, *Kul'tura khunnovi noinulinskie kurgany* (The Culture of the Hsiung-nu and the Barrows of Noin Ula). Moskva-Leningrad: Izdatel'stvo Akademii Nauk SSSR, 1962. *Artibus Asiae*, Vol. 27, No. 4 (1964-1965), p. 365-369

Mastny, Vojtech and Malcolm Byrne, editors (2005). *A cardboard castle? An inside history of the Warsaw Pact, 1955-1991.* Budapest: Central European Univ. Press.

Michalski, Ireneusz (1960). "Ekspedycja antropologiczna do Mongolii (3.VIII.—16.XI.1959 r.)" *Człowiek w czasie i przestrzeni* r.3 z.1(9) p. 9-24.

Muth, Ingrid (2000). *Die DDR-Aussenpolitik 1949-1972.* Berlin: Ch. Links Verlag.

Myšková, Eva (1959). "Bohumír Šmeral, přítel mongolského lidu" *Obrana lidu* 1.XI.1959 r.18 nr.261 p.4.

Nielipiński, W. (1936). "Charakterystyka antropologiczna szczątków ludzkich z cmentarzyska w Hulunbuir (Barga) w Mongolii" *Sprawozdania z czynności i posiedzeń Akademii Umiejętności* t. 41 nr.9 (listopad) p. 290-293.

Podepsání (1956). "Podepsání zdravotnické dohody mezi ČSR a Mongolskem" *Rudé pravo* 20.VII.1956 r.36 nr.201 p.1.

Podepsání (1957). "Podepsání čs.-mongolské zdravotnické dohody" *Rudé pravo* 24.IV.1957 r.37 nr.113 p.2.

Pokorný, Miroslav (2011). *„Nomádi" z Československa: Československé vztahy s Mongolskou lidovou republikou v 50. a 60. letech 20. století.* Plzeň. SVOČ-2011, Fakultní soutěžní přehlídka, 28. 4. 2011 Katedra historie. Studijní program: Historie se zaměřením na vzdělávání Obor: Historie se zaměřením na vzdělávání Ročník: III.

Poland and Mongolia (1954). "Umowa o współpracy radiowej między Komitetem do Spraw Radiofonii 'Polskie Radio' a Komitetem do Spraw Radiofonii 'Mongolskie Radio'." Reprinted in: *Zbiór umów międzynarodowych Polskiej Rzeczypospolitej Ludowej 1954* (published 1967) p.14-5.

Poland and Mongolia (1958). "1958 grudzień 23, Warszawa. Umowa między Rządem Polski Rzeczypospolitej Ludowej a Rządem Mongolskiej Republiki Ludowej o współpracy naukowo-technicznej" In: Kojło, Stefan, editor (1984). *Polska-Mongolia: przemiany rewolucyjne w Mongolii i problemy współpracy polsko-mongolskiej.* Warszawa: Instytut Krajów Socjalistycznych PAN, p. 303-305.

Potkanski, Tomasz and Sławoj Szynkiewicz (1993). *The social context of liberalisation of the Mongolian pastoral economy : report of anthropological fieldwork.* Brighton, UK : Institute of Development Studies at the University of Sussex ; Zaisan, Ulaanbaatar : Research Institute of Animal Husbandry : Institute of Agricultural Economics.

Rödling, J. "The possibilities and tasks of postgraduate medical education in the assistance given by the Czechoslovak Socialist Republic to the developing countries." in: J. Mirovský and K. Černý, editors. *Proceedings of the Symposium on Health Services in Developing Countries. House of Scientific Workers of the Czechoslovak Academy of Sciences, Liblice near Prague, Czechoslovakia, 9-11 October 1974.* Praha: Universitá Karlova, 1974, p.39-50.

Romania and Mongolian People's Republic (1956). *Agreement concerning cultural co-operation. Signed at Bucharest, on 8 May 1956.* (United Nations Treaty Series no. 4913) http://untreaty.un.org/unts/1_60000/10/8/00018382.pdf

Róna-Tas András (1959). "Jelentés második mongóliai tanulmányutamról" [Report on my second study-tour to Mongolia], *Magyar Tudományos Akadémia I. Osztályának Közleményei* v.14, p. 345–350.

Róna-Tas András (1961). *Nomádok nyomában. Ethnográfus szemmel Mongóliában* . Budapest: Gondolat.
Rutkowski, Edmond (1966). *Trzy dni geologa w Mongolii*. Warszawa: Wydawnictwa Geologiczne.
Sárközi Alice and Birtalan Ágnes (1997). "Hungarian explorers of Mongolia in the Twentieth Century." In: Gáthy Vera and Yamaji Masanori (eds.), *A new dialogue between Central Europe and Japan*, Budapest: Institute for Social Conflict Research, HAS, and Kyoto: International Research Centrer for Japanese Studies, p. 119-122.
Sárközi Alice (2008). Magyar-mongol népi műveltség és nyelvjárás kutató expedíció. Viewed 11 October 2012 at: http://www.otka.hu/index.php?akt_menu=3825
Schwarz, Henry G. and Sh. Bira (eds.) (1997). *International Bibliography on Mongolian Studies*, v 1. (*Mongolica: international annual of Mongol studies* v. 8)
Sokolewicz, Zofia (2005). "Polish expeditions abroad 1945-1989." In: Chris Hann, Mihály Sárkány, Peter Skalník (eds.), *Studying Peoples in the People's Democracies. Socialist Era Anthropology in East-Central Europe*, Berlin: LIT Verlag. (Halle Studies in the Anthropology of Eurasia, v.8) p.289-301.
Splisteser, H. (1975). "Spolupráce NDR a MoLR v oblasti veterinární medicíny" *Mezinárodní zemědělský časopis* r.19 č.5 p.60-62.
Studia mongolskie (1969). Wrocław: Zakład Narodowy im. Ossolińskich.
Szalontai Balázs (2004). "Tsedenbal's Mongolia and communist aid donors: a reappraisal." *IIAS Newsletter* nr 35 (November 2004) p. 18.
Szandtner Veronika. "Mongolian Prime Minister Visits ELTE BTK" *Eötvös Loránd University Faculty Of Humanities News* 11 May 2010 Viewed 10 October 2012 at: http://www.btk.elte.hu/en/article?id=NW-112
Szober, Wincenty (1965). "Architekci polscy w Mongolii" *Architektura* nr. 11 p.471-478.

Szynkiewicz, Sławoj (1986). "Монголоведение в Польше", in: Ш. Б. Чимитдоржиев (отв. редактор), *Культура Монголии в средние века и новое время, XVI-начало XX в.* Улан-Удэ : Академия наук СССР, Сибирское отд-ние, Бурятский филиал, Институт общественных наук, pp. 134-140.

Szynkiewicz, Sławoj (1981). *Rodzina pasterska w Mongolii.* Wrocław: Zakład Narodowy im. Ossolińskich.

Tinák, Benjamín (2002). *Zo sveta.* Ružomberok: Epos.

Török László (2000). "Magyar Tudományos Akadémia Régészeti Intézet" In: Glatz F (ed.), *A Magyar Tudományos Akadémia kutatóintézetei.* Budapest: Magyar Tudományos Akadémia, p. 3-24. English version available online (viewed 10 October 2012): "The Archaeological Institute of the Hungarian Academy of Sciences: The first forty-one years, 1958-1999"
http://www.archeo.mta.hu/eng/tortenet/NAS_history.pdf

Tryjarski Edward (1965). "L'inscription turque runiforme d'Arkhanen en Mongolia," *Ural-Altaische Jahrbücher*, v.36, nr3-4, p. 423-428.

Trzcianka, Janusz (1974). "Od Wisły do Toły" *Za wolność i lud* nr. 51-52 p.12.

Vašák, Václav (1968). "K činnosti čs. veterinární expedice v Mongolské lidové republice" *Veterinářství* r.18 č. 4 p. 182-185.

Vlček, Emanuel (1959). "Old literary evidence for the existence of the 'Snow Man' in Tibet and Mongolia" *Man*, v. 59 (August), p. 133-134.

Vlček, Emanuel (1965). "A Contribution to the Anthropology of the Khalkha-Mongols: (the Anthropologists and Physicians Report on the Czechoslovak-Mongolian Archeological Expedition in the Year 1958)" *Anthropologia, Acta Facultatis rerum naturalism Universitatis Comenianae*, Volume 9, Parts 6-7, 83 p.

Wanot, Elżbieta (1992). "Photogrammetric inventory of Janrajsag Temple from Gandan Monastery complex in Ulan-Bator" In: Józef Jachimski (ed.), *Numerical photogrammetry, remote sensing and spatial information systems applied to restoration of architectural and urban heritage and to archeoloty: CIPA XIII International Symposium, Cracow, 23-26 October 1990*. Cracow: International Committee for Architectural Photogrammetry, Polish National Committee of International Council of Monuments and Sites, and Polish Society for Photogrammetry and Remote Sensing. p.303-311.

Wasilewski, Jerzy (1979, repr. 1985). *Podróże do piekieł: rzecz o szamańskich misteriach.* Warszawa: Ludowa Spółdzielnia Wydawnicza.

Werner, Zbigniew (1982). "Badania polskich ekspedycji geologicznych w Mongolii" In: Kojło, Stefan, editor (1984). *Polska-Mongolia: przemiany rewolucyjne w Mongolii i problemy współpracy polsko-mongolskiej.* Warszawa: Instytut Krajów Socjalistycznych PAN, p. 135-200.

XIV

Carl Robinson's Mongolia[1]

A travel guide by a tourist for tourists.
Why do people write travel guides? For the use of travellers and tourists. In that respect Robinson's book is like all the rest. Few travel guides are written to be read from beginning to end, however, and in that respect Robinson's book is not like all the rest. The book can be read from beginning to end, just like a real book. The first 170 pages of the book offers narratives of the geography, history, people and culture of Mongolia including the section I enjoyed the most, a few pages on "Everyday Mongolian Experiences." This is followed by 300 pages of description of Mongolia that was deliberately written not as an *aimag* by *aimag* description of places to see and things to do but an actual travelogue, a narrative the author's experiences during his own two month journey clockwise around Mongolia. The book ends with Advice and facts for travelers, practical information about airlines, travel agencies, accomodations and useful sources of further information. Interspersed throughout the introductory sections and the travelogue are sections on special topics like shamanism, geology, deer stones and *naadam*, some

---

[1] Review of: Carl Robinson. *Mongolia: Nomad Empire of Eternal Blue Sky*. Hong Kong: Odyssey, 2010.

excerpted from or based upon other writers such as Mongolists Ivana Grollová and Christopher Kaplonski. Also interspersed throughout the narratives are what Robinson calls "Literary Excerpts", more selections from published works by Roy Chapman Andrews, Owen Lattimore, Natsagdorj, Thomas Barfield, Don Croner, Ben Kozel and Gaby Bamana, a Mongolist and anthropologist from the Democratic Republic of Congo, the same place where Robinson grew up.

Travel literature for the non-traveler
Robinson's book is travel literature as much as a travel guide, and a very readable account written by someone who did a great deal of reading and studying about Mongolia both before and after his sojourn there. It is not a work of scholarship but is nevertheless full of interesting information about Mongolia that even those like myself who have been to Mongolia several times may not know. The pictures are wonderful: my wife, born in Khar Chuluut near Tarialan in Khovsgol aimag gasped at the large photograph of the *vansemberuu* (snow lotus) spread across pages 366-367; my 4 year old got very excited at the picture of *aarul*—her favorite food—drying on page 118; I caught my breath at the photographs of the reclining Lady Buddha, the landscapes of Dariganga and Mongolia's incredible blue lakes. It is a very nice book to show people who may never see Mongolia except in pictures.

The book has many splendid anecdotes, such as when he relays "the apocryphal tale of the tour guide who texted a message, hit the 'Send' button and tossed it high in the air ... landing back in his hands, the phone read 'Message Sent'" (p. 160). There are also sobering statements that ring true to my own experience:

Anti-Chinese prejudice is strong and the visceral hatred expressed by some Mongolians towards Chinese--even the mere sight of them--can shock visitors. (p. 80)

And in recent times, women have pushed even further ahead as boys were kept home for herding and girls completed higher education and entered the modern workforce. Some 80 percent of college and university graduates are women; male resentment, even misogyny, is now a serious problem... (p. 120)

But too many casually discard their plastic bags, which then fly across the vast and empty steppe. You know that you're nearing an aimag or sum centre by the number of colourful bags littering the landscape hanging on every possible upstanding object. (p. 161)

The tourist's dream of Mongolia

If I could stop here after having noted all the nice things about Robinson's book, I would be much happier; no doubt Robinson would be too. But Robinson began his book with a few lines which sent this reader reeling, never to recover in spite of the interesting narratives, special topics, literary excerpts and beautiful photographs. In the first paragraph of the introduction I read this:

Some 800 years ago, people sure didn't need the Mongols when they were brutally forging the world's greatest land empire ... In today's troubled times, however, the world desperately needs what Mongolia has to offer: an uncrowded and wide-open landscape populated by friendly people where you can be totally cut off from the frustrations, depressions and annoyances of modern life. It's now time to head in the other direction. (p. 25)

This is followed by two sentences praising Mongolia's land, animals and people, and then this:

Mongolia is the ideal destination for crashed-out financiers, getting over a divorce or sorting out a midlife crisis. (p. 25)

The question is: is this what Mongolia needs? Could the Mongolia Robinson (and I) fell in love with survive hordes of frustrated, depressed, annoyed, crashed-out financiers and other people suffering from personal disasters and crises descending on its pristine natural spots in expectation of five-star hotels, good roads, four-wheel drives, first class service and ... none of the troubles of modern life? Would these hordes of tourists not do the opposite and bring all of the troubles of modern life to Mongolia? Robinson thinks not:

But even as things improve with more five-star hotels in the capital, comfortable 4WD vehicles and luxury tourist ger accommodation, Mongolia will always remain a "rustic destination"—and that is precisely its enduring attraction. (p. 26)

In fact, Robinson at one point suggests the opposite: that the biggest danger to Mongolia's natural environment arises from the cultural attitudes of the Mongols themselves:

But changing long-entrenched cultural attitudes about hunting, a very long tradition in Mongolia, is the biggest challenge. (p. 46).

Tourists in search of great hunting and fishing bring a hefty revenue to the government, but in order for there to be enough game left for the tourists it will be necessary to keep the Mongols from their own traditional ways of life. ?!?!?!
Robinson wants a scenic, traditional pre-modern Mongolia, a Mongolia that fits the frustrated modern tourist's needs. Not surprisingly for a male writer, the fact that young women outnumber boys three to one in Ulaanbaatar is seen as a blessing for the tourist (p. 479), not as a troubling problem for the people of Mongolia. Whenever Mongolia does not fit the tourist's desired image—such as the realities of the gold mines and industrial towns in the north (Erdenet and Darhan)—Robinson judges such places to be "barely worth the trip" (p. 212). But

how can one have five-star hotels, good roads, sedentary employees providing excellent service at luxury tourist attractions without building local housing for these herders who have now become proletariat? How can you develop tourism without local shops, doctors, hospitals, cell phone towers, gas stations, car repair shops, police stations and all the other necessities that a sedentary population serving demanding foreigners would require for their health and well-being? Without, that is, changing traditional Mongolian society into modern industrial society?

The massive, shiny statue certainly comes as a surprise and will no doubt become a popular tourist attraction, especially with the locals. ... Costing over US$50 million and planned to include a large tourist ger camp, the project clearly reflects the national pride, ambition and dreams of Mongolia's modern— and often still-young—entrepreneurs (Genco also runs 13th Century National Park, a replica medieval encampment with overnight accommodation some 40 kilometres (25 miles) to the southeast, and plans a spa and golf resort.) (p. 224)

So much for pristine nature, traditional hospitality, and isolation from the modern world. Mongolia will become an Asian Disneyland with amusement parks, golf courses, spas as well as a fake replica of Mongolian culture, and all of this will displace not only the gazelles (already run out of certain areas by oil drilling according to Robinson and the locals with whom he spoke (p. 257)) but local traditional communities and everything that Robinson says we should be going to Mongolia to see. And Robinson is aware of this. Writing of *Khokh Nuur* he remarks:

Surrounded by low hills, the circular-shaped lake is a lovely spot but has lost its pristine tranquility to tourism, and even private development, in recent years. (p. 229).

Yet in the very next paragraph describing *Hangal Nuur*, he writes that this is "a commnist-era Young Pioneer Camp ... no doubt waiting for an ambitious entrepreneur to revive it" (p. 229). He closes his paragraph on *Uureg Nuur* with the remark

Still undeveloped, it's only a matter of time before someone builds a tourist ger camp along its lovely shores. I can already see water skiers scooting around this lake! (p. 373)

After praising the local silversmiths in Dariganga, he notes that they have all moved to Ulaanbaatar, without saying why (p. 281). The reason is not hard to guess: no airport, permits required to visit, so there are few tourists. Tourists mean money, so if there are no tourists, the silversmiths go where the tourists are. But what happens to Dariganga if they leave? And what happens to Dariganga if they stay and the tourists do come? Robinson lets us know exactly what will happen, for it happened at Karakorum. After stating that what Karakorum "desperately" needs is "a quality showcase museum—including an open-air facility" (p. 434) he notes his shock at the place upon his arrival there, but his shock is not due to its lack of a museum:

If you've arrived from the solitude of the Mongolian Outback, however, as I did, Harhorin can't help but come as something of a shock. From capital of the Mongol Empire to Tourist City today! Scattered around the town are more than a dozen tourist ger camps, some quite large and one boasting the biggest ger in Mongolia as its dining room. Traffic is busy and everyone ends up at Erdene Zuu. Souvenir markets are everywhere—near the first turtle, the Phallic Rock and especially inside the monastery grounds. (p. 45).

And that is not the worst of it:

One of my Mongolian companions was shocked to see a European couple drinking beer just inside the main gate. Other tourists, especially those in groups, were just plain loud. Personally, I was surprised to suddenly see so many other foreigners about and didn't know what to expect. (p. 436)

My dear Mr. Robinson, if you build tourist attractions and write guide books encouraging tourists to visit them, what do you expect to attract? Gobi bears, black tailed gazelles, mute swans, snow lotuses, Przewalski horses and the stillness of the reclining Lady Buddha?

XV

A Monastery in Time[1]

I have always assumed that the reviewer of a scholarly book ought to have a background in the academic discipline(s) within which the book has been written. In the case of *A Monastery in Time*, that background would be Buddhism, Mongolian studies, ethnography, perhaps history. Yet while this reviewer took an undergraduate course on Buddhism 30 years ago and published an historical study of the Mongol naval campaign to Jawa, he can in no way lay claim to a professional or academic training in any of the above-mentioned disciplines. Linguistics and library science are the areas in which I have received advanced degrees, areas of research and employment that have occupied me the better part of my working life. Reading *A Monastery in Time*, however, directed my attention from the beginning to matters of language, and at the end towards recording, preserving and archiving written records and their role in social institutions, the sort of thing that does indeed preoccupy the attention of students of library science. *A Monastery in Time* in fact has as much to

---

[1] Review of: Caroline Humphrey and Hürelbaatar Ujeed. *A Monastery in Time: The Making of Mongolian Buddhism*. Chicago and London: The University of Chicago Press, 2013.

offer students of political science and sociology as it does to linguists and librarians, and that in addition to what it offers the specialist in Mongolian studies, Asian history, Buddhism or anthropology. So much so that specialists in Mongolian Buddhist history or Inner Mongolian ethnology might miss the depth and breadth of the arguments presented in this volume and its importance to a much wider readership. Such is my own justification for writing this review.

Right at the beginning—on page 2—the authors got my attention with their remarks on their choice of "an obscure structure in a backwater of an undeveloped part of China"—Mergen Monastery—for it presented the authors with "the utterly specific" that would allow them "to focus on what essential element in human interactions would enable a group of people to impose their own direction and sustain a particular ethical-aesthetic form of life." In an intellectual climate such as I have lived in, one in which the particular is explained by class, caste, race, gender or some other analytical category or abstraction, this orientation toward the specific was really unexpected and exciting. On the next page I read with increasing excitement that the authors found it to be "impossible to write about the monastery and the relations between the monks living there simply as a system or a culture" and on page five that "our ethnography resounds with the presence and mediating agency of particular personalities." Adieu, Niklas Luhmann. And at the top of page seven the importance of language and linguistic practices for understanding Mongolian Buddhism comes already to the fore. "The main problem for the people of Mergen" (p. 6) the authors claim, is "gathering and sustaining an assemblage of people who care enough about religion, and about one another, for them even to bother with disagreements or debates in the tradition" (p. 7). Yet language here is not the linguistics of Noam Chomsky or the systems of sociolinguistic theories, but the linguistics of Eugen Rosenstock-Huessy, for whom "Speech is the political constitution of a group beyond the life time and living space of any individual, beyond common sense and physical sense" (E.

Rosenstock-Huessy, *The Origin of Speech*. Norwich, VT: Argo Books, 1981: 31. The authors never cite Rosenstock-Huessy, but this was not the only time he came to mind as I read their book).

A few pages later in the Introduction, in the section entitled "Talking about Religion and 'Talking Religion'" the discussion again focuses on language but instead of Rosenstock-Huessy it is the late Roy Harris who comes to mind as the authors discuss "the meanings that were not in what people actually said" (p. 16). Again, Harris is not cited (Pinney, Ginsburg and Latour are mentioned), nor would he ever have allowed himself to write of language being 'used' as the authors do, but the distinction the authors make between talking *about* religion and *talking religion* illustrates one of Harris's most controversial claims, namely that science, art, religion, politics, law etc. are linguistic practices and therefore understanding them requires understanding language.

Of particular interest to me are the authors' remarks on time (Christopher Pinney and Siegfried Krakauer underwrite the discussion on pages 19-21 as elsewhere), and it is not just in the title of the book that time figures prominently. "Concerns about time have largely structured the shape of this book" the authors write on page three, but that says nothing about how differently they understand time. When they write that "time consists of many 'cataracts,' each pursuing their own trajectories" and that "disparate cultural phenomena may inhabit a given era and yet not be each other's contemporaries" (p. 21) we are far, far away from Stephen Hawking on time and I again searched the references in vain for Rosenstock-Huessy (who wrote of "distemporaries"). Next to the discussions of language, the remarks on time (and times) were, for this reader, the most interesting, and that primarily because of the importance of time in the linguistic and social theories of Rosenstock-Huessy and Roy Harris (i.e. the reading habits of a non-anthropologist and non-Buddhist). It is not just time as in 'history' that comes into play, but times that are created and sustained (wombs or cups of time, Rosenstock-Huessy called them), times within which people act and interact, times that create pasts and traditions and futures, time that is so much more than clock time or chronology.

In the first chapter (after the Introduction) the authors state that their book "is a study of the quality of institutional relations not as a pre-given structure, but as created by particular people in diverse interactions with one another" (p. 34). Here is perhaps as clear a statement as I could hope for to demonstrate the guiding orientation of this book and why I loved it so much. History, tradition, social forms and structures *are not pre-given* but are created moment by moment by people interacting. The authors pay attention to what they see and hear, and they do indeed look and listen to those people at Mergen, rather than inserting them into a pre-given theoretical structure. For me, one of the most delightful passages in the book occurs in the "Acknowledgments and a Note on the Writing of this Book": "Each year we expected a resolution into some more or less steady state (upon which we could come to an idea of the overall shape of the book)—only to find that events overtook our previous conclusions" (page xii-xiii). A book about tradition, but the tradition in question kept changing so fast that the authors could not keep up with it and finish their book... Exquisite!

There is one passage in chapter 10 (Tradition and Archivization) that reminded me of a dramatic experience of my own. On page 346 the authors write

> This sequence of events shows that the Janghan Temple did indeed come to house a spontaneous or living tradition. By this we refer to the reproduction of a given activity (worship of fierce and martial gods) under the assumption of doing "the same" ontologically, even if the actions are in fact different ... The performance of tradition in this way destroys what had gone before even as it assembles its own version. It is at work in silence about what it accomplishes and is not concerned to leave a record or an authoritative account for future reference. ... Thus although *nothing* now remains of Mergen

Gegen's original set-up in the eighteenth century, each generation bore in mind the idea that the Janghan Temple is for the worship of fierce protectors and installed the particular objects they thought most powerful.

During a trip to Mongolia in 2001 I visited Gandan several times and witnessed the destruction of the architectural decoration adorning the smaller of the temples. At first I was horrified to see monks ripping painted woodwork off the temple: Art! Sacrilege! Tradition! Defaced and destroyed! The world in ruins! And as I stood there in shock and outrage, it suddenly occurred to me that these monks were not conserving a religious monument from the past, but rather living their religion. And as they should! My whole understanding of conservation and preservation, of tradition and reverence for the past was wiped away with a monk's shovel, but I had to wait twelve more years to discover a discussion of tradition that was consonant with my own experience. And a remarkable book it is, sheer pleasure to read, and of immense value for its discussions of language, texts and archives, the politics of religion as well as the religion of politics, time, tradition and history, and making your own time in difficult times. And of course, it is also of interest if you are a specialist in Mongolian studies or Buddhism.

XVI

Imaginary Travels in Post-Socialist Mongolia

Abstract
Until recently, when the Mongols have appeared in the world's literature, they have usually appeared in the persons of chinggis Khaan or Khubilai, or as 'Mongolian hordes'. Some recent writings are unlike earlier works of the twentieth century, regardless of the political orientation and situation of the writers. In this paper I examine three works published between 1992 and 2003 that exemplify radically different instances of that difference: *Mongolski bedeker* by Serbian novelist Svetislav Basara; *Paměť mojí babičce* by Czech author Petra Hůlová; and *Mongólia* by the Brazilian writer Bernardo Carvalho. With the certainties and stereotypes of the past discarded in these novels, contemporary Mongolia provides the setting for the authors' encounters with the strangeness of the world at the turn of the millennium.

Introduction: The Mongols in literature
Throughout the twentieth century, literary treatments of Mongolia and the Mongols in the western world were predictably either about the imperial era – tales of Chinggis Khaan,

Khubilai, the invasions of European and Asian lands – or they were adventure tales for children, with the addition of stories in praise of the glorious new Mongolian communist society found in socialist literatures. Vasilii Yan's trilogy *Нашествие монголов* (*Nashestvie mongolov* 1955–1960) in Russian, Harold Lamb's *Genghis Khan: Emperor of all men* (1927) and Taylor Caldwell's *The Earth is the Lord's* (1940) in English, Zofia Kossak-Szczucka's *Legnickie pole* (1930), Michel Eristov's *L'empire mouvant* (1948), Kadir Tisna Sujana's *Babad Madjapait* (1935) and C.C. Bergius's *Dschingis-Chan* (1958) are all examples of the former, while children's literature included such varied fare as L.P. Wyman's *The Hunniwell Boys in the Gobi Desert* (1930), Kurt David's tale of Chinggis Khaan and his companions in *Der schwarze Wolf* (1966), G.V. Leclercq's tale of horses and riders *Va comme le vent* (1960) and geologist Maciej Kuczyński's *Gwiazdy suchego stepu* (1965): mysteries, adventures, spies, horses and the Gobi. Those few works for adult readers that dealt with modern Mongolia were largely about the glorious new communist Mongolian citizen-hero (such as Ma Jia's 开不败的花朵 (*Kai bu bai de hua duo*, 1950)), the Second World War (K.M. Simonov's *Товарищи по оружию* (*Tovarishchi po oruzhiiu*, 1954) or the horrors of communist persecution (J.P. Leynse's *Gobi, Prince of Moving Sand*, 1973). Although present in a few travel books, the everyday life of the Mongols in the twentieth century was rarely the focus of any non-Mongolian literary work during the period between the Second World War and the opening up of Mongolia in the early 1990s.

During that long period, some writers from Eastern Europe–Konstantin Simonov, Kurt David and Maciej Kuczyński, for example–wrote their works after spending time in Mongolia, but most twentieth- century fictional accounts of Mongolia and the Mongols are works of the imagination uninformed by firsthand experiences. The situation changed after 1990: not only writers from the former socialist countries but writers from the rest of the world could visit Mongolia, and this largely without the restrictions of government supervision.

The earlier emphasis on the imperial period and children's literature continued: Tor Age Bringsvard's *Gobi* series in the 1980s (*Barndommens måne*, 1985, *Djengis Khan*, 1987, and *Djevelens skinn og ben*, 1989) kept going with two volumes published in the 1990s; Chinggis Khaan and Mongolian warriors appeared in scores of historical novels and children's books, and the same themes appeared on television and in films. While some of these authors may have travelled to Mongolia, they clearly were not writing about thirteenth-century Mongols from first-hand experience, any more than writers of science fiction and children's magical adventures were. What is new after 1990 is the appearance of narratives of modern Mongolia as part of *our* world and understood from the perspective of personal experiences at home and in Mongolia.

In this article I examine three works published between 1992 and 2003 that exemplify radically different instances of that difference: *Mongolski bedeker* by Serbian novelist Svetislav Basara, *Paměť mojí babičce* by Czech author Petra Hůlová and *Mongólia* by the Brazilian writer Bernardo Carvalho. Written and published under the conditions of late socialism (Serbia in 1992), Svetislav Basara's *Mongolski bedeker* has been described as a handbook on how not to travel in Mongolia and as a book about Serbia (or Basara) rather than Mongolia. In 2002 Petra Hůlová published her début novel *Paměť mojí babičce*, intimate stories of five women in one Mongolian family and one of the most widely read czech books of the decade. The book won the Discovery of the Year prize of Magnesia Litera and was voted Book of the Year by the Prague daily *Lidové Noviny*. In *Mongólia*, published in 2003, Bernardo Carvalho describes the journey of a diplomat who goes to Mongolia to find a Brazilian photographer who has disappeared. *Mongólia* won the prize of the Associaçao Paulista dos Críticos de Arte for novels in 2003.

Svetislav Basara: *Mongolski bedeker*

Reading *Mongolski bedeker,* Basara's travel guide to Mongolia written in 1991 and published the following year, it is impossible to tell whether the author has or has not been to Mongolia. In fact, unlike the authors of the other two works discussed later, Basara has never been to Mongolia.[1] While his knowledge of Mongolia is not at first hand, he claimed in an interview that 'certain techniques of post-modern games that the author plays with his readers, and the narration – so convincing that socio-political life from Mongolia "can be used for granted"' (Basara in an interview with Dejan Vasilevski, 2010).[2] Yet he is not interested in presenting the reader with a realistic Mongolian setting, but an exaggeration, for 'The art of fiction is the art of exaggeration, but in that exaggeration is much truth' (Basara in an interview with Vesna Roganović, 2012).

The book opens with a conversation in the Ulaanbaatar Hotel bar. a friend of the narrator has committed suicide after agreeing to write a travel guide to Mongolia, but before committing suicide he writes to the narrator asking him to write the travel guide for him in order to fulfil his obligations. With this introduction out of the way, the travel guide begins. The second chapter opens thus:

> Bügd Nayramdakh Mongol ard Uls – The People's Republic of Mongolia – 1,565,000 square kilometres, 1,710,000 inhabitants. a remote country of central asia, populated by the descendants of Chingis Khaan, some ghosts and a few european colonial settlers. Bounded by the People's Republic of China and the Soviet Union. anywhere you go in this country you are only a day's journey from nowhere.

---

[1] In an email sent to the author on 23 october 2012, Basara wrote 'nikada nisam bio u Mongoliji. Zato sam i napisao tu knjigu' [I have never been to Mongolia. That is why I wrote that book].
[2] I thank Nada Petković for her help in translating this awkward passage.

But what is it that brought me to Mongolia? I asked myself at the same time as the customs officer asked me the same question. officially I had come to write a travel guide at the request of the review *Epoch*, whose first issue will be published in a few years. If of course they can find someone to promote and finance the review, which I doubt. ... Ultimately, I have an obligation to my deceased friend, and Mongolia is sufficiently far from that pile of shit in which I live. And then? Arriving in Ulaanbaatar I realized that here was another pile of shit, just further away.

With that, the travel guide is pretty much over, and the reader then follows Basara, not through Mongolia as a tourist would, but through the fantasies, drunkenness and absurdities of a Serbian man's life in a hotel that happens to be in Ulaanbaatar. Yet, in spite of that limited view of Mongolia, Basara's satiric presentation of late socialist society – whether Serbian, Mongolian or both – is hysterical, and I suspect it offers some glimpses of Mongolia or Serbia that few more sober writers would ever encounter. an example:

> The morning that I arrived in Ulaanbaatar they had executed the meteorologist on duty. The day before he had forecast sunshine with wind, but since dawn it had been sleeting. The tribunal had no pity. Tsedenbal refused to sign a pardon. Such cruelty! But real socialism is like that. After the war didn't they execute people in our country for having a house and a little money? In the end, this is an internal matter of Mongolian sovereignty. ... meteorological conditions do not depend upon monsoons, cyclones and depressions but on the pronouncements of the central Directorate of the Meteorological Service. Nothing can be left to chance.

Much of the absurdity, humour and truth of Basara's remarks about Mongolia are of just this kind: propaganda and misinformation are satirised precisely by being presented as facts in a tourist manual. In Ulaanbaatar, Basara writes,

> statistics are sacred. Inflation is zero, production grows annually at 2 per cent, unemployment is zero. And it has been this way for centuries. It will be this way forever. This is the secret of the radiant serenity and spontaneity one sees in Mongolian faces, of their inner strength that conquered the rest of the world in a few weeks under Chinggis Khaan. For a little while. Those wise riders of the steppe immediately realized that there was nothing good in the West. So just like they came, they went back. Remembering their yurts, they got on their horses and went back to their steppe.

Towards the end of the novel the protagonist reads some poems, one of which contains the lines 'I would feel even better were I nowhere. Or in Mongolia. Under the tent of some bloodthirsty hunter with bone ornaments in his hair.'

Basara gives us Mongolia as just more of the same absurdities that one finds everywhere else:

> It has been said that all places are equally shitty and absurd, and that travel only benefits travel agents. People run around looking for emotions, beauty ... What am I trying to say here? It is the devil they're looking for. and they will always find him.

Serbia or Mongolia, late socialist society or America, all the world is the same for Basara's character. *Mongolski bedeker* has been called a guide for how not to travel in Mongolia, but it is probably one of the better – certainly one of the most amusing – guides to late socialism hitherto written. The final pages of the book describe the contents of another letter written to the main character during the political changes of 1991:

> They have abolished many of those anachronistic and absurd laws that so exasperated you and life has become much more agreeable, but – unfortunately – also much more European. The Government has promulgated a law according to which the Republic of Mongolia will be relocated 8,500 kilometers to the southwest in order to be closer to what is happening in the world today and to integrate themselves more quickly into the general decadence.

Bernardo Carvalho: *Mongólia*

Bernardo Carvalho's *Mongólia* is not at all like Basara's novel, and in one respect it is the opposite. Whereas Basara gives us a character with keen insight into the absurdities of life in a land which is both completely strange and all too familiar, Carvalho's main character (not the narrator) strides through the narrative thinking he understands everything, asking all the pertinent questions and getting frustrated at the manners and customs of the Mongols who do not proceed in the manner which he desires. Mistrust, suspicion and incomprehension surround him and it is only at the climax of the book that he – like the narrator in the epilogue that follows – realises he has understood nothing. Also unlike Basara, Carvalho gives us a glorious ride from Tsagaannuur to Dalanzadgad and from Altai to Ölgiy, but one that does not correspond to the geographer's Mongolia. Although written as fiction, it is based on the author's actual travels in Mongolia in 2002.

In response to an interviewer's question, 'Why Mongolia?' Carvalho answered, 'In my head, it was the place which would have the greatest difference from what I am and what I know, the opposite, the antipodes' (Almeida 2003). The reality that he encountered was radically different from what he had 'in his head' prior to arrival:

> When I left for Mongolia I imagined the best and most liberal country on earth, judging by everything I saw in the guidebooks. I had understood that it was a classic place inhabited by Mongols, noble savages in reality who, since they were Buddhists, never killed anything, having a love for life and nature. But, when I arrived, it was clear that it was nothing like that. (Carvalho, quoted in Alves 2003)

Instead of writing a travel book as he had planned, he decided to write a book about a country that does not exist – the country of 'the travelers responsible for the reproduction of myths of the Orient in the Occident' (Carvalho, quoted in Alves 2003).

Carvalho's main character is a diplomat stationed in China, who, against his will, has been engaged by the Brazilian government through the narrator (also a diplomat stationed in China) to try to locate a photographer who disappeared while in Mongolia. All he has to go on is the diary of the disappeared man, describing his travels immediately preceding his disappearance. Carvalho lets us read the disappeared person's diary, in which we are treated to a description by someone attentive and intensely interested in the life around him, followed by the description of the diplomat sent in search of him, written while attempting to retrace the steps of the disappeared. The two narrators have completely different perspectives and observations, giving the reader two views of Mongolia side by side, with the view of the diplomat always being one of someone trying to guess the motions and unwritten thoughts of the other. This quest gives rise to much of the tension between the diplomat and his Mongolian guides. At one point the exasperated guide argues with his employer:

> You are asking me to make the same trip that he did six months ago. I am telling you that the course depends upon the people that we meet *en route*. In a country of

nomads, by definition, the people are never in the same place. They move with the seasons. The places are the persons. You are not looking for a place. You are looking for a person.

The descriptions in this novel must all be read with that tension in mind: the diplomat thinks and acts as a Brazilian diplomat, and the facts and interpretations given are never simply descriptions of facts. But what he narrates is just as often the beautiful as it is the troubling and disconcerting things that strike an outsider, but are simply the humdrum and everyday for those native to the place. It is therefore just as difficult to know how to respond to his descriptions of the behaviour of Buddhist monks and the treatment of women – topics that stand out in the book – as it is to judge the descriptions of environmental conditions and the behaviour of his Mongolian guides. Of *Mongólia* and another of his novels (*Nove noites*), Carvalho stated in an interview, 'These books are works of fiction. They are not chronicles of preceding realities, even though they deliberately generate a lot of confusion between fact and fiction' (Brizuela 2008). The reader eventually discovers that the book contains not merely two descriptions of Mongolia, but one which was written by a man lost, on the run and illegally in Mongolia, the other written by a man confident of his powers of observation and understanding, yet who never sees the obvious and understands nothing. Yet the differences between these two narratives go deeper:

> To a certain extent the disappeared and the occidental have a sinister affinity in their ethnocentric ideas. The difference, as I am coming to understand, is that the disappeared goes about trying to treat the world as his ally. He was more ingenious or optimistic. The occidental did not make that effort. The discomfort led him to assume as a matter of course an adversarial stance. He struggled with the world. (Carvalho 2003: 50)

Both narrators have left their descriptions and interpretations of the Mongolia of their encounters in diaries which the narrator of the novel then uses to reconstruct the story many years later – a third narrative.

In his brief remarks on *Mongólia*, Óscar Checa (2005) wrote

> The guiding idea, the compass, in this book is communication seen from multiple points of view: How to enter into relation with that which is strange to us? Are we capable of truly understanding? "We see only what we are disposed to see." Thus the search is an attempt to decipher and understand the Mongolian world that leads the characters to discover their own identity.

Granted that Carvalho's book is fiction, as much so as Basara's travel guide, any reader with experience in contemporary Mongolia will recognise Carvalho's Mongolia. While the reader may object that Carvalho's narrative voices have not understood the experiences they described, the question this book – as well as Petra Hůlová's *Paměť mojí babičce* – raises is whether the perspective of the foreigner and the traveller can lead a Mongolian reader to understand his/her own world better. It is not just the characters who discover themselves in their encounter with a foreign world, but that world also comes to see itself differently through the same encounter.

Petra Hůlová: *Paměť mojí babičce*

Petra Hůlová studied Mongolian civilisation at Charles University in Prague and lived in Mongolia in 2000–2001. *Paměť mojí babičce* was her first novel – which she published at the age of 23 – and it catapulted her to fame, garnering for her a reputation as a great writer that each of her subsequent novels has confirmed. It is a very disturbing book. Comprising autobiographical narratives of five women in one family, it provides intimate but fictional portraits of life in Mongolia now. In an interview, the author remarked 'No-one in Mongolia would have told me these things' (Anonymous 2012), but much of what she wrote is far too recognisable to dismiss as simply fantasy. In the narratives of their lives, these women reveal a world of family dynamics, generational conflicts, love, marriage, sex, the predicaments of being a woman, the life of children, ethnic conflict, poverty, violence, rape, prostitution, rural-urban migration and the trouble with being *erliiz* [of mixed parentage].

In an interview with radio Prague, Hůlová commented on her status as an outsider, noting that she was writing about how she understood the world in a way that she could not write about in a Czech setting–deciding to place the narrative in Mongolia was more a way of enabling her to write than a decision to write about Mongolia.[3] In an interview with Miroslav Balaštík (Balaštík & Hůlová 2006), Hůlová explained that she could not write about life as she did in a Czech setting because she needed some distance, a distance that Mongolia provided. 'It is not just "local colour" that inspires me, it has to do above all with the fact that as a stranger I perceive things in a more alert and more intense manner' (Hůlová in an interview with Sarah Flock and Richard Vacula, 2009). To the question 'Why was this story about important decisions in the life of women set in Mongolia?', she replied, 'Well, probably because I was there and had a strong experience with it' (Vohryzková & Hůlová 2002). In another interview, she stated:

> I think that I was always there as a foreigner, and they took me as a foreigner always, so, although I spent a year there I didn't break that wall that divides Mongolians from foreigners generally. I had a lot of friends there, and still I have a lot of friends there, but, I think I will always be for them something other, something

---

[3] Her latest novel is set in the Czech Republic and was 'inspired by a cleaning lady and my Mongolian friends who are trying to get by in the Czech Republic' (Kadlecová 2012).

strange, something that they may accept. But never as a part of their culture.

This book is my opinion in a certain time, now or a year ago, how the life is, how the world is. And for me it is about relations, about love, about disappointment, about bitterness, about such feelings, basic feelings for me, and in Mongolia I think life isn't polluted – maybe not the proper word – polluted by artificial phenomena like in Europe. Media, advertising, career maybe, so, if I set the story in a Czech setting I couldn't avoid writing about such things. But, I'm not interested in that, and I wanted somehow to write a rough, simple story about what life means to me. (Hůlová in an interview with Jan Velinger, 2003)

The question, then, is whether we are dealing with Mongols who are as unreal and imaginary as those populating a Clive Cussler novel, a government-dictated piece of propaganda or a children's cartoon. Basara was accused of writing about Serbia rather than Mongolia in *Mongolski bedeker*,[4] and the same accusation was made in regard to Hůlová. She responded to the accusation thus:

> It's not about the Czech Republic. It's about Mongolia, but – it's not only about the people and the characters. It's about the time, the era, the transition period that is similar for the whole region of post-Soviet countries. (Hůlová in an interview with Lisette Allen, 2009)

That explanation seems to fit her book well, and is probably just as true of Basara's. Hůlová also responded to questions from interviewers about her sincerity and the authenticity of her exposition of the points of view of others:

---

[4] http://www.calmeblog.com/article-basara-svetislav-guide-de-mongolie-mongolskibedeker-1992-traduit-en-2006-pour-les-editions-les97306693.html

I have nothing but myself and the possibility of imaging what others think and feel. obviously, I understand, see and imagine things too. (Hůlová in an interview with Sarah Flock and Richard Vacula, 2009)

As to Hůlová writing about Mongolia, the first two paragraphs of her book make her point clear:

When the shoro hits, plastic sacks go whipping round and round the ger. Sometimes I sit outside and watch the sand swirl as the horizon turns golden-brown and through the whirl of yellow dust the sun is dim and trembly. My shoes turn gray under the buildup of dust, a dust that stings people's eyes and crunches under the horses' hoofs, setting the whole herd on edge and making it hard on the yelping nochoi whose job it is to separate the in-foal mares with young from the rest.

When the shoro hits and there's nothing to do, since I can't see a step ahead and I'd choke to death outside, or not be able to find my way back, I sit out in front of the entrance to our ger, on the right, and wonder what it used to look like here in the days before there were plastic sacks, when families like us didn't have even a decent knife and couldn't improve their lot by selling crackers and cigarettes, the way our father did whenever someone happened to stumble across us. (Hůlová 2009: 1)

In another interview with radio Prague, Hůlová stated, 'While writing it I realized how much of Mongolia got into me during that stay and how many things I actually discovered there' (Vaughan 2007), and that seems to be exactly what happened: she experienced Mongolian social life as few travellers ever do. certainly there is nothing like her narrative in either Basara or Carvalho. Basara sees only the familiar old absurdities during his imaginary sojourn in Mongolia, while Carvalho offers the otherness of the world that impresses and often irritates the foreign tourist. Hůlová offers us Mongolia through the eyes of someone peering into the soul of Mongolia and seeing, not an exotic mystery, but the hard, harsh, and mostly unpleasant realities of the modern world, moving the reader to feel that Mongolia is indeed part of our world.

In Hůlová's Mongolia, love, disappointment, poverty, failure, conflict, prostitution and rape tear the families – and the reader – to pieces. Yet the most astonishing surprise of her novel is that none of the narratives of the five women are laments of lost and destroyed women. all of the women present their stories as how things were, as who they are. The narratives are full of judgments – this was bad, I hated these things, I will never forgive this person, I failed miserably, etc. – but all of the women accept themselves and their lives. The greatest failure of them all – Zaya, the *erliiz* – returns alone at the end of the book to her home out on the steppe, a grey-haired, middle-aged woman with nothing, completely rejected by her daughter for having been a prostitute and not welcomed by her sister. She sits in what used to be her deceased mother's *ger* and surveys the sun, the sand, the red mountains, the animals, the plants, the children, everything from her feet to the horizon, and says to herself: 'all this belongs to me'. She is at home: 'I know it here'. It is a stunning affirmation of life by a complete failure, and in that affirmation one understands the whole of her narrative, as also the narratives of her relatives: the 'all this' is not just what she sees, but who she is, 'all this' is her story. 'All this belongs to me. Zaya of Bashkgan *somon*'.

Mongolia orientalised? Fictional Mongols and real readers
In *Orientalism* (2003), Edward Said argued that occidental orientalists have consistently reproduced the viewpoints expressed in the writings of their predecessors, rather than allowing their scholarly opinions to be formed through their encounters with the object of their research, the Orient and its peoples. In its simplest form, Said's argument was that orientalists had read too much while loving too little. It was a devastating critique that

many of his readers quickly realised applied to every branch of study, not just the study of Asia. It was an immensely influential argument which went well beyond the confines of academic life and looked at the connections among scholars, travellers, poets, government and business. Of particular importance for present purposes was his appraisal of the representation of oriental peoples and civilisations in western literary works.

Said insisted that literary representations were an important element in the construction and maintenance of Orientalism, this being understood as a discourse that had long silenced the voices of those represented, and continued to do so. The writings of poets and novelists consolidate and reproduce that discourse in ways that scholarship rarely does, embedding the orientalist discourse ever more deeply within occidental culture. Roy Harris (2004) made a related claim when he argued that literary representations were important for our understanding of history, since they play a significant role in the assumptions and orientations of the historians themselves: Shakespeare, Harris claimed, has long been and remains the most influential historian of England.

Said opened *Orientalism* with the claim 'I believe no one writing, thinking, or acting on the Orient could do so without taking account of the limitations on thought and action imposed by Orientalism' (2003: 3). He further insisted that 'for a European or American studying the Orient there can be no disclaiming the main circumstances of his actuality: that he comes up against the Orient as a European or American first, as an individual second' (2003: 11). Yet he immediately qualified the earlier statement with the note 'This is not to say that Orientalism unilaterally determines what can be said about the Orient' (ibid.) adding on the next page, 'if we eliminate from the start any notion that "big" facts like imperial domination can be applied mechanically and deterministically to such complex matters as culture and ideas, then we will begin to approach an interesting kind of study' (2003: 12). With these statements he introduced an extraordinary tension into the practice of reading as well as writing, and left an enormous opening for discussion and debate.

In the preface to the 25th anniversary edition of *Orientalism*, Said recounted his two main arguments. His first argument was

> that history is made by men and women, just as it can also be unmade and rewritten, always with various silences and elisions, always with shapes imposed and disfigurements tolerated, so that 'our' East, 'our' Orient becomes 'ours' to possess and direct (Said 2003: xviii)

and his second

> that there is a difference between knowledge of other peoples and other times that is the result of understanding, compassion, careful study and analysis for their own sakes, and on the other hand knowledge – if that is what it is – that is part of an overall campaign of self-affirmation, belligerency, and outright war. There is, after all, a profound difference between the will to understand for purposes of coexistence and humanistic enlargement of horizons, and the will to dominate for the purposes of control and external domination. (Said 2003: xix)

If, as Said argued

> Orientalism is premised upon the exteriority, that is, on the fact that the orientalist, poet or scholar, makes the Orient speak, describes the Orient, renders its mysteries plain for and to the West. He is never concerned with the Orient except as the first cause of what he says ... The exteriority of the representation is always governed by some version of the truism that if the Orient could represent itself, it would; since it cannot, the representation

> does the job, for the West, and *faute de mieux*, for the poor Orient. (Said 2003: 20–21)

then we can indeed read an author with our minds open and actively searching for this exteriority and the concerns he associates with it. However, if we wish to understand writing, writing is only half of the story: there remains another side of the story, and that is the reader. Said himself has opened the door to such an orientation with his remarks concerning the reception of his own book:

> Nine years ago I wrote an afterword for *Orientalism* which, in trying to clarify what I believed I had and had not said, stressed not only the many discussions that had opened up since my book appeared in 1978, but the ways in which a work about representations of 'the Orient' lent itself to increasing misinterpretation. (Said 2003: xv)

In his insistent focus on the claims to authority implicitly or explicitly made among the authors he studied, Said rarely discussed the readers' attitudes to those claims other than to argue over and over again – as in the quotations above – that the authority was accepted, promulgated throughout the culture and perpetuated up to our time. In only one passage – a passage that reveals a great deal – Said offers a brief note on language and representation:

> Another reason for insisting upon exteriority is that I believe it needs to be made clear about cultural discourse and exchange within a culture that what is commonly circulated by it is not 'truth' but representations. It hardly needs to be demonstrated again that language itself is a highly organized and encoded system, which employs many devices to express, indicate, exchange messages and information, represent, and so forth. In any instance

> of at least written language, there is no such thing as a delivered presence, but a *re-presence*, or a representation. The value, efficacy, strength, apparent veracity of a written statement about the Orient therefore relies very little, and cannot instrumentally depend, on the Orient as such. On the contrary, the written statement is a presence to the reader by virtue of its having excluded, displaced, and made superogatory any such *real thing* as 'the Orient'. (Said 2003: 21)

If, indeed, language must exclude, displace and make superogatory the real world, and if it is language – rather than the writer or speaker – that employs, expresses, indicates, exchanges messages and represents, then all authors are off the hook, as are all readers. Yet of course this cannot be the case, for we know that readers misunderstand and thus must be involved in the creation of meaning, not merely in its transportation or 'circulation'. Said himself noted that he found it 'ironic' that his book 'lent itself to increasing misinterpretation' (2003: xv). If readers interpret what they read, then the authority claimed by a writer or a critic writing of the writer is always a matter the reader must deal with as an individual in the first instance, rather than after having matters determined by a socially determined identity: we are human beings before we are Americans or Mongolians.

In *Orientalism*, Said presented a very unpleasant – and largely convincing – account of many scholars, statesmen and literary figures who have accepted the authority of a text about the Orient and let that authority override their actual experience in and of the Orient, which is the real moral evil that Said decried. There is, Said noted, 'a rather complex dialectic of reinforcement by which the experiences of readers in reality are determined by what they have read' (Said 2003: 94). Those readers who prefer the authority of what they read, of 'Orientalism' (or 'science') over their own experience, have read too much and loved too little. If readers are not passive agents reproducing a language that speaks for them – as Said's Orientalist speaks for the Oriental who cannot him or herself speak – then the measure of how much 'authority' a text carries and how much it attempts to silence the represented other through representation is a matter that can be easily studied by reading the responses of readers of that text. We can ask of the writers: Is experience 'dislodged by a dictionary definition' (Said 2003: 155)? Does an author 'form a circle sealing off him and his audience from the world at large', as Said (2003: 125) wrote of Sacy? Is her purpose 'dominating and mediating everything we are told about the Orient' (Said 2003: 168)? Or does the author strive to give 'a lively sense of an Oriental's human or even social reality – as a contemporary inhabitant of the modern world' (Said 2003: 176)? While these are the questions Said asked, there is a further question that literary works present to the reader, namely, is the work 'about' the Orient (or Mongolia) at all?

These questions are not simply questions to put to the authors; if we are to understand an author's actual influence and authority we must attend to that author's readers. Said did this for his authors and their readers and was not happy with what he found. Do the authors considered here fare better? For Basara, Carvalho and Hůlová, are 'the racial, ethnic, and national distinctions ... less important than the common enterprise of promoting human community' (Said 2003: 328)? Do their readers reproduce that discourse or question and criticise it?

It is in Said's recognition of the possibility of knowing 'other peoples and other times' for purposes of coexistence rather than domination that I see the best manner in which to understand the novels of Basara, Carvalho and Hůlová. It would no doubt be possible to select certain passages from the novels (and other writings and interviews) of Basara, Carvalho and Hůlová which could then be presented as evidence of more of the same old Orientalism.[5] Yet, if we wish to understand a book in relation to its readers, it is necessary to consider responses to

---

[5] Some readers of these novels have posed the question in other terms, but I found no references to Said in any publications related to these three books.

each book read as a whole. If the claim is to be made that the authors are 'sealing off the audience from the world at large' and 'dominating and mediating everything we are told' about Mongolia, then such a claim needs to be supported by evidence that the readers of these works understand them to be representing 'the real Mongolia' and doing so with a voice claiming authority. In the pages that follow, responses to these three novels in the writings of academics, literary critics, book reviewers, bloggers and one anonymous orientalist will be examined, with an eye to how they read, prior assumptions, expectations, and attitudes towards Mongolia, fiction and the authority of the authors. The object of the following survey of readers will be to see whether there is any evidence of Mongols silenced by authoritative representation, or whether there is evidence of a wide range of engagements and understandings.

Reading Basara's *Mongolski bedeker*

> What is great about Basara's fiction is that, like any truly new advent, it arrives as if detached from any world outside its own, yet simultaneously it proves an organic outgrowth from the most hidden recesses of our reality. (Davis-Van Atta 2012)

The reader of travel literature, and especially of travel guidebooks, assumes a presentation of facts relevant to the time of travel, either the author's or the reader's. No one seeks an outdated travel guide in order to prepare for a journey, though one may well peruse old travel guides in order to acquire some knowledge of the particulars pertaining to a particular time. Basara's *bedeker* is however of another sort: those portions of his novel that read like a travel guide serve principally to ensure that the reader understands that the book contains no description, no facts, in fact, that it is no guide book at all.

Mongolia is one of those places about which we have so little knowledge that when someone explains anything at all we have no other option but to believe it. Playing with this advantage, the Serbian author Svetislav Basara wrote this delirious, absurd and apparently philosophical guide to Mongolia that is complete nonsense. For in reality it is not a guide but a novel. (Mas 2010)

The first thing then is to see whether this description of Mongolia, its steppes, its camels, its horses, its yurts, its laments and its mountains, is accurate. ... In the end, there is no travel guide. Of Mongolia, there is nothing. Nor are there any Mongols. Its significance is elsewhere. (Josse 2007)

Writing in a blog devoted to travel literature, Briongos warned the readers:

> regarding this *Guide to Mongolia* I shall say simply that it has nothing to recommend it as a source of information for travellers and that it is inappropriate for anyone hoping to find advice and knowledge for taking a trip to that country. (Briongos 2010)

Any reader who approaches *Mongolski bedeker* with assumptions appropriate to a handbook for travellers will respond in a manner similar to the anonymous orientalist who reviewed the novel in *Observatorio Asia Central* (the only review that I could find in an academic publication devoted to oriental studies):

> In light of this, what could be the reason for a subscriber to *Observatorio Asia Central* to read this guide to Mongolia? The reason would be, like the novel, metaphorical: Mongolia is the great forgotten place in central Asia. In light of this novel, it does not even seem that the author tried to produce an unusual guidebook, but that he had a

contract with a publishing house [to write a guidebook] but decided not to write it, writing something else instead, keeping only the title. (Anonymous 2010)

That review in *Observatorio Asia Central* was the only review that criticised the book for not being a factual account of Mongolia (as the orientalist reviewer understood it). In every other review I read, Basara's Mongolia was understood to be a country of the imagination:

> Basara has not written a travel book, he has written about the reality that we believe we see ... Basara speaks of fishmongers hiding in brothels, of communist governments, of reality distorted. (Elchicoanalogo 2012)

> By definition, something that calls itself a guide one supposes to be real and truthful. Nevertheless, there are parts of this book that appear to belong to the literature of fantasy. Thus, Basara refers to some laws and customs of the country that we would describe as pertaining to the realm of the absurd. (Artacho Reyes 2012)

> Mongolia is not a country situated between the former Soviet Union and China and having two million inhabitants ... Nor is its capitol Ulan Bator that one found on maps. It is a territory between the chaplinesque and the dark ... Furthermore, *Mongolski bedeker* is not a guide to Mongolia. It is of little importance if the world described no longer exists because it never existed beforehand. (Pinedo 2010)

If Basara does not give us a guidebook nor even a travelogue, if what he presents to the reader is a book in which the real Mongolia and real Mongols do not appear at all, then what is the significance of *his* Mongolia and Mongols? 'We have a right to ask what truth value we can assign to what the narrator relates',

Landry (2009) remarked, 'because the narrator is obviously making it all up'. Those who have reviewed and commented on *Mongolski bedeker* differ widely on how to interpret the book. For some, like Monasevda (2012) and Paquin (2007), Basara's Mongolia is 'a Mongolia that is nothing but pretext and subterfuge' whose author 'the darling child of Serbian literature poses the question of mimesis and that grand illusion that is the world we see', suggesting to Paquin that 'Basara realizes that fictions have influenced human evolution more than the so-called facts of history' (Paquin 2007).

Both Boer and Lévrier point out that within the novel the narrator (Basara himself) claims that his trip to Mongolia was finally undertaken not simply in deference to his deceased friend's wishes, but that 'it was nothing but a matter of finding material for writing his novel' (Lévrier 2009). And at this point in the novel, Lévrier notes, 'the delirium begins ... Where is the dream, and where does reality begin? Basara goes even further than Murakami in that game' (Lévrier 2009). Boer claimed that the book 'led me to ask myself where I had landed' (Boer n.d.).

A frequent remark is that the book blurs the boundaries of dream and reality, and not only through the consumption of alcohol. '*Mongolian dreams* is no realistic story' Peter (2012) remarked in reference to the title of the Dutch translation *Mongoolse dromen*. Hérault (2009) acknowledged that 'as to Mongolia, it quickly becomes a very improbable kind of country', but insists that Basara offers us 'magnificent digressions on the decadence of our societies rotting from consumerism ... and the comic ineptitude of communist bureaucracy'. Frieling (2008) described *Mongolski bedeker* as gonzo journalism, claiming that Basara's parody of socialism among the heirs of Chinggis Khan is a fiction that is 'is closer to the truth and more convincing in every sense'. Boisvert (2009) urged the reader to 'take the time to savour this book and not be distracted by this imaginary world that Basara offers us', for that would distract us from the truth that is hidden behind his text.

If the Orientalist claims to speak as an authority on behalf of the oriental other, what sort of authority do Basara's readers ascribe to Basara? Basara's Mongolia is the pure product of a dream, Rossini (2012) concludes, and if the book states that 'Mongolia is a pile of shit we must remember that its author is an expert' [on shit], adding that 'In reality, Basara does not speak of anything but Basara'. For Monasevda, Basara is an expert on late socialism and vodka is his muse: 'This is not a travel guide, but ... a lucid reflection on the absurdity of a system (communist) and an ode to vodka' (Monasevda 2011).

Perhaps the clearest indication that Basara's Mongolia is not the closed representation of the other resting upon the author's claims to authority – the situation that Said objected to – is the existence of such radically different interpretations as those of Menéndez Salmón (2010), Jongeling (2010) and Bonnargent (2011):

> *Mongolski bedeker*, as its exotic label seems to suggest, is not a Baedeker for a traveler. Nor does it hide a bucolic pastoral, ecojournalism, a philosophical treatise, a novel of local color or a compendium of demonology ... Basara's text hides a wise reflection on the direction that literature can take ... [a] ferocious, caustic and extremely original book that, one more time, in case it has not already become clear, refutes the verdict that hell is other people (Menéndez Salmón 2010)

> [Basara's] concerns are real political and religious systems that are made by human hands. (Jongeling 2010)

> *Mongolski bedeker* is not at all a tourist guide; it is nothing other than a violent pamphlet against humanity ... For an occidental, Mongolia is a non-place, it is beyond the world and [it may seem that] this is where Basara begins. This is also what those Basara meets in Ulaanbaatar think. But this would be a great deception.

> Mongolia appears above all as a place like any other ... In the end Mongolia is revealed as the worst of places, for it is the delusional substance of the world. (Bonnargent 2011)

Basara's readers disagree on how to understand *Mongolski bedeker*, and it is precisely that disagreement and the questions that readers asked of his book which suggests that Basara was not engaged in 'orientalizing Mongolia', of silencing Mongolia through some authoritative representation. What Basara once claimed to be writing about is chaos:

> I do not know a better definition of chaos. Uncombinables are combined, and what could be united is split apart everywhere around the world; among us overreaction and extremism. And this is the result of endemic Orientalism. (Basara in an interview with Zoran Radisavljević, 2010)

What that may or may not have to do with Mongolia, Basara leaves entirely up to the reader to think about. The best thing one can say about the book is that readers have been thinking about what it means rather than accepting it as a representation of some facts about Mongolia.

> Svetislav Basara refreshes our view of the world and rudely shakes our comfortable Western ways. (Argoul 2009)

Reading Carvalho's *Mongólia*

Every edition and translation of Carvalho's *Mongólia* that I consulted includes a map of Mongolia, a map similar in every respect to one that could be consulted in any atlas except for indications of the routes of Buruu nomton and The Occidental as they are narrated in the novel. Despite this, Carvalho insists that the Mongolia of his novel is an imaginary country.

> With *Mongólia*, readers thought that what was there was a real country. In a lecture in Goiânia, there was a teacher who had printed a handout with all the geographic data of Mongolia: population, per capita income, etc. I told her that the Mongolia of the novel is an imaginary country, that I invented it. My guide, for example, hated the book because it was not Mongolia. It's the same if a foreigner were to come to Brazil and write a fantasy about this country. (Carvalho, quoted in Araújo 2009: 91)

With his novel *Mongólia*, Taufer writes, 'Carvalho elicits the most different reactions in his readers because of the themes which he treats – travel, cultural shock and the sense of alterity, among others – depending upon the aesthetic tastes and literary maturity of each reader, he can elicit loathing, censure, criticism, praise and ecstasy' (2007: 4).

Like the teacher in Goiânia, Belém Barbosa (2004) described *Mongólia* as 'a novel that mixes travelogue, research on the history, economy and politics of Mongolia with the detective novel' and the Italian edition was even published in a series of travel books (Feltrinelli Traveller). Other readers have understood the book to be much more about the possibilities and difficulties of encounter and cross- cultural understanding than a book of travel or a narrative of Mongolia.

> It is a revision of the 'serene' concepts of the other, stripped of all forms of romanticism or of the banal fruit of travel as the bourgeois discovery of distant lands ... the traveler is marked by a curious and tragic inability to comprehend the other. (D'angelo 2008: 89)

Bewilderment, incomprehension and 'a certain humility before the foreign' (Döbler 2007) are the chief matters noted by many readers.

> Inverting the associations that link 'orientation' to 'Orient,' in *Mongólia* the Orient disorients the [character called] Occidental. (Nunez 2008)

Mata (2005: 1) argued that for Carvalho 'It is impossible to narrate facts, since reality is incomprehensible and "to remember is to imagine"'. Whereas Naves (2011) writes of Carvalho's 'obsessive search for the exotic', D'Angelo claims (2008: 88–9) that 'Carvalho parodies the manner of mystical, exotic travels in order to open up a space for reflection on nomadism and the allegorical meaning of the philosophical search'. There are descriptions of Mongolia, but instead of a travelogue readers of *Mongólia* find a drama of incomprehension. Rettig (2007) understood the narrative to circle round 'the ambivalence of violence, the incomprehensibility of the stranger, the search for the absent'. Given the structure of the novel as one where a narrator tries to reconstruct the past events through the two diaries of travel in a land where the narrator has never been, Ferreira suggested that 'a reading of *Mongólia* (and in general, of Bernardo Carvalho), is an incitement to redescription' (2009: 22).

In essay after essay, blog after blog, readers of *Mongólia* noted the contrasting situations and attitudes of the photographer (called Buruu nomton by the Mongols who knew him) and the diplomat trying to find him (called The Occidental by the Mongols):

> The lost photographer is called *Buruu nomton* (the maladjusted) because he does not conform to either the Mongolian order of things nor to the occidental order. (Mata 2005: 10)

> The Occidental –as the nomads call him– displays his ignorance about the Orient. (Giron 2003)

> The other awakens horror in the Occidental, whose hands are almost always tied due to his inability to adapt

> himself to cultural differences, differences of language and culture above all. (Taufer 2007: 8)
>
> If the Occidental privileges the monologue, the photographer prioritizes the dialogue. (Taufer 2007: 10)
>
> Combining distinct narratives (of the disappeared photographer, the Occidental and the diplomat who sent the Occidental on his journey) [the narrator] does not present a truth, but in his effort at understanding the narratives, becomes convinced of it. (Mata 2005: 17)

Carvalho does not give 'a lively sense of an oriental's human or even social reality – as a contemporary inhabitant of the modern world' (Said 2003: 176). What he does instead is to 'demonstrate what one could call a typical ethnocentrism of Occidental civilization' (Taufer 2007: 5). While Carvalho's Brazilians in Mongolia are recognisably real and recognisably ethnocentric westerners, his Mongolia is not – at least not for many readers. 'The country of the book [*Mongólia*] is fictitious' (Chaves 2009). Bruno Brasil (2007) took great offence, comparing Carvalho's Mongolia to Rio de Janeiro in *The Simpsons* television show: 'The Mongolia presented in his pages is only an imaginary country (on the level of Rio de Janeiro appearing in a polemical episode of The Simpsons, except without the irony)'. Carvalho's Mongolia is 'a no-place that literature attempts to "situate" fictitiously' (D'angelo 2008: 92).

> To this conception of space, as an indefinite and non-defined place, corresponds a disarticulation of plot and of writing: three narrators, three typologies of different writing, three subjective views on Mongolian reality aim to dissolve and alter the fictional representation. There is no longer a center nor a destiny ... The distance between the occidental and the Mongolian reality is revealed as unbridgeable. (D'angelo 2008: 93)

Araújo (2009: 22) reported that, during a talk at Universidade Federal de Minas gerais in 2007, Carvalho claimed 'that his displacements around the world did not follow the tradition of the writer-traveller who relates what he saw, but insisted that his creative project makes a short-circuit provoked by contact between his subjectivity and the place visited'. As Frateschi Vieira read *Mongólia*, it is this real encounter that underwrites Carvalho's novel, producing 'a lucid and intelligent view that does not succumb to an easy fascination with other "exotic" alternatives' (Frateschi Vieira 2005: 219).

Reading Hůlová's *Paměť' mojí babičce*

According to her own testimony, in this novel Hůlová was writing about how she saw life, in particular the dynamics of family life. Eriksson (2012) wrote of the novel that it is 'based on a couple of conflicts at the thematic level: between generations, and between urban and rural areas', seeing in it not a book about Mongolia but a book about these social relations. Gregorová (2003) asked, 'What is the reason that her book reads so easily, naturally and almost in the same breath?', answering her question with the remark 'Perhaps because the author hit the nail right on the head for the reader who is looking between the lines for the eternal, unchanging truths [about life]'. Bigosowa and Ready also understood the novel in that way, emphasizing that Hůlová has not offered a detailed look at local colour:

> The author does not spin tales of the culture and customs of Mongolia. She shows us modern life, the contemporary modern pursuit of happiness, difficult relationships between family members. This makes the novel universal and does not focus only on introducing the reader to the intricacies of a different culture. (Bigosowa 2011)

> *Czas czerwonych gór* [Time of the red Mountains, the title of the Polish translation], however, is not a documentary about Mongolian customs, but a story about

> family relationships, full of tension, arguments, and often ill-concealed secrets ... objective truth is not the important thing. What counts are the emotions and prejudices that mothers, daughters and sisters feed themselves, because they shape the outlook of the heroines. (Ready 2009)

The personal interests and attitudes clearly determined what some readers found in the book and how they interpreted it:

> For me, it is a book with a magical touch, it enabled me to think about how to create a bond between people. (Kmentová 2002)

> Hůlová examines female identity in a society that is still tied to its patriarchal functions, a world where violence against women perpetrated and perpetuated appears as something 'normal' to the women themselves. (More 2012)

In his review of the German translation *Kurzer Abriss meines Lebens in der mongolischen Steppe* [A brief summary of my life in the Mongolian steppe], Wilde (2007) used the marvellous phrase 'against the simplification of the world' to describe the novel, adding that 'the longer you follow the melody of the novel, the more the impression of naivety fades ... Hůlová does not give in to the seductively simple contradiction of alienated urban life and happier country idyll'. His understanding of the novel as being a novel 'against the simplification of the world' seems to go against Hůlová's statement that she wanted to write a simple tale, but only apparently, for a simple tale need not require the simplification of the world and perhaps requires a profound complexity.

Yet other readers *have* seen in the novel straightforward representations of contemporary Mongolia, or have assumed or believed that the novel depicts social relations as they are in Mongolian society today.

> Petra Hůlová's writing is very fluid, dynamic and able to carry the reader through worlds that do not belong to him, accompanying the reader inside a ger, a diner and brothels in the city, she succeeds in giving voice to different characters. (Francesca 2012)

> Hůlová offers a penetrating look at relationships between mothers and daughters, and between sisters. great bonds, but also tension and antagonism, exist between the women as their secrets and silences feed countless misunderstandings and misconceptions. The book is candid about the devastating effects of alcoholism, prostitution, and social and racial alienation in the old Mongolia in the mountain, and in the modern evolving Mongolia in the city. (Gaibie-Dawood 2010)

> A friend of mine, who was also in the country [Mongolia], said she recognized it in the book, and that's what makes it worth writing about – it's not exactly often that we can get an insight into ordinary people's lives on the other side earth, in a part of the world we rarely even hear about on the news – Mongolia. (Elmerot 2011)

> Praised for its compelling depiction of a part of the world that remains both geographically and culturally remote, Hůlová successfully pulls off the feat of writing in the first person as a Mongolian woman while herself being Czech, a fact seen by some as 'puzzling ? weird and suspicious', Hůlová says. ... Although based in Mongolia's main city, she also made trips into the countryside; indeed, one of the strengths of her novel is its vivid portrayal of the clash between the two opposing

worlds of the remote steppe and the nightmarishly bleak city. (Allen 2009)

> There is no doubt that Petra Hulova knows Mongolia in every detail – the fragrant, tough, rugged life in the white tents on the steppe, yurts heated by fire from manure, as well as the equally harsh life in the country's only city, Ulaanbaatar. But it is a totally convincing, extremely empathetic portrayal of women entrenched in its culture and its geography … touching the core of existence. … And you sit there and stare at the meaning of life straight in the eye. (Arnald 2012)

In her thesis, Pavla Soukopová stated that the novel 'shows the reality of contemporary Mongolian society, built upon the contrast between good and evil' (2007: 33), but followed this statement a few pages later with the remark 'it might seem that the text is mainly based on the exotic environment of Mongolia, but the opposite is true. This asian country has become a mere backdrop' (2007: 44).

One blogger provided just the kind of reading that Said traced throughout the history of Orientalism. Mandżuria (the blogger's pen name) acknowledged reading the book due to an old desire to learn about Mongolia, and set forth her existing ideas about Mongolia, her attitude toward the Mongolia presented in the novel and her re-description of what she has read. She also notes her deferential attitude towards Hůlová as a mongolist:

> I have long been attracted to Mongolia, still wild and inaccessible, yet so little known. I wanted to know more about Mongolian culture and customs, and an additional incentive [for reading the book] was the fact that 'Red Mountain Time' is a novel of manners, showing the everyday life of the residents of Mongolia and trying to penetrate into their mentality. Ideally, this would be a

book written by a native Mongolian, but this debut novel is by Petra Hůlová, a mongolist who spent a lot of time in this country, so I think you can trust her when she writes about the realities of the modern steppe and the city of Ulaanbaatar.

Mongolia in 'Red Mountain Time' is an inaccessible country, of ravishing beauty and rugged landscape, but also a land of overwhelmingly strict customs, lack of respect for human dignity and where everyday life is full of harsh realities. (Mandżuria 2009)

The question that this reader raises is how much her attitudes were formed by her reading of Hůlová's novel and how much were they formed by other elements of her experience? Mandżuria was not the only reader to refer to Hůlová's authority as a mongolist and visitor to Mongolia (see Strebel (2008) and Imani (2012) among others), but she was the only reader to associate such descriptions as 'strict customs' and 'lack of respect for human dignity' to the real Mongolia rather than to the novel. In more detail than Mandżuria, Bigosowa (2011) also described the ideas about Mongolia which she entertained prior to reading the novel:

When I think of Mongolia I see the vastness of Mongolia and the earth, the horizon on one side sets up the sky on the other. I see smiling small eyed people, colorfully dressed, riding small horses and rushing ahead. My image of Mongolia, as I imagine it, comes from watching documentaries on the Travel Program and deep-rooted stereotypes: Mongolia–steppe–round tents–smiling people–time that is not flowing–a world that does not change. (Bigosowa 2011)

Unlike Mandżuria (2009), Bigosowa (whose response to the novel was quoted above) did not have her preconceptions about

Mongolia confirmed, nor did she take from her reading a new image of Mongolia, but of 'modern life'.

Certain readers, rather than seeing accurate depictions of Mongolia in the novel, have asked just how accurate these depictions might be:

> Czech Petra Hůlová who studied Mongolian and cultural studies and spent a lot of time in Mongolia, has decided to take the risky approach of showing us another country through the eyes of native inhabitants of those lands. Does she do this accurately? I have mixed feelings ... (Imani 2012)

In an interview, Hůlová mentioned a review that appeared in the Mongolian press which was highly critical of her for writing about prostitution and poverty, but she noted also that she had 'also received some positive responses from Mongols who told me that it would be magnificent if a Mongol were to write such a book' (Flock & Vacula 2009).[6]

A more critical group of readers have asked, not how closely her characters reveal Mongolian society, but how well they reveal Czech society, a question arising inevitably for any reader who has encountered the author's own remarks on this subject.

> Yet while this european author's novel may seem to reinforce Western assumptions about the oppressed lives of women in developing countries, the representations here are not straightforward. Hůlová has said that her characters and the realities they face were modeled on Czech subjects, transported in fiction to a distant setting, where their emotions and relationships might be pursued

---

[6] Without having located that Mongolian review, the only further comment that I can make regarding it is that the Mongolian author of that review could not have criticised the book on the basis of the absence of prostitution and poverty in Mongolia.

in a purer form uncluttered by European ephemera. The seemingly authentic Mongolian characters, European projections onto an Asian landscape, are in fact ambiguous cultural hybrids. Their experiences of racism and sexism reflect not only on the Mongolian society Hůlová appears to scrutinize, but also on the Czech one that informs her subject matter. (Clements 2010)

How much more difficult to invent characters in a culture not your own, and keep them true to themselves. Unless you don't. Unless, these are actually Czech women and men in essence, transported to exist in a faraway land ...

By and about women, yes, but is this all real? It's a fiction of course, but fiction for most of us is a way of revealing the real, a way to enter into stories about those things that are not so visible or which tighten up the diffuse until a shape and a substance appears to that which was only dimly known before ... It kept gnawing at me: are these actually Mongolian women? These many women in a family gone to prostitution? Another one, also a love-child, a lesbian? A man without any described qualities – Mergen – the love object, and kept man for at least three of them? Do these conditions actually exist in the big cities of Mongolia? Or is Petra Hulova talking about Czech experiences? And if so, why dress them as Mongols? ...

Some Mongolian readers might, of course, feeling [sic] misrepresented by her images. But art is art. Art is always a mixing of the un-familiar with the familiar. Where would we be had Picasso and Matisse not stolen Japanese and African art and integrated it into their own? (Kirkland 2011)

Some readers of Hůlová's novel have asked themselves – and the author herself – if her stories of Mongolian women were based on interviews. one blogger wrote that she suspected that 'Petra Hůlová listened to more than one woman's story during her stay in the Mongolian steppe' (chiara76 2012), but asked directly in an interview, Hůlová claimed that she had made no interviews, that she began writing the novel because she 'was not in good shape psychologically' and had so much free time while in Mongolia that she needed to orient herself to keep her thoughts from turning round and round upon themselves (Flock & Vacula 2009).

To ask whether the characters in the novel were based upon interviews is a question about the real Mongolia more than a question about the fictional Mongolia. The question requires an approach to the novel which desires either to discern the real Mongolia as the origin of the fictional Mongolia, or to deny it. At least one reader assumed that the novel must be a 'testament' concerning the real Mongolia, and criticised the novel on precisely that point:

> Yet here the novel stumbles upon a major pitfall that is hard to avoid: that of ethnocentrism. Not that the world painted by the author is inconsistent or that it seems to betray the Mongolian cultural reality, but the psychological dimension of the narrative strongly places the reader in a difficult situation: he must trust the author, who claims to offer raw testament, a deeply rooted experience in the culture, one not mediated through the occidental thinking of a young czech woman. (Meunier 2006)

Another reader felt that Hůlová had avoided the 'pitfall' of ethnocentrism:

> Books written about any culture, about the 'foreign', the outsider, always arouse my attention. It is extremely difficult to resist evaluation, explaining through the imposition of patterns and filtered through the lens of the writer's own culture. Hůlová managed to avoid that.
> (Anonymous 2007)

In her comments on Clements (2010), a review of the English translation, Hüblová (2010) saw Hůlová as a postcolonial writer, but her comments on Clements' review reveal something even more interesting: readers of Hůlová (and of Basara and Carvalho) are not simply reading Hůlová and thereby restricting themselves to her view and her authority as a writer, however they may understand that. Readers are reading these novels and reading critical appraisals of them at the same time; reading and understanding do not occur in isolation from the world of experience and cultural debate.

Hüblová's remarks are also interesting for noting what no others among those I consulted mentioned: the legitimacy that European (white) writers from postcolonial countries have as postcolonial writers about 'the other' postcolonial countries. She suggests that there is an imbalance between 'writers from former colonies, who are allowed to write – if possible colorfully and folkloristically – about their own environment' (Hüblová 2010) and what readers and critics allow the postcolonial writers of Europe to write.

Conclusion

Every encounter is an encounter with an Other, and every encounter made influences how we approach every subsequent encounter. This applies to our reading as much as to our everyday life. The Other is not just the Oriental; the Other is everyone else in our history and experience. It is not true that we encounter the Other first as an American or a European; we encounter the Other as a being constituted by a lifetime of encounters unique to ourselves and no other. And every encounter with the Other is an encounter on both sides, an encounter in which all involved have the opportunity to see themselves in a way that is only possible through encounter, through the world with an Other. To refuse that encounter is to refuse life, to deny the existence of the world beyond oneself. The value of each encounter, its meaning and consequences for all involved is never determined by one person alone, but unfolds over time through histories of interaction. Some encounters are fruitful, producing creative responses, children and entire civilizations, while other encounters produce death and devastation. Dialogue and monologue, love and hate, birth and death: these are the extremes between which our encounters take place. Different as they are, the three novels discussed above are all exemplary cases of responses to an encounter with Mongolia and the Mongols, even if only – as in the case of Basara – the Mongols of hearsay and historiography. Those who have read these novels and written about them have provided ample evidence that they did not encounter a closed discourse that authoritatively represented the Mongolian Others; rather they encountered three books that set their minds and imaginations to reflecting on life, love, family, communism, and what Mongolian society might be like.

What originally interested me about these three novels and led me to write of them is that in them Mongolia is not some place far away and long ago, nor is it the superficial background for an adventure, a socialist morality tale, a pot-boiler romance or a bedtime story for christian boys and girls. Mongolia is a place here and now, in a world that we inhabit together. Yet the Mongolia of these novels is in every case a fictional Mongolia, not a description of that land between Russia and China. In spite of that, and unlike most earlier literary works set among Mongols, those unacquainted with contemporary Mongolia no less than those familiar with it can recognise many things in these imagined Mongolias, for the otherness of Mongolia and the Mongolian people has become the otherness of our contemporaries in Basara, our neighbours in Carvalho, and our family in Hůlová.

References

Светислав Басара. *Монголски бедекер.* Београд. Нолит, 1992; reprinted: 1993 (Нолит), 1997 (Народна књига), 1998 (*Дерета*)
Dutch: *Mongoolse dromen*. Breda: De Geus, 2010.
English: *Mongolian Travel Guide*. Dallas: Dalkey Archive, 2019.
French: *Guide de Mongolie*. Montreal: Les Allusifs, 2007; Paris: 10-18, 2008.
German: *Führer in die innere Mongolei*. München : Antje Kunstmann Verlag, 2008.
Italian: *Mongolski bedeker*. Macerata: Quodlibet, 2009.
Spanish: *Guía de Mongolia*. Barcelona: Minúscula, 2010.

Bernardo Carvalho. *Mongólia*. São Paulo, Brazil: Companhia das Letras, 2003; Lisboa: Cotovia, 2003
French: *Mongolia*. Paris: Métailié, 2004.
German: *Mongólia*. München: Luchterhand, 2007.
Italian: *Mongolia*. Milano: Feltrinelli, 2005.
Serbian: *Mongolija*. Beograd : Laguna, 2008.

Petra Hůlová. *Paměť mojí babičce*. Praha: Torst, 2002.
Dutch: *Mijn Grootmoeder*. Amsterdam: Prometheus, 2004.
English: *All this belongs to me*. Evanston: Northwestern University Press, 2009.
French: *Les montagnes rouge*. Paris: Editions de L'Olivier, 2005.
German: *Kurzer Abriss meines Lebens in der mongolischen Steppe*. München: Luchterhand, 2007.
Hungarian: *Nagyanyám emlékezete*. Budapest: Európa Könyvkiadó, 2004.
Italian: *Tutto questo mi appartiene*. Milano: Baldini Castoldi Dalai editore, 2012.
Polish: *Czas Czerwonych Gór*. Warszawa: Wydawnictwa WAB, 2007.
Swedish: *Allt detta tillhör mig* . Malmö: Rámus förlag, 2011.

Allen, Lisette. 2009. Telling a foreign tale in a foreign tongue. *The Prague Post* September 30, 2009. http://www.praguepost.com/tempo/2383-telling-a-foreign-tale-in-a-foreign-tongue.html (accessed 23 October 2012)

Almeida, Cláudia. 2003. Encontros desencontrados: entrevista com Bernardo Carvalho. *CEM Reflexões* Janeiro 2003 http://www.c-e-m.org/reflexoes/019/4.htm (accessed 29 January 2013)

Alves, Rogério Eduardo. 2003. Bernardo Carvalho desmitifica a Mongólia. *Folha de S. Paulo* 11 October 2003. http://www1.folha.uol.com.br/fsp/ilustrad/fq1110200309.htm (accessed 17 January 2013)

Anonymous. 2007. Petra Hulova "Czas Czerwonych Gór" *Independent.pl* 19 June 2007 http://independent.pl/n/6766 (accessed 23 January 2013)

Anonymous. 2008. Svetislav Basaras furioser Höllenritt "Führer durch die innere Mongolei": der neue Roman der serbischen Autors. *Die Berliner Literaturkritik*, 28 Oct. 2008 http://www.berlinerliteraturkritik.de/index.php?id=26&tx_ttnews[tt_news]=19280&cHash=51850b9c19 (accessed 17 Jan. 2013)

Anonymous. 2010. Guía de Mongolia. *Observatorio Asia Central-- Boletín bimestral* 8 (Marzo-Mayo). http://www.asiacentral.es/docs/fitxa_svetislav_basara_mar10.pdf (accessed 16 January 2013)

Anonymous. 2012a. Petra Hůlová introduces 'All of This Belongs to Me' in Sweden. *Czech Literature Portal* 6 May 2012. http://www.czechlit.cz/news2/petra-hulova-introduces-all-of-this-belongs-to-me-in-sweden/ (accessed 23 Oct. 2012)

Araújo, André Luís de. 2009. *"Eu existo pelo nome que te dei": Ana C. por Bernardo Carvalho.* Thesis, Universidade Federal de Minas Gerais, Belo Horizonte. http://www.bibliotecadigital.ufmg.br/dspace/bitstream/handle/1843/ECAP-7QQJGM/tese_corrigida.pdf?sequence=1 (accessed 30 January 2013)

Argoul. 2009. Svetislav Basara, Guide de Mongolie. *Paperblog* 30 October 2009. http://www.paperblog.fr/2462950/svetislav-basara-guide-de-mongolie/ (accessed 16 January 2013)

Arnald, Jan. 2012. Petra Hulova: "Allt detta tillhör mig." *DN.se* 2012-02-06. http://www.dn.se/dnbok/bokrecensioner/petra-hulova-allt-detta-tillhor-mig (accessed 23 January 2013)

Artacho Reyes, Jesús. 2012. Guía de Mongolia: Svetislav Basara. *La Biblioteca Imaginaria* 5 June 2012. http://www.labibliotecaimaginaria.com/2012/06/guia-de-mongolia-svetislav-basara.html (accessed 16 January 2013)

Balaštík, Miroslav & Petra Hůlová. 2006. Je pro mě těžký napsat knihu o současnejch Čechách… *Host* 22(2): 6.

Barbosa, Belém. 2004. Bernardo Carvalho: Mongólia. *Nova cultura* março 2004. (accessed 17 January 2013) http://www.novacultura.de/0403carvalho.html

Bergius, C.C. 1958. *Dschingis-Chan*. Gütersloh: Mohn.

Bigosowa. 2011. Czas Czerwonych Gór, Petra Hulova. *Bigos Kulturalny* 3 August 2011 http://bigoskulturalny.blogspot.com/2011/08/czas-czerwonych-gor-petra-hulova.html (accessed 23 January 2013)

Boer, Nicole de. N.d. Een roman of een delirium? *Prospekt-online* (accessed 23 January 2013) http://www.prospekt-online.nl/ablak/ablak_recensies/delirium.html

Boisvert, Christian. 2009. Livre "Guide de Mongolie" de Svetislav Basara: Folie pure! *Voir: blog de Christian Boisvert* 29 November 2009. (accessed 16 January 2013) http://me.voir.ca/christianboisvert/2009/11/29/livre-guide-de-mongolie-de-svetislav-basara-folie-pure/

Bonnargent, Éric. 2011. Broyer le monde: Svetislav Basara, Guide de Mongolie. *L'anagnoste* 18 November 2011. http://anagnoste.blogspot.com/2011/11/svetislav-basara-guide-de-mongolie.html (accessed 16 January 2013)

Brasil, Bruno. 2007. É tudo mentira. *Overmundo* 22 November 2007 http://www.overmundo.com.br/banco/e-tudo-mentira (accessed 30 January 2013)

Bringsværd, Tor Åge. 1985. *Barndommens måne*. Oslo: Gyldendal.

Bringsværd, Tor Åge. 1987. *Djengis Khan*. Oslo: Gyldendal.

Bringsværd, Tor Åge. 1989. *Djevelens skinn og ben*. Oslo: Gyldendal.

Briongos, Miguel. 2010. Guía de Mongolia. *Libros y viajes* 23 May 2010. http://librosyviajes.blogspot.com/2010/05/guia-de-mongolia.html (accessed 16 January 2013)

Brizuela, Natalia. 2008. Bernardo Carvalho. *BOMB* 102/Winter. http://bombsite.com/issues/102/articles/3038 (accessed 23 October 2012)

Caldwell, Taylor. 1940. *The earth is the Lord's : a tale of the rise of Genghis Khan*. New York: Charles Scribner's Sons.

Chaves, Teresa. 2009. Estilo de Bernardo Carvalho passeia entre cinismo e coragem. *Folia de S. Paulo, Folha Online* 29/06/2009 (accessed 30 January 2013)
http://www1.folha.uol.com.br/folha/ilustrada/ult90u587494.shtml

Checa, Óscar. 2005. Literatura, identidad y autores del Brasil actual. *Paralelo Sur: Revista de literatura* nr.2.
http://www.paralelosur.com/revista/revista_dossier_017.htm
(accessed 23 October 2012)

chiara76. 2012. Czas Czerwonych Gór. Petra Hulova.
http://chiara76.blox.pl/2012/08/Czas-Czerwonych-Gor-Petra-Hulova.html (accessed 23 January 2013)

Clements, Madeline. 2010. What belongs. *TLS* January 8: 21.

D'Angelo, Biagio. 2008. Escritas circulares: a viagem e a morte em Mongólia, de Bernardo Carvalho. *Scripta*, revista do Programa de Pós-graduação em Letras e do Centro de Estudos Luso-afro-brasileiros da PUC Minas Belo Horizonte. 12(23): 84-97. (Accessed 17 January 2013)
http://periodicos.pucminas.br/index.php/scripta/article/view/4414

David, Kurt. 1966. *Der schwarze Wolf*. Berlin: Verlag Neues Leben.

Davis-Van Atta, Taylor. 2012. Structuring madness: notes toward an understanding of Svetislav Basara. *Numéro Cinq Magazine*, 3(12). (accessed 16 January 2013)
http://numerocinqmagazine.com/2012/03/19/structuring-madness-notes-toward-an-understanding-of-svetislav-basara-taylor-davis-van-atta/

Döbler, Katharina. 2007. Eine Materialsammlung macht noch keinen Roman. *Deutschlandradio* 20 March 2007.
http://www.dradio.de/dkultur/sendungen/kritik/606049/

Elchicoanalogo. 2012. Guía de Mongolia (Svetislav Basara). *Espacios en blan co...* 14 Junio 2012. http://despuesdelnaufragio.blogcindario.com/2012/06/01096-guia-de-mongolia-svetislav-basara.html (accessed 16 January 2013)

Elmerot, Irene. 2011. En flicka i en jurta blir en kvinna i Ulan Bator. *Dagensbok.com* 2011.11.03. http://dagensbok.com/2011/01/03/petra-hulova-all-this-belongs-to-me/ (accessed 23 January 2013)

Eriksson, Magnus. 2012. Skarpa porträtt i laddat samspel. *Svenska dagbladet* 16 January 2012. http://www.svd.se/kultur/litteratur/skarpa-portratt-i-laddat-samspel_6771405.svd (accessed 17 January 2013)

Eristov, Michel. 1948. *L'empire mouvant*. Paris: B. Grasset.

Ferreira, Nuno Miguel Félix. 2009. *Testemunho e historiografia em Nove noites e Mongólia: conflitos morais na representação discursiva do passado*. Tese de mestrado, Estudos Comparatistas, Universidade de Lisboa, Faculdade de Letras. http://repositorio.ul.pt/handle/10451/357 (accessed 17 January 2013)

Flock, Sarah & Richard Vacula. 2009. Entretien avec Petra Hůlová. *Slavica bruxellensia* 2:49-55. http://slavica.revues.org/171 (accessed 17 January 2013)

Francesca. 2012. Tutto questo mi appartiene: recensione. *Life in Technicolor* 23 April 2012. (accessed 23 January 2013) http://bondgirlintechnicolor.blogspot.com/2012/04/tutto-questo-mi-appartiene-recensione.html#.UQCB0_Kijco

Franco, Adenize. 2012. Narrativas em trânsito: deslocamentos em *Mongólia*, de Bernardo Carvalho e em *A Luz do Índico*, de Francisco José Viegas. In *Anais do XXIII Congresso Internacional da Associação de Professores de Literatura Portuguesa (ABRAPLIP)*. São Luís: UFMA. p.1140-1152. http://www.abraplip.org/anais_abraplip/images/stories/sessoes/Adenize%20Franco.pdf (accessed 17 January 2013)

Frateschi Vieira, Yara. 2005. Diante do espelho: refração e iluminação em Bernardo Carvalho. *Portuguese studies* 21: 210-223.

Frieling, Wilhelm Ruprecht. 2008. Svetislav Basara, Führer in die Innere Mongolei. *Literaturzeitschrift.de* 02.09.2008. http://www.literaturzeitschrift.de/rezension/lesen.php5?page=detail&id=343&search=xt&item=reviewer&id_reviewer=27&PHPSESSID=hlwsydwll (accessed 17 January 2013)

Gaibie-Dawood, Akeela. 2010. All this belongs to me. *Belletrista* 4 (March/April). (accessed 23 January 2013) http://www.belletrista.com/2010/issue4/reviews_2.php

Giron, Luís Antônio. 2003. Labirinto sem paredes. *Época* 282 (13 October).http://revistaepoca.globo.com/Epoca/0,,EPT615495-1661,00.html (accessed 17 January 2013)

Gregorová, Bára. 2002. Hůlová, Petra: Paměť mojí babičce. *Musiq* 4/11/2002. Viewed on *iLiteratura.cz* 9.4.2003. http://www.iliteratura.cz/Clanek/10817/hulova-petra-pamet-moji-babicce (accessed 17 January 2013)

Harris, Roy. 2004. *The Lingusitics of History*. Edinburgh: Edinburgh University Press.

Hérault, Pascal. 2009. Svetislav Basara. Guide de Mongolie. *Encres vagabondes* 01/02/2009. http://www.encres-vagabondes.com/magazine/basara.htm (16 Jan. 2013)

Hüblová, Magda de Bruin. 2010. Hůlová, Petra: All This Belongs to Me, komentář k recenzi. *iLiteratura.cz* 7.2.2010. http://www.iliteratura.cz/Clanek/25835/hulova-petra-all-this-belongs-to-me-komentar-k-recenzi (accessed 17 Jan. 2013)

Ян, Василий. 1955-1960. *Нашествие монголов*. Москва: Гослитиздат.

Imani. 2012. Czas Czerwonych Gór, Petra Hulova. *Myśli Czytelnika* 11 Listopada 2012 (accessed 23 January 2013) http://mysliczytelnika.blogspot.com/2012/11/czas-czerwonych-gor-petra-hulova.html

Jongeling, Ann. 2010. Svetislav Basara – Mongoolse dromen. *NU.nl* 23 March 2010. (accessed 23 January 2013) http://www.nu.nl/boek/2210917/svetislav-basara--mongoolse-dromen.html

Josse, Jacques. 2007. Svetislav Basara / Guide de Mongolie. L'étonnant séjour de Svetislav Basara à Oulan-Bator. *Une Revue* 25 February 2007. (accessed 16 Jan. 2013) http://remue.net/spip.php?article2119

Kadir Tisna Sudjana. 1935. *Babad Madjapait*. Batavia: Bale Poestaka.

Kadlecová, Kateřina. 2012. Hrdá pravdoláskařka Petra Hůlová: Člověk si nesmí nechat ucpávat hubu. *Reflex* 21.03.2012. http://www.reflex.cz/clanek/zpravy/45587/hrda-pravdolaskarka-petra-hulova-clovek-si-nesmi-nechat-ucpavat-hubu.html (accessed 17 January 2013)

Kirkland, Will. 2011. All This Belongs To Me: a novel of Mongolian sisters; or is it? *All in one boat—and heading through the Straits of Messina (Will's blog)* 4 August 2011. http://www.allinoneboat.org/2011/08/04/all-this-belongs-to-me-a-novel-of-mongolian-sisters-or-is-it/ (accessed 23 Jan. 2013)

Kmentová, Jitka. 2002. Petra Hůlová: Paměť mojí babičce: poznámky k četbě. *Kritické listy* 9 (podzim). http://www.kritickemysleni.cz/klisty.php?co=klisty9_hulova (accessed 23 January 2013)

Kossak-Szczucka, Zofia. 1930. *Legnickie pole*. Kraków: Nakładem Krakowskiej Spółki Wydawniczej.

Kuczyński, Maciej. 1965. *Gwiazdy suchego stepu*. Warszawa: Nasza Księgarnia.

Lamb, Harold. 1927. *Genghis Khan : emperor of all men*. New York: Bantam.

Landry, Pierre-Luc. 2009. "Est-ce un roman, ou le délire?": petit voyage dans une Mongolie fabulée. *Salon double* 8 September 2009. Accessed 16 January 2013 at: http://salondouble.contemporain.info/lecture/est-ce-un-roman-ou-le-delire-petit-voyage-dans-une-mongolie-fabulee

Leclercq, Gine Victor. 1960. *Va comme le vent, ou Les aventures d'un jeune cavalier mongol*. Paris: Bourrelier.

Lévrier, Sébastien. 2009. Manuel de l'absurdité : Svetislav Basara – Guide de Mongolie. *Le globe-lecteur* 29 December 2009. http://www.leglobelecteur.fr/index.php?post/2009/12/29/Svetislav-Basara-Guide-de-Mongolie (accessed 23 January 2013)

Leynse, James P. 1973. *Gobi, prince of moving sand*. Westchester, Ill.: Good News Publishers.

馬加. 1950. 開不敗的花朵. 北京: 新华书店. [Ma Jia. 1950.

Kai bu bai de hua duo. Beijing: Xin hua shu dian]
Mandżuria. 2009. "Czas Czerwonych Gór", Petra Hůlová. *Herbatniki* 27 September 2009
http://mandzuria.wordpress.com/2009/09/27/czas-czerwonych-gor-petra-hulova/ (accessed 23 January 2013)
Mas, Ramon . 2010. Guía de Mongolia (Svetislav Basara, 1992) *Les Males Herbes, blog de la revista de terror i fantàstic* 26 July 2010. http://lesmalesherbes.blogspot.com/2010/07/guia-de-mongolia-svetislav-basara-1992.html (access 16 Jan. 2013)
Mata, Anderson Luís Nunes da. 2005. À deriva: espaço e movimento em Bernardo Carvalho. *Fênix – Revista de História e Estudos Culturais* 2(2: Abril/ Maio/ Junho). http://www.revistafenix.pro.br/PDF3/Artigo%20Anderson%20da%20Mata.pdf (accessed 17 January 2013)
Menéndez Salmón, Ricardo. 2010. Bilis balcánica. *La Nueva España* (online) 18 March 2010. 16 January 2013 at:
http://www.lne.es/cultura/2010/03/18/bilis-balcanica/888414.html
Meunier, Benoit. 2006. Les montagnes rouges. *Bohemica, littérature tchèque* (site of the Association Bohemica)
http://bohemica.free.fr/auteurs/hulova/montagnes_etude.htm
(accessed 17 January 2013)
Monasevda. 2012. Guide de Mongolie, roman de Svetislav Basara. *Boudoir Moderne* 4 March 2012.
http://boudoirmoderne.org/2012/03/04/guide-de-mongolie-roman-de-svetislav-basara/ (accessed 16 January 2013)
Moody, Sarah. (2005). Locating Brazil: notions of place and nation in Bernardo Carvalho's *Nove Noites* and *Mongólia*. Center for Latin American Studies, University of California Berkeley website.
http://clas.berkeley.edu/Research/graduate/summer2005/tinker/Moody/index.html (accessed 17 January 2013)
More, Erminio Fischetti. 2012. Tutto questo mi appartiene. *Fuori le Mura: il primo settimanale online di Roma* 14 maggio 2012. http://www.fuorilemura.com/2012/05/14/tutto-questo-mi-appartiene/ (accessed 23 January 2013)
Naves, Santuza Cambraia. 2011. O ofício do tradutor como etnógrafo-escritor e como escritoretnógrafo: a propósito

de Lévi-Strauss e Bernardo Carvalho. *ArtCultura, Uberlândia* 13(23): 49-56. (accessed 17 January 2013) http://www.artcultura.inhis.ufu.br/PDF23/santuza_naves.pdf

Nuñez, Carlinda Fragale Pate . 2008. "Mongólia" de Bernardo Carvalho: romance de espaço e imagologia, in *XII Congresso Nacional de Lingüística e Filologia* (Círculo Fluminense de Estudos Filológicos e Lingüísticos). http://www.filologia.org.br/xiicnlf/textos_completos/Mong%C3%B3lia,%20de%20Bernardo%20Carvalho-%20%20romance%20de%20espa%C3%A7o%20e%20imagologia%20-%20CARLINDA.pdf (accessed 17 January 2013)

Paquin, Éric. 2007. Svetislav Basara: La part du rêve. *Voir* 19 April 2007. http://voir.ca/livres/2007/04/19/svetislav-basara-la-part-du-reve/ (accessed 16 January 2013)

Peter. 2012. Mongoolse dromen. *Mijn Novi Sad-Dobrodošli!* 5 February 2012 (access 23 Jan. 2013) http://mijnnovisad.blogspot.com/2012/02/mongoolse-dromen.html

Pinedo, Jorge. 2010. El principio de la historia: Una disparatada muestra de literatura serbia que transcurre en un país tan irreal como casi todos *Página 12* 9 May 2010. http://www.pagina12.com.ar/diario/suplementos/libros/10-3829-2010-05-09.html (accessed 16 January 2013)

Radisavljević, Zoran. 2010. Poslove trežnjenja Srba ostavljam Pelagiću i policiji. *Politika online* 23 October 2010. http://www.politika.rs/rubrike/Kulturni-dodatak/Poslove-trezznjenja-Srba-ostavljam-Pelagicu-i-policiji.sr.html (accessed 16 January 2013)

Ready, Ania. 2009. Petra Hůlová - Czas czerwonych gór. *Tygiel* 17 sierpnia 2009. http://magamara.blox.pl/2009/08/Czas-czerwonych-gor-Petra-Hlov.html (accessed 23 January 2013)

Rettig, Maja. 2007. Neun Leben. *Tagesspiegel* Online 25 August 2007. http://www.tagesspiegel.de/kultur/literatur/roman-neun-leben/1023650.html (accessed 17 January 2013)

Roganović, Vesna. 2012. Intervju Svetislav Basara. *Politika Online*, 15.9.2012. http://www.politika.rs/rubrike/Kulturni-dodatak/Intervju-Svetislav-Basara.lt.html (accessed 16 January 2013)

Rosa, Luís Carlos dalla. 2010. *Educar para a sabedoria do amor: a epifania do rosto do outro como uma pedagogia do êxodo.* Tese de doutorado, Escola Superior de Teologia, Instituto Ecumênico de Pós-graduação em Teologia. São Leopoldo.

Rossini. 2012. Basara Svetislav, Guide de Mongolie (Mongolski bedeker (1992)). *Calmeblog* 17 January 2012.
http://www.calmeblog.com/article-basara-svetislav-guide-de-mongolie-mongolski-bedeker-1992-traduit-en-2006-pour-les-editions-les-97306693.html (accessed 16 January 2013)

Sacco, Marcello. 2011. "Mongolia" di Bernardo Carvalho. *Sul romanzo* 25/08/2011. (accessed 17 January 2013)
http://www.sulromanzo.it/blog/mongolia-di-bernardo-carvalho

Said, Edward. 2003. *Orientalism.* London: Penguin.

Симонов, Константин. 1954. Товарищи по оружию. Москва: Молодая гвардия.

Soukopová, Pavla. 2007. *Spisovatelé na jeden rok? Aneb češtíliterární debutanti 2001 – 2005.* České Budějovice: Jihočeská Univerzita v Českých Budějovicích Pedago-gická Fakulta, Katedra Bohemistiky. Diplomová prace.
http://theses.cz/id/2e82p2/downloadPraceContent_adipIdno_4125 (accessed 31 January 2013)

Strebel, Volker. 2008. Kinos und Konservenwürstchen: Kein westlicher Feminismus in der mongolischen Steppe: Petra Hulovás tschechischer Frauenroman. *Literaturkritik.de* 1(January).
http://www.literaturkritik.de/public/rezension.php?rez_id=11466&ausgabe=200801 (accessed 23 January 2013)

Taufer, Adauto Locatelli. 2007. Os eus e os outros: a viagem e o senso de alteridade em Mongólia, de Bernardo Carvalho. *Nau Literária* 3(1: jan/jun). (accessed 17 January 2013)
http://seer.ufrgs.br/NauLiteraria/article/view/4891

Vasilevski, Dejan.. 2010. Basara pod svetlom petrolejki. *Spona: kulturno-informativni centar Srba u Makedoniji* 19 December 2010. (accessed 16 January013)
http://www.srbi.org.mk/index.php?option=com_content&view=article&id=1897%3Abasara-pod-svetlom-petrolejke&catid=72%3Asrbija-makedonija&Itemid=96&lang=sr

Vaughan, David. 2007. Petra Hulova: a rising star of the young generation of Czech writers. *Český rozhlas* 14 January 2007. http://www.radio.cz/en/section/books/petra-hulova-a-rising-star-of-the-young-generation-of-czech-writers (accessed 23 October 2012)

Velinger, Jan. 2003. Petra Hulova - to Mongolia and back again. *Czech Radio 7, Radio Prague*. January 13, 2003. http://www.radio.cz/en/article/36378 (accessed 23 Oct. 2012)

Vohryzková, Tereza & Petra Hůlová. 2002. Tradice a ztráta jistoty. *Tvar* 13(19): 5.

Wilke, Insa. 2007. Sehnsuchtsorte eines mongolischen Mädchens. *Die Zeit* 27.12.2007 nr.1. http://www.zeit.de/2008/01/L-Hulova (accessed 23 January 2013)

Wyman, Levi Parker. 1930. *The Hunniwell Boys in the Gobi Desert*. New York: A.L. Burt.

www.ingramcontent.com/pod-product-compliance
Lightning Source LLC
Chambersburg PA
CBHW071220080526
44587CB00013BA/1437